PATTON IN MEXICO

PATTON IN MEXICO

*Lieutenant George S. Patton, the Hunt for
Pancho Villa, and the Making of a General*

MICHAEL LEE LANNING

STACKPOLE
BOOKS

Essex, Connecticut
Blue Ridge Summit, Pennsylvania

STACKPOLE BOOKS

An imprint of Globe Pequot, the trade division of
The Rowman & Littlefield Publishing Group, Inc.
4501 Forbes Blvd., Ste. 200
Lanham, MD 20706
www.rowman.com

Distributed by NATIONAL BOOK NETWORK

British Library Cataloguing in Publication Information available

Library of Congress Cataloging-in-Publication Data

Names: Lanning, Michael Lee, author.
Title: Patton in Mexico : Lieutenant George S. Patton, the hunt for Pancho
  Villa, and the making of a general / Michael Lee Lanning.
Description: Essex, Connecticut : Stackpole Books, [2023] | Includes
  bibliographical references. | Summary: "Serving under General John
  Pershing in the hunt for Pancho Villa in Mexico, Lieutenant George S.
  Patton learned leadership, logistics—and how to promote himself. These
  are the roots of the World War II general"— Provided by publisher.
Identifiers: LCCN 2022016215 (print) | LCCN 2022016216 (ebook) | ISBN
  9780811770729 (cloth) | ISBN 9780811770736 (epub)
Subjects: LCSH: Patton, George S. (George Smith), 1885–1945. | United
  States. Army—Officers—Biography. | United States.
  Army—History—Punitive Expedition into Mexico, 1916. | Patton, George
  S. (George Smith), 1885–1945—Diaries. | Pershing, John J. (John
  Joseph), 1860–1948—Friends and associates. | Generals—United
  States—Biography.
Classification: LCC E745.P3 L36 2023 (print) | LCC E745.P3 (ebook) | DDC
  355.0092 [B]—dc23/eng/20220518
LC record available at https://lccn.loc.gov/2022016215
LC ebook record available at https://lccn.loc.gov/2022016216

∞™ The paper used in this publication meets the minimum requirements of American National
Standard for Information Sciences—Permanence of Paper for Printed Library Materials, ANSI/
NISO Z39.48-1992.

CONTENTS

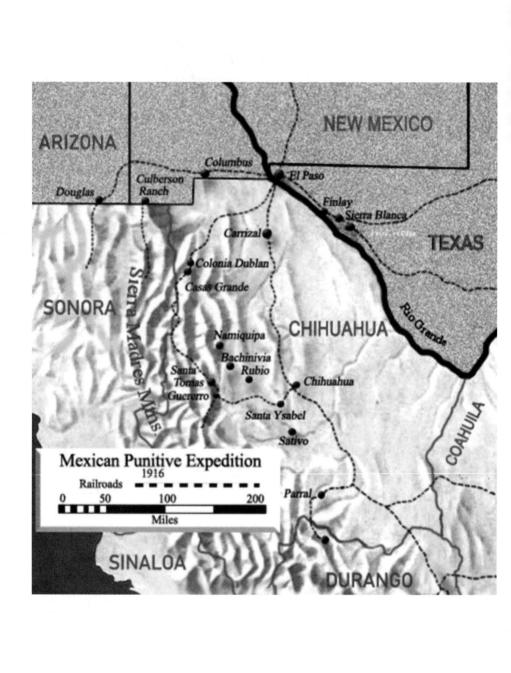

Introduction

Dozens of biographies and military history books have George S. Patton as their topic. Without exception, these writings focus on the mature man at the peak of his performance. While his exploits were indeed noteworthy and often breathtaking, he did not arrive on the battlefields fully formed and informed. He reached his pinnacle and his power because he had prepared for his moment in time by being in the right place at the right time—though he did not always clearly understand exactly where his path was leading.

He did, however, arrive on the scene of his glory determined that it was his destiny. He always believed that he would be great, and he ensured that biographers and other writers would have ample material on his life from which to work. Patton obsessively kept journals and notebooks. He also was a prolific writer of personal letters to his wife, father, and others.

On July 11, 1913, in one of his earliest notebook entries, he prophesied that he would be remembered, writing that he included "facts, dates, and incidents in my life which I hope will be of interest to posterity."

In a letter to his sister, Nita, in 1930, he wrote, "I am certainly giving my future biographer—if there ever is one—an easy job with all my papers on war so nicely arranged."

Patton's foresight was on target. A host of writers have mined the treasure of his papers to produce biographies, instruction on leadership principles, and vignettes on all other aspects of his life. A two-volume tome of nearly two thousand pages includes a "summary" of the *Patton Papers*. Most, if not all, of these publications mention Patton's service in the Punitive Expedition to some degree. None, however, emphasize the immense influence the time in Mexico had on his future career. True to form and habit, Patton kept a personal journal during his time in Mexico (March 13–November 26, 1916), making daily entries that varied from ten to one hundred words. His notes include mentions of operations, interactions with General John J. Pershing and other notable military officials, combat with the enemy, and personal observations.

Patton originally wrote his diary for himself. However, shortly after his return to the United States from Mexico, he sent a copy to Pershing at Fort Sam Houston, Texas. In the cover letter, dated April 23, 1917, from his in-laws' home at Prides Crossing, Massachusetts, he wrote, "The enclosed diary is not so good as I could wish because I had no time to typewrite it myself and had to read it into a Dictaphone and when the man wrote it he made a great many mistakes."

He continued in the letter by noting that he had departed El Paso abruptly to accompany his wife, Beatrice, to her father's deathbed. Patton apologized for the edited diary, writing that it "was not completed when I left and had to follow me here hence the delay in reaching you." He also noted that all the people were "war mad" and that Beatrice would stay at Prides Crossing if his unit went to France.

The edited version of the diary he sent to Pershing differs little from Patton's handwritten notes composed in the field in Mexico. Both were consulted for this writing, but only the edited version is included in its entirety. No previous publication has offered the complete diary kept by the future American military icon during the operation or attempted to analyze the Expedition's influence on what made Lieutenant Patton into General Patton. It clearly shows that Patton had already determined his destiny.

CHAPTER ONE

The Legend

Patton. The name says it all. Audacious. Flamboyant. Brave. Victorious. Tough. Single-minded. Heroic. These—along with brilliant, bold, and defiant—are but a few accurate descriptions of the man who perfected U.S. armored warfare and became America's best-known military leader.

A man of destiny. He was also privileged, arrogant, egomaniacal, profane, quick-tempered, and racist, all while he fought to master his two main personal challenges: a weak voice and dyslexia. True to character, he turned both distractions to his benefit. He cloaked his scrawny voice in epic speeches that inspired his troops, and he concentrated on conquering the difficult learning and writing tasks in order to maintain dairies and write multitudes of letters for his entire life, accomplishments that augment the telling of his life's story even until today.

Thus, Patton learned early to convert adversarial situations into inordinate opportunities. Other American heroes—Washington, Jackson, Grant, Marshall, Eisenhower—also served bravely in the military and rose in the ranks to great acclaim. Yet, for most of the best-known, their lasting reputations are the result of accomplishments achieved after leaving behind their uniforms. Patton stands alone as a great American leader known singularly for his military prowess, rivaled only by John J. "Black Jack" Pershing, who was, in fact, his mentor and most influential role model.

Had *Lieutenant* George S. Patton not served with Pershing on the southern border during the Mexican Expedition of 1916, there might never have been a *General* George S. Patton to take the world by storm as a notoriously bold leader and daring commander of the U.S. armored forces during World War II a quarter of a century later. But Patton did participate in the mission to Mexico as part of the Punitive Expedition, serving as aide-de-camp for Pershing. In that position, he understudied leadership techniques from the man who would become the senior American commander in World War I.

As Pershing's aide, Patton came into contact with almost every important senior officer of the period, officers who had experienced the Indian Wars, fought in Cuba, and put down the Philippine Insurrection. Of equal significance, he was exposed to the latest technical advances that were about to be applied to modern warfare. Because he was there, Patton grasped the advantages of motorized vehicles over horses for moving men and supplies, he benefited from intelligence gathered by some of the first military aerial reconnaissance, and he personally wrestled with setting up early wireless radio equipment that would change the way the military communicated. For Patton, the Expedition was all about learning how to integrate new technology—automobiles, planes, and radio waves—into logistics and military operations.

This service on the border formed Patton's vision of why and how to convert troops of cavalry-mounted soldiers into battalions of armored tanks and other mechanical vehicles. This vision ultimately transformed modern warfare and set the stage for America to be prepared to face the Axis powers when needed. The Punitive Expedition into Mexico also presented Patton with his first confrontation with an armed enemy. When faced with belligerent Mexicans, Patton charged, wielding his pistol skills to slay two of Pancho Villa's bandits.

This daring action brought Patton to the attention of the press again. While he had enjoyed publicity as an army Olympian athlete before the Expedition, it was in Mexico that Patton discovered not only how much he liked the media attention but also how to manipulate events to get more of it. It was in the Mexican desert that he developed that growing affinity for fame into the art of self-promotion.

Another facet of Patton's development as a soldier that is often overlooked was that field operations of the Expedition exposed the twenty-nine-year-old lieutenant to real physical hardships for the first time in his life. Having grown up in affluence and all creature comforts, Patton had to adjust to primitive settings in the desert in all seasons. He had to sleep on the ground, endure inclement weather without shelter at times, push automobiles out of mud puddles—all the while running menial errands for General Pershing.

It was all these factors—his belief in his own destiny, his introduction to influential leaders and innovations, his reintroduction to the media, and his personal hardships—that shaped and informed the young soldier in his formative ranks. They made the man.

CHAPTER TWO

Patton's Boyhood

In a notebook begun in 1913, George S. Patton Jr. wrote, "I was born on the eleventh of November 1885 in my family house in San Gabriel, California. I was born in the same room in which my mother had been born."

On his arrival, George Patton entered the world of wealth and privilege of a family who combined the Southern tradition of military service with the enterprising spirit of Western pioneers. His was a story of influential "begats" that could rival the book of Genesis, an analogy he would find fitting, for he saw himself as the product of prominent ancestry and the vessel of greatness yet to come.

Indeed, the family was affluent when the future general arrived, but such status had not always been the case. The first Patton in America arrived from Scotland and landed in Virginia in 1770 as an indentured servant bound to the Scottish merchant magnate William Cunninghame of Fredericksburg. Robert Paton (who later added a second *t* to his name) marketed various goods, including wine, coal, salt, coffee, and sugar, on his own after he completed his servitude, becoming a successful merchant in his own right. During the American Revolutionary War, he continued with his business activities with no apparent loyalties to either the Tories or the rebels.

In 1792, Robert married Anne Gordon Mercer, daughter of Brigadier General Hugh Mercer, who served in the French and Indian War before being mortally wounded in the Battle of Princeton during the Revolution. Anne Patton gave birth to seven children, including John

Mercer Patton, who practiced law and engaged in Virginia politics. John's marriage to Margaret French Williams, in turn, produced twelve children, including nine sons. One of these boys, George Smith Patton, born in 1833, attended the Virginia Military Institute and then taught school for two years before joining his father John's law practice.

The bloodline thickened when this first George Patton married Susan Thornton Glassell—who claimed a lineage that included George Washington, English and French nobility, and at least sixteen signers of the Magna Carta. From the 1855 marriage, they produced four children, including the future General Patton's father, George William Patton, born in 1856. The family settled in Charleston in what is now the state of West Virginia.

At the outbreak of the Civil War, the senior Patton joined seven of his brothers in the ranks of the Confederate army. One of the brothers, Tazewell, was wounded first at the Second Battle of Bull Run in August 1862 and then again in Pickett's Charge at the Battle of Gettysburg in July 1863. George Patton fell mortally wounded at the Third Battle of Winchester on September 19, 1863. His mother, Margaret French Patton, supposedly remained stoic despite the loss of her sons. The first time she cried was when still another son was wounded in battle. According to family remembrances, she cried not for his wounds but "because she had no more boys to send to fight the Yankees."

After the death of her husband George, Susan Glassell Patton moved her family of four children in with her brother William, who was a Confederate navy veteran. A year after the war concluded, Susan sailed with her brood for California, where they briefly lived with another brother, Andrew, whom family lore describes as "a man of means." The widow then set up her own household in a small adobe house by teaching school while her son George helped support the family by cleaning the schoolhouse and a local church. According to his son, George "developed an intense aversion to poverty."

In 1870, Susan married George Hugh Smith, a cousin and VMI classmate of her late husband. Smith, a Civil War veteran, was such a devoted husband and father that George William Patton changed his name to George Smith Patton Jr. to honor his stepfather.

When it was time for his university education, George Patton returned to Virginia, where he graduated with the class of 1877 from VMI. He remained there for a year as a French instructor, but he apparently found himself craving a more adventurous life and was in the process of seeking a commission in a British-led Egyptian mercenary army when he learned his mother was dying of cancer. He returned home.

Back in Southern California, George Smith Patton studied law under his stepfather and became involved in politics. While his education and position as an attorney afforded him some social distinction, he remained far from wealthy. This changed on December 28, 1884, when he married Ruth Wilson, daughter of Benjamin D. Wilson and Margaret Short Hereford.

Benjamin Wilson, Ruth's father and a Tennessee native who as a teenager had gone to South California in 1841, was one of the first Anglo-American settlers. Because Wilson's own father had fought as a major in the Revolutionary War, it is not surprising that his son Ben joined the local California militia to fight the Indians and Mexican bandits in order to establish a general store and a cattle ranch. In between the sporadic clashes, the young Wilson acquired additional properties, eventually owning land where Westwood, San Gabriel, San Marino, and Pasadena would one day be built. In addition to being a merchant and rancher, Wilson was an innovator, bringing orange groves and vineyards to Southern California and using wood gathered from a nearby mountain—later named Mount Wilson in his honor—for the construction of orange crates and wine barrels.

In 1854, Don Benito Wilson, as he was locally known, purchased 128 acres in what would become San Marino and built a lavish, two-story adobe mansion with a tile roof overlooking a lake. Construction of the estate structures, complete with an elaborate wine cellar, cost an exorbitant $20,000. Don Benito surrounded the house with vineyards and citrus trees and called it Lake Vineyard.

Wilson had first married Ramona Yorba, the daughter of a wealthy Mexican landowner, in 1844. After Ramona died in 1849, he married Margaret Short Hereford, a widow from Virginia, four years later. The latter union produced two daughters, Annie and Ruth. Don Benito, who died in March 1878, did not live to see his daughter Ruth marry George Smith Patton or celebrate the birth of his grandson George Smith Patton Jr., the second Patton to be so named as Junior.

George Smith Patton and Ruth Wilson Patton made a powerful couple. She brought the wealth and social prestige of the founding California Anglos while George contributed vestiges of the Old South aristocracy. The heritage and assets of Ruth Wilson Patton would be just as instrumental in shaping her son as was the lineage of the Pattons' military service. Their marriage melded peaches and magnolia blossoms with oranges and palm trees.

Thus, George S. Patton Jr., known to his family as Georgie or simply as "the boy," grew up in Lake Vineyard, an experience about which he later wrote, "We never wanted a thing we did not get." He spent his time hunting, fishing, and exploring his family's vast holdings, which included not only the family estate at Lake Vineyard but also a vacation home on Santa Catalina Island. In keeping with the Pattons' strong emphasis on traditions, George Jr. learned to ride horseback in the McClellan saddle on which his grandfather had been killed in the Civil War. Patton described it in his journal, writing, "[O]n the pommel was a stain which I thought was his blood. Papa had also learned on this saddle."

The saddle was but a part of the great influence the Civil War and its veterans had on young George. Steel engravings of Robert E. Lee and "Stonewall" Jackson hung prominently on the walls of the family home. His daughter Ruth Ellen later wrote, "Until he was 15 years old, my father thought those steel engravings were of God and Jesus Christ." She also noted:

> *The Civil War stories he heard right from the men who had fought in it: his step-grandfather, Colonel Smith, and the Confederate guerilla, J. S. Mosby, who migrated to California and was practically supported, in his old age, by the Pattons. Georgie lived and played in the company of heroes, dead and alive.*

Another strong influence was his sister Anne, known to family and friends as Nita, who was born in 1887 when George was two. The brother and sister were close for all their lives, both benefiting from the strong hold of familial bonding that included their father's active participation in their childhoods. The younger George later recorded that his father read aloud to them the *Iliad* and the *Odyssey* while their mother traveled back east in 1892.

The Pattons homeschooled George Jr. until age eleven, when they enrolled him in the Classical School for Boys in Pasadena headed by Stephen C. Clark. Over the next six years, Clark and his faculty became the first major influencers on the young Patton outside his family. Included in the curriculum were the standard reading, writing, and arithmetic along with ancient and modern history. Patton particularly liked his history classes, especially the study of the military operations of the Persians, Greeks, and Romans. He closely studied and admired the careers of Julius Caesar and Alexander the Great.

Patton was well behaved in school and enjoyed learning. However, he had difficulties in the classroom due to dyslexia—a condition not defined until 1896 and little known in the United States until the 1920s. It was generally defined as a learning disorder marked by the mental reversal of letters and numbers, resulting in difficulties in reading and writing and, in Patton's case, mood swings, hyperactivity, and boastfulness. Despite his disability, Patton studied hard and eventually loved to read—especially stories of warfare and military leaders.

In the summer of 1902, the Patton family retreated to their vacation home on Catalina Island. There, on August 26, the seventeen-year-old George met sixteen-year-old Beatrice Banning Ayer, who, along with her family, had come west for the season on their private railcar. Beatrice—heir to a multimillion-dollar New England textile industry conglomerate established by her father, Frederick, and daughter of Ellen Barrows Banning, an actress Ayer married in 1883 after his first wife died of cancer in 1878—brought with her the lineage of the influential Southern California Bannings. She was also a distant relation to George's father's half-sister.

Initially, George was impressed with neither Beatrice's family tree nor her manner of "Belle of Boston" dress. By summer's end, however, the two had developed a deep affection that they continued by mail over the following years. Beatrice would remain the principal female influence on the future general for the remainder of his life.

In addition to courting Beatrice during the summer of 1902, George was considering his future and which profession he should pursue. With his family's wealth and influence, he could have chosen any career, but no one was surprised when he declared his desire to become a professional soldier. The Patton tradition of serving in uniform, combined with his interest in military history and great leaders, culminated in his plan to become a regular army officer.

A regular army commission, however, was not easily attained regardless of wealth and influence because the small army relied primarily on the United States Military Academy at West Point to supply its officers. Reserve commissions could be more readily acquired, but they did not guarantee a career track.

George's father supported his son's choice by pursuing an appointment to the Academy from California U.S. senator Thomas R. Bard. While Patton and Bard differed in their politics, the senator recognized the power and influence of George's family—especially when he began receiving letters supporting an appointment from many prominent Californians—but, unfortunately, Bard had already made his selection for 1903. He could only promise that he would strongly consider George in 1904.

Neither son nor father intended to wait for a possible appointment. Despite his learning disability, George studied for and scored well enough on his entrance exams to be accepted to Princeton University. Meanwhile, his father contacted a cousin who was a modern language professor and commandant of cadets at the University of Arizona to ask whether he could expedite George's admission to the Academy. Failing all else, the senior Patton believed he could get his son into his and his family's old alma mater, the Virginia Military Institute (VMI), from which a regular army commission might be secured. More important, being enrolled at VMI would greatly increase George's chances of being accepted to West Point.

George agreed with his father that VMI was the best course of action, and he spent much of the summer of 1903 at Lake Vineyard and Catalina studying to prepare himself for college. His normal self-confidence prevailed, though he did experience self-doubts that he recalled in a letter written in 1927 when he stated, "Just before I went away to the VMI I was walking with Uncle Andrew Glassell and told him that I feared that I might be cowardly. He told me that no Patton could be a coward. He was a most reckless man. I told this to Papa and he said that while ages of gentility might make a man of my breeding reluctant to engage in a fist fight, the same breeding made him perfectly willing to face death from weapons with a smile. I think that this is true."

In September 1903, George departed Lake Vineyard by rail for Virginia accompanied by his parents, sister, and aunt. In 1927, he recalled the ending, writing, "Papa went with me to report. The First Captain, [Reuben] Ragland, was in the room on the left of the sally port which had been Papa's when he was Sergeant Major. When I signed up Ragland said, 'Of course you realize Mr. Patton that now your son is a cadet he cannot leave the grounds.' Papa said, 'Of course.' I never felt lower in my life."

What George was experiencing was the culture shock from having left his familiar pastoral Southern California orchards and vineyards behind to step into a world best described thirty-five years later by the opening words of David O. Selznick's 1939 epic rendition of Margaret Mitchell's masterful novel *Gone with the Wind*: "There was a land of cavaliers and cotton fields called the Old South. Here in this pretty world gallantry took its last bow." Its voice-over concluded, "Look for it only in books for it is no more than a dream remembered. A civilization gone with the wind."

The civilization may have been "gone with wind," but many of the deeply instilled traditions and customs of that Old South lived on at the Virginia Military Institute, founded in 1839, which saw 92 percent of its graduates fight in the Civil War. One of the war's most famous officers, Confederate general Thomas "Stonewall" Jackson, who actually graduated from West Point in 1846, taught at VMI from 1851 until 1861 before he joined the rebel army and marched off to glory. VMI would forever claim him as one of their own.

The Institute's proudest moment came when the entire Corps of Cadets left their classrooms on May 15, 1864, to reinforce Confederate forces at the Battle of New Market. Nearly a quarter of the students fell wounded or dead in the fight. By the time Patton arrived at the Lexington campus, the tradition of annually honoring the occasion on "New Market Day" was well established—a ceremony that included the roll call of each dead cadet's name and the "died on the field of battle" accounting by a current cadet.

Such was the world in which the young Patton found himself. Although a Californian by birth, he was a Virginian by family heritage, and so he now turned to that background to lead his way through the maze in which entering cadets, known as "rats," faced harsh discipline, difficult classes, long drills, and general hazing by upperclassmen. Patton adapted well, quickly feeling comfortable with his fellow classmates whom he found to be mostly sons of former graduates and "Southern gentlemen." He proudly noted in his remembrances of the time that, when he reported for uniform fittings, the school tailor informed him that his measurements were identical to those on file for his father and grandfather.

Patton gave his all at VMI. He performed adequately in the classroom despite his struggles with dyslexia. He went out for the football team, an effort where he found himself, according to his later writings, "probably the world's worst football player, but I did begin to inherit there—or one might say 'inhale' the fighting spirit of that great institution."

While George endured the challenges of being a "rat" at VMI, his father continued his efforts to secure an appointment to West Point for his son. On March 4, 1904, he received a telegram from Senator Bard stating, "I have today nominated your son as principal to West Point."

George welcomed the news despite the additional hazing he received from his upperclassmen when they learned of his appointment. Undeterred, he spent much of his final weeks at VMI touring and studying the Civil War battles of the Shenandoah Valley. Before departing Virginia for New York and West Point, Patton wrote Senator Bard, "I hope that I shall be able to maintain the reputation of California and by my conduct there repay you at least in some small measure for your goodness in appointing me."

Cadet George S. Patton Jr. reported to the U.S. Military Academy at West Point on June 16, 1904, where over the next several weeks he participated in "Plebe Camp," later known as "Beast Barracks" for its hardships, discipline, and out-and-out hazing. With his experiences as a "rat" at VMI, Patton had no difficulties enduring the challenges, and, in a letter to his mother dated June 21, he wrote, "West Point is pretty nice and so far I have been treated a lot better than at VMI."

He also wrote to his father about his initial reactions to life at the Academy. Despite his appreciation for his VMI experience, Patton wrote on July 17 that he somewhat regretted attending the Institute because "two rat years in succession are very depressing."

A week later in a second letter to his father, assessing his Academy brothers with his typical elitist bias, he wrote, "Most of the men here are nice fellows but very few indeed are born gentlemen; in fact, the only ones of that type are Southerners."

Just after completing Plebe Camp and beginning regular classes, Patton again wrote to his father, saying, "When you get this letter, it will have been just a little over a year . . . since I started to learn the profession of killing my brothers. . . . And in this year of contact with the world my respect for man has dwindled instead of increasing. For even among the best and the best are I take it those who devote themselves to the service to Mars, there is not the self-sacrificing love of fame or self-denying selfishness which I feel and which I had expected in others but rather a languid lassitude careless indifference or hazy uncertainty not becoming in my estimation a soldier or a man. But let this be: the fewer of the species there are for the greater is its individual worth. And if my nature proves incapable of the task I have set myself, or if the opportunity never comes I can at least die happy in my own vanity knowing that I stood alone and that alone I fell."

Of all of Patton's early letters and notebooks, this entry best foreshadows the future general's ideas of being a military leader. Although his messages were somewhat morose, he nevertheless concluded, "In spite of this letter I am quite well and happy."

In other early correspondence from West Point, Patton revealed three things that were important personal characteristics then and would continue to be so in his future. First, he cared deeply about the impressions his appearance made. At the Academy, he was so enamored with the quality of the West Point uniforms that he ordered additional ones at his own expense. He later wrote his father, "I got a new blouse and dress coat so I will always be the spooniest [best-dressed] man in my class even if I do have to spend an hour pressing my trousers."

Second, Patton exhibited the affinity for expressing opinions publicly that were better kept private. In a letter to his father on July 3, 1904, he wrote that he had been "catching a great deal of hell lately because in an unguarded moment I said that we braced harder at VMI than here. All the Corps have been trying to show me my error and they have succeeded."

Third, Patton honed his own personal traits to conform with what he thought were the characteristics of a strong military leader. He adopted an all-but-permanent facial scowl to look fierce, he generously laced his speech with profanities for their shock effect, and he became autocratic in his demands of others.

Patton excelled in his military subjects, as might be expected, but he continued to struggle with his academic courses. His excellence with the sword in his fencing class could not compensate for the problems his dyslexia caused him in French and mathematics. Long hours of studying and memorization could not overcome his learning disability. Patton wrote his father on June 12, 1905, "Did not pass math turned back to next class."

"Turned back" was much better news than "turned out," as the former meant that, although he would have to repeat his plebe year academics, he would not be dismissed from the Academy. Signing Patton's paperwork for the "turn back" was Lieutenant Colonel Robert L. Howze, commandant of cadets and future commander in the Eleventh Cavalry Regiment during the Punitive Expedition that would so pivotally impact Patton.

With this turn of events, Patton became a cadet-without-a-class for all practical purposes, a situation that would taint his relationships both at West Point and throughout his career because traditionally a cadet's closest friends for life are those with whom he bonds during those critical four years. Academically, Patton would have to repeat all the first-year classes with the incoming plebes during his second year at the Academy, though he would not have to endure a second round of the harassment and hazing with them. The result was that the young men who had entered the Academy with Patton would graduate a year earlier than he did, and the class of plebes with whom he shared his repeated first-year classes never accepted him as one of their own, viewing him instead as some kind of hybrid upperclassman who did not share their particular hardships and hazing. As a result, Patton had few good friends at West Point. His most constant companions were the several cadets, including Henry Ayers, who had also attended VMI. Even among them, Patton found rifts. He and Ayers often disagreed on many subjects, and, on occasion, their arguments even came to physical blows.

When Patton returned to West Point in the fall of 1905 to repeat his first-year academics, he brought with him a notebook in which he recorded his thoughts for his remaining years at the Academy. "Do your damnedest always" was his first entry.

The diary served as a surrogate friend with which Patton presided over one-sided conversations with himself as he wrote his thoughts. One such observation, written in the early months of his second year, reads, "It is better to live in the limelight a year than in the wings forever. Fame never found a man who waited to be found. Do everything possible to attract attention. Always be very neat and when you get new clothes let everyone know it."

Despite his academic and social challenges, Patton was undeterred. He committed to improving himself physically by joining the football team only to find his abilities could take him no further than the third string. Even then, his propensity for accidents and injuries would lead him to a dislocated right arm, which ensured he remained on the bench.

Whether it was through sheer determination or incredible arrogance—or a combination of the two—Patton tamed his academic demons sufficiently to put himself in the top third of his class by the end of his second year. More important to the future general, though, was that on June 13, 1906, he received promotion from private to second corporal, meaning only one cadet in his 1909 class exceeded his military appearance and conduct.

As second corporal, Patton had a leadership role in Plebe Camp the following summer. At the conclusion of training, however, Patton's superiors reduced him from second corporal to sixth corporal. In a letter to Beatrice he wrote, "Why I don't know unless I was too d------ military. For I certainly am the only man who can march this class."

The demotion was but a symptom of the situation Patton created in his efforts to project himself as the stern, exemplary military cadet he had envisioned for the role. What Patton did not include in that letter to Beatrice was that he had developed a reputation for severe hazing and excessive demands of the plebes and that he had several disagreements with his fellow classmates. When Patton had formally become an upperclassman after repeating his plebe year, his classmates acknowledged his overall military dress and bearing, but they simultaneously labeled him a "quilloid" for his demands for perfection and hazing of plebes, as well as his being a "bootlicker" constantly seeking favor from his superior officers. He further eroded his popularity by frequently and openly stating that he intended to become a general, a common goal of cadets but one that was to remain unspoken.

Nevertheless, neither his rank reduction nor his lack of social acceptance dented Patton's determination or ambitions for future Corps and army leadership positions. "I think there must be destiny," he wrote in his notebook.

From the moment Patton decided on a military career, he had been seeking the assistance of anyone who could advance his objective to achieve his perceived destiny. Everything he did was to that end, including within his family. He had, of course, relied on his father's influence to secure an appointment to West Point and to curry favor with the staff after he entered the Corps of Cadets. In an April 29, 1905, letter to his father prior to the senior's impending visit, the relentless son reminded his father not to "forget to cultivate the Tacs [U.S. Army tactical officers who supervised the Corps and taught military subjects]." Such was the support through personal relationships Patton exercised for the remainder of his life.

With his class now having only 114 members, Patton remained in the middle academically while continuing to excel in all matters military. He easily advanced to his third year and, just before departing for summer leave in California, was informed that he had been promoted to cadet sergeant major.

Back home he enjoyed the social activities opened to him by virtue of his family status. He also would write in a 1927 essay that "we bought a White Streak Buick and drove quite a lot."

At the end of the summer, after a ten-day stay with Beatrice's family in Massachusetts, Patton returned to West Point, where he reveled in his position as cadet sergeant major, solidifying his beliefs and disciplining his own personal conduct. In his notebook he wrote, "Never, never, never stop being ambitious . . . you have but one life, live it to the full glory . . . nothing is too small to do to win." Later he added, "Never stop until you have gained the top or the grave."

The year passed fairly uneventfully for Patton, with much of his journal writings focused on concern about what rank he would attain for his First Class and final year. With his mid-level academic ranking, the cadet captain positions were not available to him, but promotion to lieutenant and adjutant of the cadet battalion remained within his reach.

While Patton continued to write in his notebook and in letters to his parents and to Beatrice about his ambitions, he included little information on what influences he experienced from his fellow cadets, Tac officers, and academic instructors. These men, as individuals and as a group, must have contributed to the ideas and psychic of the future general; however, he wrote only of his own thoughts and analysis.

One characteristic that Patton's writings—journal and letters— exposed was his prejudice toward minorities that were typical of White Americans, military and civilian, of the time. These were prejudices against Blacks and Jews that he would obliviously but firmly hold for the rest of his life. In a letter to Beatrice on February 22, 1908, he described a horsemanship exercise in jumping obstacles: "Four of us succeeded in clearing four feet eight and could have gone higher but they made us stop. Each man had a nigger soldier to hold his horse. My nigger was named Lee, he was the blackest thing you can imagine but a very good orderly."

At year's end, Patton happily learned that he had been successful in his pursuit of the adjutant position. After home leave, he returned to the Academy to take center stage before the Cadet Corps as he read daily orders and formed the battalion for his cadet captain. He wrote Beatrice about changing uniforms as many as fifteen times a day to always appear sharp and clean. Along with his Corps duties and academic challenges, Patton practiced on the rifle range to improve his marksmanship and competed in fencing to sharpen his skills. He also joined the cadet polo team, discovering firsthand how this sport could give him an automatic entry into the elite world of senior officers and high-ranking civilians. Despite suffering a small bone fracture in his left arm that put him on the sidelines for five weeks and prevented his making the team, Patton learned the value of polo.

As he had worried about his senior year's rank during his junior year, Patton now, in his senior final year, strategized about his branch selection after graduation. To Beatrice on October 2, 1908, he wrote about the difficulty in deciding whether to choose the infantry or the cavalry. He wrote, "There are so many considerations each way I stay awake during many hours drifting first one way and then another. . . . There seems to be a nicer class of people in the cavalry than in the infantry but in time of war the infantry is best and promotion faster." Ultimately, Patton sided with the cavalry.

Patton courted Beatrice primarily by letters during his days at VMI and West Point, but he visited her at the opulent Ayers family home in Massachusetts during summer and Christmas breaks. Beatrice, in turn, occasionally joined him at West Point for dances and other social events.

Despite having limited free time, given his cadet duties and Beatrice commitments, Patton did find opportunities to date several other women. The only one who made a significant impression was a wealthy Vassar coed identified in his writings only as "Kate." He wrote that, despite her "$40,000,000" family assets, he would stay with Beatrice, not mentioning the fact that Beatrice would come into her own fortune.

As it turned out, "Kate" was Kate Fowler, daughter of Eldridge M. Fowler, owner of iron and timber assets in Minnesota and a senior officer of the International Harvester Company. Because those with like backgrounds tend to gravitate to each other, it is not surprising that Beatrice and Kate Fowler later met and became lifelong friends. Even though Kate would marry Van S. Merle-Smith—a New York lawyer, banker, and

National Guard officer—Patton would resume his correspondence with Kate while serving on the Mexican border and remained in contact with her for the rest of his life. Near the end of World War II, Kate's son, Van Merle-Smith Jr., would serve as Patton's aide.

In the meantime, Patton contemplated his marital future, which he detailed in an essay about his father in 1927, writing, "The winter before I graduated Papa was at West Point and I had a long talk with him in the library. I said that I was in love with Beatrice but was afraid to propose. Papa encouraged me to do so, I did, only to be accepted."

Patton rarely made decisions that he was not sure would have a positive effect on his future military career. He had reservations about just how a wealthy socialite would adapt to being "a good army wife" when confronted with austere postings and long separations. For once, Patton acted from his heart rather than his head and wrote Beatrice's father declaring his intention and asking permission to marry his daughter.

Mr. Ayer approved of Patton but not the idea of his daughter marrying a professional soldier. He tried to entice Patton to join him in business after completing his military obligation. With Ayer in his eighties and an assured short pathway to the top of the business in sight, there may have been some temptation for Patton to become a part of the Ayer family enterprises. Yet Patton remained true to himself and his desire to be a soldier, noting his convictions in a letter to his parents on January 17, 1909: "I am different from other men my age. All they want to do is live happily and die old. I would be willing to live in torture, die tomorrow if for one day I could be really great."

From his youth, Patton believed that his destiny lay in the uniform of an officer in the U.S. Army. His greatest fear when he was younger was that he would get "the call" to become a minister of the faith like his father's first cousin, Robert Patton. According to the book *The Button Box*, written by Patton's daughter Ruth Ellen, Robert had been the "worst" boy at the University of Virginia before receiving "the call" while kneeling beside his bed to say his prayers. Robert, according to the story, claimed that Jesus touched him on the shoulder and said, "'Robbie Patton I want you to come and work for Me.'"

When asked how he knew it was Jesus, Robert is said to have replied, "When Jesus speaks to you, you just know who it is." Robert switched from law school to the seminary and became a minister of the Gospel, spending the remainder of his days in service to God.

According to Ruth Ellen, "Georgie had been brought up with this story, and every night when he was a little boy, saying his prayers on his knees, he would pray that Jesus would not call him because he wanted to be a soldier." Jesus did not call, and Patton continued down the path to his destiny.

CHAPTER THREE

Lieutenant Patton

Cadet George S. Patton Jr. became Second Lieutenant George S. Patton Jr. on his graduation and commissioning at West Point on June 11, 1909. He ranked number 43 out of the 103 graduates. On May 16, he had written his father, "It is the end of a long and not unhappy period. A period which has seen great changes in me. In fact all that is left of the boy who entered here . . . are the aspirations."

Looking back on that occasion in 1927, Patton wrote, "The day after graduation Papa, Mama, and I went to Tiffany and they bought me a watch. It has a stop watch repeater priced at $600.00 but we got it for $350.00 [more than $10,000 in current value] because it was thicker than the then style. I carried it in Mexico and France."

After spending the summer in California, Lieutenant Patton reported to the Fifteenth Cavalry Regiment, which was located at Fort Sheridan, just north of Chicago, while other parts of the regiment were stationed at Fort Leavenworth, Kansas, and Fort Myer, Virginia. Although he had been in uniform for six years as a cadet at VMI and West Point, this was his first extended experience with the regular army. Excited and motivated to have finally become an officer, Patton, writing his early letters from Fort Sheridan, nevertheless noted the austerity of his social and political prospects. On September 20, 1909, he wrote to his father about his fellow officers and their wives, saying, "Most of the people here are nice, not very nice, but nice." His definition of "nice people" was "ladies and gentlemen." He added, "There is also a bunch here that are not even decent," explaining they were part of the "sin of 1898" that allowed militia officers to enter the regular army after the Spanish-American War. Patton also noted that he found the ordinary enlisted men poorly educated, who had difficulty properly expressing themselves.

Patton rarely wrote about being impressed by or having any great admiration for his senior officers. The exception was his Fort Sheridan troop commander, Captain Francis C. Marshall, a veteran of the Sioux Indian Campaign of 1890 to 1891 and the China Relief Expedition of 1900 to 1901. Marshall had also taught military tactics during four of the five years Patton was a cadet at West Point. In the same letter of September 20 to his father, Patton declared, "I am certainly glad that I got into Capt. Marshall's troop as he teaches me things that the other two [new lieutenants] never hear about from their troop commanders."

Routine duties soon bored Patton, but he filled his extra time studying military history, practicing his rifle and pistol marksmanship, playing polo, and attending the many social events sponsored by local officials. He corresponded with Beatrice as they discussed marriage. Patton also continued writing to Mr. Ayer, who had not yet given his blessing to the nuptials.

On Patton's graduation from West Point, his father had provided him with information about his family's financial situation, which had somewhat surprised him by its tally. Now, in the winter of 1910, Patton sent the family financial statement to Ayer. On March 7, Ayer wrote, "My dear George, I thank you for your letter and [financial] statement." He added that he had not known that Patton had "such a nice nest egg." Without ever admitting that the statement influenced his decision, Ayer gave his approval for the marriage. Included in the letter giving his blessing, Ayer added, "It has been my custom when my children have married and left our home to give them a monthly income and shall do the same to Beatrice." He concluded, "I admire your firmness of purpose in sticking to the army until more strongly tempted by another occupation and with every good wish for your early and steady advancement."

In his last letter to Beatrice on May 22 before their wedding, George wrote, "Darling, since I wrote my first letter to you almost eight years ago, I have grown older and wiser and thus been enabled to better understand and more clearly see your infinite perfection. So that in a way I may be said to love you more now than then. . . . May our love never be less than now and our ambition as fortunate and as great as our love."

On May 26, 1910, at Avalon on the Massachusetts North Shore, George and Beatrice became husband and wife in a wedding that had all the grandeur the Ayers family wealth could lavish and all the traditional touches, including fresh orange blossoms brought from California, that the Pattons required. The newly married couple spent their wedding night in Boston and then traveled to New York, where they boarded the luxury liner SS *Deutschland* to cruise to England for their honeymoon. With five weeks' leave, Patton was not due back at Fort Sheridan until June 29.

Patton intended to keep a diary of their tour of England but made little more than brief mention of the sights they visited. Always singular of mind, though, he did make note of the purchase of a book on military theory.

George and Beatrice arrived at Fort Sheridan on June 29 as scheduled and moved into Quarters 92A. With its few small rooms, the housing was far from what Beatrice had become accustomed to, and she found that she had little or nothing in common with the wives of her husband's fellow officers. Thus, when George departed for maneuvers in Wisconsin, Beatrice returned to Massachusetts to stay with her parents during his absence. When they reunited in September, Beatrice announced she was pregnant.

Beatrice Smith Patton, later renamed Beatrice Ayer Patton, joined the family on March 11, 1911. According to letters later written by a family member, George observed the birth of his daughter and became so distraught that he hurried from the birth room to throw up in the kitchen sink. All that military training had not prepared the young soldier for certain aspects of his future.

The Pattons did not live like their military counterparts, nor did they appear to apologize for being different because of their ample additional funds from their families along with his junior officer salary. They hired a full-time nurse for their new daughter, for example, and George purchased a horse. He then bought a new automobile after reviewing publications and attending a car show in Chicago, his interest in vehicles powered by internal combustion engines increasing as time went on. Later he wrote his Aunt Nannie, "We traded our auto for a bigger one that holds four or five people. It is a very handsome machine indeed and easy to look after too."

Although he still had difficulties with spelling and punctuation because of his dyslexia, Patton learned to type and began translating French military articles, as well as writing original documents in English. In an article titled "National Defense!" he wrote, "Attack push forward, attack again until the end"—an axiom he would follow for the rest of his life.

Because he found most of his official duties tedious, Patton wanted a posting where he could continue to learn his craft and, more important, be in a position to meet influential military and civilian leaders. But where? He considered the Philippines, but the insurrection there was over and, therefore, reassignment to the islands offered no more challenges and excitement than he found in Fort Sheridan. The one current trouble spot that piqued his interest was the Mexican border, where tension between the two countries was intensifying. While he was intrigued enough to predict that the United States would soon become involved, Patton did not appear to intuit the impact that situation would have on his destiny. In a letter to his father on April 12, 1911, he assessed his less-than-inspiring options of either being reassigned to West Point or serving as a liaison—perhaps to the French Cavalry School at Saumur— writing, "There seems to me to be but two jobs open to me. Namely a Tac at West Point or an Attaché somewhere."

Patton was restless and without direction but leaving no stone unturned. On July 2, he wrote Beatrice, who was visiting back at Pride's Crossing to avoid the Illinois heat, about his future assignment. He mentioned knowing Major General Fred Ainsworth, the adjutant general of the U.S. Army, who might help him get a proper assignment and suggested that her father might "work the Mass. people for me and that Papa would try to fix it in California." In a September 18 letter to his Aunt Nannie, he reported that Kay Ayer, his sister-in-law, had an officer friend "doing all he can in Washington and he is quite influential."

Whose influence triumphed in delivering the prized transfer remains unknown, but the Pattons reported to Fort Myer across the Potomac River from Washington, D.C., on December 3. Assigned to A Troop of the Fifteenth Cavalry Regiment, George welcomed the opportunities to meet important people as he served as an escort to dignitaries visiting the capital. He, as an Academy graduate, became a member of the Army-Navy Club, which offered even more chances to intermingle with those in power.

Beatrice was extremely happy to return to "civilization." Quarters at Fort Myer, even for junior officers, were spacious. Her monthly stipend from her father allowed the Pattons to employ a full-time maid and chauffeur.

Soon after he arrived in Virginia, Patton—by either luck or design—met Secretary of War Henry L. Simson while the two were out on an early morning ride on their horses. Simpson admired Patton's élan and horsemanship, and the two developed a professional and personal friendship that resulted in the secretary having the lieutenant serve as his aide at several Fort Myer social events.

Patton remained in A Troop for only three months before transferring to squadron quartermaster, a reassignment more likely based on Patton's additional exposure to the members of the Fort Myer polo team and his competing in steeplechase races than on his administrative abilities. While the new position presented still more opportunities for him to meet the influential, Patton quickly recognized that the horses he had brought from Fort Sheridan were inferior to those of the riders in Virginia. Without hesitation, he searched nearby horse farms as well as those in Kentucky until he had a stable of seven polo and steeplechase ponies.

Early in 1912 came the announcement that the Fifth Olympiad, to be held in Stockholm, Sweden, would include the Modern Pentathlon, an event focusing on military skills and requiring all-round athletes to engage in swimming, running, shooting, fencing, and riding. Army leaders initiated a search for a likely competitor, and, with several West Point officers familiar with Patton's demonstrated athletic abilities and the new cadre recognizing his active-duty skills, the service selected Patton for the competition.

Patton immediately began a comprehensive training program that ended only when he sailed for Sweden on June 14, accompanied by Beatrice, his parents, and his sister Nita. Of the forty-two entrants in the Pentathlon, Patton finished in fifth place. He might have finished with a medal had it not been for two shots in the pistol competition that did not score on his target even though the others were tightly targeted. Legend now explains that the scored shots were so precise that the missing rounds had gone through holes from those previous bullets—at least, that was the story spread by his family and conceivably by Patton himself.

Despite not earning a medal, the Games were pivotal for the future general because they were when Patton received his first national and international media recognition. The August 7 edition of the *Los Angeles Times* reported, "Young Patton has carried off honors in fencing, shooting, riding, and swimming and according to the reports that are coming out of Stockholm his athletic versatility is attracting considerable attention." Patton found he enjoyed the acclaim, and he likely would have received even more attention if not for accolades heaped on fellow American Olympian Jim Thorpe, who won gold medals in the Modern Decathlon, the civilian track-and-field equivalent of the Pentathlon.

After the games concluded, the Pattons toured the major cities of Germany before going to Saumur, France, where George observed and participated in fencing instruction at the French Cavalry School. Then, shortly after his return to Fort Myer, Patton topped off his trip with a dinner with Army Chief of Staff Major General Leonard Wood and Secretary of War Henry Stimson on August 23. During the meal, Second Lieutenant George Patton briefed the army's two highest-ranking military and civilian officials on the Olympics and his visit to Saumur.

Throughout the following fall, Patton played polo, competed in steeplechases, and participated in fox hunts. In letters to his family, he frequently mentioned the problems along the Mexican border but wrote that he did not think the United States would become involved any time soon. The Metropolitan Club of Washington, where "all the big men were," according to his writings, admitted Patton into its membership on November 6.

On December 14, Patton transferred to General Wood's office as an aide to the Chief of Staff and Secretary Stimson. His primary duties were researching, writing staff studies, and preparing correspondence for Wood. More important, he exercised some control over who gained entrance to the general's office and strengthened his relationships throughout senior officers. On March 5, 1913, Patton rode alongside Wood down Pennsylvania Avenue in the inauguration parade of President Woodrow Wilson. Patton was in his element.

While he continued to write articles for military journals, Patton also authored papers for the army staff on his ideas for a new design for the cavalry sword, one that promoted thrusting rather than slashing. His concept met with approval from Wood, who, on February 24, ordered the Ordnance Department to produce twenty thousand sabers according to Patton's precise specifications. The lieutenant was then dispatched to the armory in Springfield, Massachusetts, to oversee the manufacture of what was officially the U.S. Saber, M-1913—but more commonly to be known as the "Patton sword."

Patton returned to the Fifteenth Cavalry Regiment at Fort Myer on March 22, 1913, with a letter from General Wood stating, "I wish to express my appreciation of the satisfactory manner in when you have discharged the duties assigned to you." Although not lengthy or overly laudatory, such a missive from the army's top general to a lowly second lieutenant was highly unusual.

On his request, on June 25, Patton received orders instructing him to "proceed to France for the purpose of perfecting yourself in swordsmanship. You should adjust your time as to be able to arrive at Fort Riley, Kansas by October 1." The orders continued, "[I]t is understood that in conformity with your suggestion no expense to the Government will be incurred on your visit abroad."

The Pattons could afford not only to pay their own way but also to travel in style. For the six-week trip, they took along their own automobile at an expense equivalent to two months of George's military salary. On their arrival at the Port of Cherbourg, the Pattons drove through the hedgerow country of Normandy to Saumur—much of the same territory he would traverse some three decades later with his Third Army.

In addition to learning swordsmanship at Saumur, Patton paid close attention to the school's teaching methods, beginning to conceptualize his own curriculum for taking his knowledge back to the United States.

During George's off time, the couple used their automobile to tour the battlefields of Europe that Caesar and Attila had once conquered. Daughter Ruth Ellen later wrote that her father reported that he claimed to have fought in those very fields in a previous life and that his intention was to study the terrain "for the next time around." She concluded, "He said that the battles had been lost and won in these fields and hills through knowledge of the country; that history had already picked the battlefields, and that history was the greatest teacher."

In late August, the Pattons began their journey home via Paris, where George ordered fifty swords, masks, and vests to be sent to Fort Riley. Before their departure, he also resumed his contact and relationship with General Wood by sending him a fine saddle.

The Pattons arrived in New York on September 17 and immediately went to Fort Myer, where they supervised the packing of their household goods for transfer to Fort Riley. Beatrice then relaxed in Massachusetts while George journeyed to Kansas to report to the Mounted Service School, where he became first a student and then an instructor. In his letters about what he found at Fort Riley, George described the post as remote, austere, and dirty. Perhaps most telling was his relaying the message found on a sign on the drill field: "By order of the Commanding Officer. Officers will not shoot buffalo on the parade ground from the windows of their quarters." But, as always, Patton's real concern was what this posting would do for his career, and, despite the rugged conditions, he concluded that Fort Riley was "the place to be" for a cavalry officer.

In a letter to his father on October 16, 1913, Patton said, "This is the most strict army place I have ever been in and also the most strictly business. We start at eight o'clock and get through at three thirty which is more work than I have done in the army."

On March 23, 1914, the army authorized the printing of Patton's *Saber Exercise 1914 Training Manual*. He also received the title of "Master of the Sword," the first officer in the U.S. Army to be so designated. On May 8, he graduated from the First Year Course of the Mounted

Service School and was selected to attend the Second Year Course, continuing as Master of the Sword. In June, the American Olympic Committee selected Patton to again be a member of the U.S. team in the pending Sixth Olympiad—games that were soon canceled because of the First World War.

Patton closely followed the increased hostilities in Europe, and on August 3, the same day France and Germany declared war against each other, he wrote General Leonard Wood, stating, "I would like to get a year's leave on some pretext and go to France and take part in this war."

Three days later, Wood responded, "Don't think of attempting anything of the kind, at present. We don't want to waste youngsters of your sort. . . . Stick to the present job . . . I know how you feel, but there is nothing to be done. I also am required to look on with patience, but I hope to get over there some later time."

In a letter to his father on November 12, Patton expressed his frustration: "I certainly am aging . . . I fixed twenty-seven as the age when I should be a brigadier and now I am twenty-nine and not a first lieutenant."

Despite his angst, Patton continued to perform well as a student and as a teacher. In his year-end officer's efficiency report, however, Major Charles D. Rhodes not only evaluated the young soldier's overall performance, swordsmanship, and horsemanship as "excellent" but also recorded accurate insights into his development status. Rhodes wrote, "Lieutenant Patton, though lacking experience with troops, is a most promising young officer of high ideas, devotion to duty, and marked industry. He is somewhat impulsive and intolerant of the opinion of others and needs a period of service duty with troops to counter-balance his protracted duty away from troops and to round out his efficiency as an all around officer."

The new year brought major changes for the young Patton family. On February 28, 1915, Beatrice gave birth to their second daughter, whom they named Ruth Ellen. About that time Patton learned that the Fifteenth would soon rotate to the Philippines to replace the Eighth Cavalry Regiment, which was bound for Fort Bliss, Texas. Remaining strong in his conviction that the islands would be a boring, backwater assignment, he began efforts to find another posting despite being injured when his horse stepped into a hole, fell, and rolled over on him, causing a head laceration.

Even while convalescing, and certainly after he returned to his regular duties, Patton increased his reading of military history while closely following the war news from Europe and the increased disturbances along the Mexican border. In letters to his father, he criticized President Wilson for not declaring war on Germany. On May 16, he wrote, "If Wilson had as much blood in him as the liver of a louse is commonly thought to contain he would do this." He concluded, "There is but one International Law—the best army."

Although a student and instructor at the Mounted Service School, Patton remained assigned to the Fifteenth Cavalry Regiment. On June 1, the Mounted Service School Press published Patton's *Diary of the Instructor in Swordsmanship.*

After graduation on June 17, Patton delivered his family to Pride's Crossing before going to Washington to seek a transfer out of the Fifteenth Cavalry. In a letter to Beatrice dated July 1, he described his reactions to the city and re-avowed his intentions of making the most of his opportunities, writing, "I certainly like Washington. Even its whiskey smell at the theater charms me and I was gratified that the nigger door keeper at the Club knew me. No one else did. Someday I will make them all know me."

Despite his assessment that he was an unknown, Patton obviously found friends in the right places, for he secured orders to be transferred out of the Fifteenth Regiment and its move to the Philippines, though he never recorded in his letters or notebooks just how he managed this task. Whatever his means, at the end of July, he received his assignment to join the Eighth Cavalry Regiment at Fort Bliss, where now Lieutenant Patton would develop and hone the abilities and characteristics of the future General Patton.

CHAPTER FOUR

Fort Bliss

Despite his impatience with what he considered his lack of progress during his initial six years in the army, George S. Patton Jr. had actually accrued an impressive list of accomplishments by the time he reported to Fort Bliss, Texas, in the fall of 1915. His efficiency reports were all "excellent," he had completed the two-year Mounted Service School, redesigned the army's saber, written a manual and book on the use of that weapon, and become the army's only Master of the Sword. More important, he had developed close relationships with military and civilian leaders—individuals most second lieutenants would be fortunate to see across a parade field, not to mention become friends with and personal confidants for.

Patton had few duties after arriving at Fort Bliss, as the Eighth Cavalry did not arrive from the Philippines for several weeks. He spent his time studying for his pending promotion board and organizing the post polo team. In a letter to Beatrice on September 23, 1915, he wrote, "Things here are quiet and un war like."

Things might have been "un war like" when Patton arrived on the Texas–Mexico border, but that was not its normal state. After Mexico achieved its independence from Spain in 1821, the country went through various internal rebellions while losing Texas to a revolution in 1836 and much of what is now the Southwest of the United States in the Mexican-American War of 1845–1846. Then the Mexicans had to repel an invasion by the French in the 1860s.

When dictator Porfirio Díaz seized control of the country in 1876, he was able to rule with only brief disruptions until 1910. In order to stimulate economic development—and to build his personal fortune—Díaz initiated incentives and enacted laws that allowed foreign companies as well as individuals to assume control of large sectors of the Mexican economy. By early in the twentieth century, foreign investors controlled much of Mexico's farmland while the native peasants owned none. U.S. companies controlled 97 percent of mining interests and 90 percent of the emerging oil industry.

In 1908, Díaz announced he would not seek reelection in 1910, but he changed his mind when it appeared Francisco I. Madero, a political moderate, might win control. Díaz arrested Madero, who then escaped to Texas and issued his Plan de San Luis Potosí from San Antonio, a proposal that called for a national uprising against the Díaz government. A people's revolt, led by Pancho Villa and Pascual Orozco, rose to successfully oust Díaz and make Madero the new president of Mexico in 1911.

Conflicts erupted across the country even after Madero took charge and continued throughout the next decade, with most of the outbreaks occurring near or along the border with the United States. The border at this time was little more than "a line in the sand" established by the Treaty of Guadalupe Hidalgo of 1848, with only the splotchy Rio Grande River and no official fence or wall separating the two countries. Local citizens on both sides, along with bandits and cattle rustlers, moved back and forth across the border with little notice.

Military presence on the American side was minimal at the time, with most of the soldiers defending a chain of isolated forts that had been established in Texas to lay claim to the land and to protect pioneers heading west from San Antonio to El Paso en route to California. Not until 1911, when the Díaz–Madero forces began skirmishing and fighting along the border, did President Wilson deploy what was called "the Maneuver Division" to safeguard American interests along the Rio Grande. The troops remained in the area only a few months before being withdrawn once Madero stabilized his government.

Peace was not to last, however. General Victoriano Huerta assassinated Madero in a coup in 1913 and assumed the office of president.

His Federalist regime was immediately challenged by rebel forces led by Venustiano Carranza, known as Constitutionalists. Among Carranza's supporters was the same Pancho Villa—former supporter and now opponent of Madero—who would be riding his way into legend with the largest army in Mexico, the Division del Norte, of thirty thousand to fifty thousand men.

President Woodrow Wilson attempted to placate both sides of warring Mexicans in order to keep the United States out of their conflict. However, he was forced to act in the spring of 1914 when a small party of sailors from the USS *Dolphin* went ashore on April 9 in Tampico on Mexico's east coast to secure supplies. Mexican officials detained the sailors on the pretext that they had entered a restricted area. When U.S. State Department officials complained, the Mexicans released the sailors and apologized. American naval officers deemed the apology insufficient and demanded a twenty-one-gun salute be made to the U.S. flag.

When the Mexicans refused the salute, the U.S. Navy stood off Tampico awaiting further instructions from the United States. President Wilson elected to take no action until he learned that a German freighter delivering arms and ammunition to the Huerta government was inbound for Veracruz, located 280 miles south of Tampico. The president ordered the marines aboard the *Dolphin* to occupy the Veracruz Custom House to prevent the landing of the shipment. The force went ashore on April 21 and, with little resistance, occupied the town for the next seven months.

All the various factions in Mexico were suddenly united in their outrage at the U.S. occupation of Veracruz. Carranza used the situation to overthrow Huerta, assuming the presidency on July 15. The Carranza government drafted the Plan of San Diego, which called for a race war against the United States to secure the return of all territories previously claimed by Mexico. That set off a series of Mexican raids across the border into Texas, New Mexico, and Arizona. The attacks stopped only when Wilson recognized Carranza as the lawful Mexican president on the condition that he would punish the raiders and those supporting the plan.

CHAPTER FIVE

Sierra Blanca

When George Patton arrived at Fort Bliss in September 1915, he joined the command of Brigadier General John J. "Black Jack" Pershing, who had been transferred from the Presidio in San Francisco on April 14 to Texas to command the five thousand soldiers guarding the border from Arizona to the Sierra Blanca Mountains that lay ninety miles southeast of El Paso.

The posting of these two men in the same unit at this point in time was providential, both because Pershing—a veteran of the Indian Wars, the Spanish-American War, and the Philippine Insurrection—would become Patton's most influential mentor and role model and because the frontline experiences Patton was exposed to under Pershing would mold the visions and strategies of the man who would lead one of America's greatest armies and win one of America's greatest victories.

In many ways, to understand Patton, one also has to understand the man who did the most to shape him into the great soldier he always believed himself destined to be. Despite the twenty-five-year difference in their ages, the two soldiers had much in common, both being graduates of West Point, both having finished in the middle third of his class, and both having attained high rank in the Corps of Cadets (Pershing having attained its highest rank of first captain).

Like Patton, Pershing had married well when in 1905 he joined the family of Helen Francis Warren, the daughter of Wyoming Republican senator and Civil War Medal of Honor recipient Francis E. Warren, who at various times chaired the Senate Military Affairs and Appropriations Committees.

Other characteristics the two men had in common were that both Pershing and Patton were highly energetic and dedicated to their craft. Pershing had the combat experience that Patton envied. The younger officer also admired the elder's no-nonsense style of discipline, his impeccable manner of dress, and his angry fixed stare that intimidated subordinates and peers alike. During Pershing's tour as a tactical officer at West Point in 1897, he had been so strict and rigid that the cadets referred to him harshly as "Nigger Jack" because of his former service with the Black Tenth Cavalry Regiment. Although the cadets eventually softened the name to "Black Jack"—a moniker that identified him for the remainder of his life—it did not dampen their hostility toward him.

In addition, Pershing, like Patton, understood the value of networking, receiving support not only from his father-in-law but also from other high-ranking government officials. In 1903, when a fellow Spanish-American War veteran, President Theodore Roosevelt, sought to revamp the officer promotion system to advance officers in rank by merit rather than seniority, he encountered so much opposition from the army as well as Congress that he took no further action until 1905. This time he was successful, and he advanced three captains and one major to the rank of brigadier general. Pershing, as one of the captains, skipped three ranks and jumped over 835 officers who outranked him.

Pershing's meteoric rise in rank had made him instantly unpopular, but by the time he reached Fort Bliss in 1914, he had earned the respect of peers and superiors alike for his leadership and organizational abilities. El Paso civilians and those in towns and villages along the border also quickly took a liking to Pershing for his military bearing and the fact that he was their protector from bandits and revolutionist raids.

Pershing appeared to have risen above his critics and have his career on track when tragedy struck in his personal life. His wife and their four children had remained in California while he settled into his new command. A few days before they were to depart for Texas, a fire, intensified by a flammable varnish Pershing himself had applied to the floors, swept through the house on August 27, 1915. Helen and three of the four children died of asphyxiation. Only six-year-old Warren survived.

Pershing immediately set off by rail to California, where Frank Helm, a civilian friend, met him in Bakersfield to escort him the remaining distance. As a professional soldier, Pershing was accustomed to casualties on the battlefield, including close associates, but nothing could have prepared him for the deaths of his wife and children. Helm later recalled that the usually stoic general screamed and cried, saying, "I can understand the loss of one member of the family, but not nearly all." After a brief service at the Clark and Booth Funeral Home on Geary Street in San Francisco, Pershing escorted the caskets containing his wife and children to her native Wyoming, where they were buried in the family plot in Cheyenne.

Patton had little interaction with the grieving general during the first months after his arrival at Fort Bliss. Assigned to Troop D of the Eighth Cavalry Regiment, Patton assisted in the unit's arrival from the Philippines and supervised the grooming and feeding of their mounts. In a letter to Beatrice, who was still in Massachusetts, he wrote on October 8 that his troop would soon be replacing the Thirteenth Regiment at Sierra Blanca to provide security along the border. Two days later, he again wrote Beatrice, telling her about preparation for the mission: "I went downtown and got a fine lantern and a coffee pot and an alcohol lamp yesterday. The lantern is the best I have seen and gives a good clear light. It also packs in a tin box so will be easy to put in the bedding roll." The lantern would play a later role in Patton's time in Mexico by adding to his tendency toward accidents.

A and D Troops departed by horseback for Sierra Blanca, a small settlement ninety miles southeast of Fort Bliss, on October 13. They reached Finley, described by Patton as "one house and a station in the middle of a desert," by nightfall and arrived in Sierra Blanca the next day. On October 20 he reported, "This is the funniest place I have ever been. It is supposed to be very tough and at least half the men wear boots and spurs and carry guns. I met a Mr. Dave Allison yesterday. He is a very quiet looking old man with a sweet face and white hair. He is the most noted gun man here in Texas and just at present is marshal. He alone killed all the Orozco outfit [Pascual Orozco, a Mexican revolutionary turned bandit] about a month ago. He shot Orozco and his four men each in the head at sixty yards. He seemed much taken with me and is going hunting with me."

Patton was not exaggerating Allison's accomplishments. Born in Ohio in 1861, he arrived in Texas at age twenty-seven and became the youngest sheriff in the state when he was elected to that position in Midland in 1888. He later moved west and became an Arizona Ranger and the chief of police in Roswell, New Mexico, before returning to Texas to become a Ranger. The young Patton made an impression on the old gunfighter, and Allison spent many hours telling him about his experiences.

Patton wrote of Allison and Sierra Blanca, "I would not miss this for the world. I guess there are few places like it left."

Duty at Sierra Blanca was not all visiting with Allison or hunting in the adjacent hills. Patton made inspection trips to outposts spread across the countryside, riding as much as one hundred miles in three days. In an October 26 letter to Beatrice, he wrote, "It is the most desolate country you ever saw. Rocks and these thorny bushes. We slept on the ground taking off only our boots. It was quite cold but we were comfortable."

Patton concluded the letter saying, "I made the darndest shot with a pistol you ever saw. I hit a jack rabbit at about fifteen yards while riding at a trot. My reputation as a gunman is made."

On October 29, Patton took a detachment to Hot Wells to guard the rail line that was to carry forces of President Carranza of Mexico west to confront the army of his former comrade, and now opponent, Pancho Villa—a most unusual accommodation to a foreign army that President Wilson had authorized on October 15 after recognizing the Carranza government.

Founded in 1912 as a resort and railroad community twenty-four miles southeast of Sierra Blanca, Hot Wells was little more than a ramshackle hotel and the mineral springs from which it got its name. The Mexican army, which Patton described as a "circus," "a sideshow," and "hungry," passed safely though the area.

Patton himself described his Hot Wells adventure in an essay titled "Earning My Pay" that was included in his posthumously published book *War as I Knew It*:

> *During the border troubles in 1916, I was on duty in charge of a patrol of twenty men at Hot Wells, Texas. My mission was to protect from attacks by the Villistas some forty miles of Southern Pacific Railroad, over which the Carranzista trains were operating. Hot Wells was the center of my sector. I sent a sergeant with half my command to the west and took the remainder to the east, having previously telephoned the Commanding Officer of the 13th Cavalry that I would take over to include a certain bridge. As we approached the bridge in the dark, the point came back and reported to me that he heard voices on the bridge speaking Spanish. I therefore presumed that the Villistas were mining the bridge. It has always been my belief that a surprise attack is correct. I therefore formed my group in line and gave the command, "Raise pistols, Charge!" Just as we got under the very shadow of the bridge, we ran into a wire fence and had to stop. At the same time a number of rifles stuck over the top of the bridge. I challenged with much profanity, demanding who was there, and was greatly relieved when a voice replied, "Patrol, 13th Cavalry." They had missed the bridge where they were supposed to stop and were in my bailiwick. This instance convinced me of the value of adhering to a plan.*

Patton met several men who impressed him while he was in Hot Wells. One was a long-haired Texan with whom he had a shooting contest. Another was "very dark." Patton quoted this man as saying, "Damn it a fellow took me for a Mex and I had to shoot him three times before he believed I was white." Patton demonstrated his insightfulness as well as his sense of humor, adding, "This impressed me very much and I assured him that he was the whitest man I ever had seen."

On November 13, Patton made a brief visit back to El Paso, where, he described in a letter to Beatrice, he had spent most of the day in a gun store and purchased "a new rifle and knife and two carved leather holsters."

While he did not name the business in his letter, most likely these purchases were made at the city's Shelton Payne Arms Company. And, most likely, this is the time he ordered his infamous 4¾ inch, .45 caliber Long Colt Single Action 1873 Army Model revolver, Serial Number 332088, from the Colt factory in Hartford, Connecticut.

Patton bought the revolver for a couple of reasons. First, he did not like the army-issued M-1911 .45 automatic pistol—one of the safest handguns ever built, complete with multiple safeties—because he had earlier managed to accidentally fire a round that grazed his leg. And, more objectively, he believed that the spring-loaded magazine was subject to jamming. It is also reasonable to assume that Patton had been so impressed with the revolvers carried by the lawmen and others in Sierra Blanca that he wanted to emulate these memorable characters.

Whatever the reason or the exact date, the .45 arrived in El Paso with sufficient time for the initials *GSP* to be intertwined with the raised American eagle on the smooth, white ivory grip before Patton departed on the Punitive Expedition into Mexico. He would carry this revolver for the remainder of his life.

Patton hoped to engage Mexican bandits along the border, but despite much patrolling on long rides, he failed to make any contact. The nearest he came was late in the month. In a letter to his father on November 24, he wrote from Sierra Blanca:

> *About six o'clock I got a wire from El Paso from some D[amn] F[ool] that 200 Mexicans were going to raid this place. I don't believe it at all but have had the men put their guns beside their beds and told them where to form in case of alarm.*
>
> *I wish they would come. I have about a hundred men or more and could give them a nice welcome. Well, if this is the eve of battle it is not at all interesting nor as exciting as a polo game.*

Later that night Patton received a telegram from Pershing informing him that noted bandit Chico Cano would raid Sierra Blanca with about eighty men. Mexican Federal troops had also crossed the Rio Grande into Texas fleeing from Villa's army. Patton, in command because of the absence of more senior officers who had gone to El Paso, prepared defenses and dispatched patrols.

On November 24, Patton wrote his father, "I . . . decided that to act with vigor meant to attack first and ask questions later. So, I decided that if possible I would make a saber charge on the [enemy] camp. I thought I had a Medal of Honor sewed up."

Patton's column departed south at 3:30 a.m. In his letter to his father, he wrote that under "a fine moon . . . we started and the men were in great spirits. They were tickled to death at the chance of a fight."

After four and a half hours and more than thirty miles in the saddle, Patton and his troop had found no threats. As he wrote to his father in his next letter, "There was nothing to meet." The presence of bandits or Federal troops was only rumors. Patton would have to wait for another day to find his glory.

And wait he did—even though that was not his choice. His end-of-year efficiency report noted that he was "an excellent field soldier," but Patton was restless again even after he welcomed Beatrice, along with her maid from Massachusetts, and the girls back to Fort Bliss before the end of the year.

He continued to monitor the progress of the war in Europe and to maintain his relationships with senior officers. On March 27, he wrote General Wood to remind him that he was still available for service on the Continent and to declare his opposition to the current study on the feasibility of converting cavalrymen into mounted infantrymen. Wood responded on March 3, concurring with Patton on ideas against transforming the cavalry, but on the subject of Europe and Patton's wish to go to France, he offered no help.

In early 1916, Patton's sister, Nita, arrived at Fort Bliss for a visit. Her niece, Ruth Ellen Patton, later described her aunt as looking exactly like her brother George, as she also stood six feet tall and had yellow hair and blue eyes. At a social function on the post, Nita met "Black Jack" Pershing, the fifty-five-year-old now-widower. The twenty-eight-year-old spinster and the general were immediately attracted to each other. Although their relationship was to be interrupted by the Punitive Expedition, it would eventually blossom into a full-blown love affair.

Meanwhile, Patton and his saber design had the attention of army officials at Fort Riley, who were studying changes to the sword. On March 8, Patton wrote his father, "I am very much excited and will probably have to go to Rock Island Arsenal to convince them what D[amned] F[ools] they are."

Pancho Villa, however, had other plans for the impatient soldier. He was about to raid Columbus, New Mexico, and set in motion the Punitive Expedition into Mexico, where Lieutenant George Patton would face his first combat and apply his developing warfare theories that would eventually elevate him to the rolls of all-time great military leaders.

CHAPTER SIX

Columbus

As part of a compromise with President Wilson, President Carranza agreed to rid his country of Villa and his army. The accord also permitted the legal import of American arms and ammunition into Mexico and the use of American railways to move Mexican troops, their safe passage ensured by the likes of Patton and his troops.

By the final months of 1915, Villa had suffered multiple defeats that reduced his once mighty army to fewer than one thousand men—many of whom were his elite guards known as Dorados. Villa blamed his losses on the U.S. support of the Carranza government, including American rail troop transport. Villa also blamed his defeat when he attacked Agua Prieta on large U.S. searchlights that illuminated the battlefield from across the border from Fort Douglas, Arizona.

Prior to the Wilson–Carranza agreement, Villa had generally been friendly to Americans, who looked on him as some kind of revolutionary hero. During his early years of command, he invited American and other reporters to accompany his "army" and regularly gave interviews to news correspondents. Villa himself occasionally crossed the border into El Paso, where he enjoyed eating ice cream at the Elite Confectionery. On one of his visits, he met and had his picture taken with General Pershing.

Born José Doroteo Arango Arámbula to sharecroppers in the Mexican state of Durango in 1878, Villa claimed to have worked as a farmer, mule skinner, butcher, bricklayer, and foreman for a U.S. railway company before killing a wealthy ranch owner for raping his sister. After serving only briefly as a conscript in the Federal army in 1903, he killed an officer, stole his horse, and took to the hills to become a bandit, changing his name to Pancho Villa after his paternal grandfather, Jesus Villa.

The charismatic Villa usually wore ammunition bandoliers cross his chest and a wide *sombrero*. He could be gentle on occasion but was murderous to his enemies and prisoners. Although nearly—if not completely—illiterate, he often carried a large fountain pen in his jacket pocket. Villa was also adept in handling public relations and recognizing the importance of the news media.

Villa instinctively understood the potential for personal fame and profit in the emerging motion picture industry. On January 3, 1914, he signed a contract with the California-based Mutual Film Company, founded by Harry E. Aitken, for $25,000—nearly $680,000 in today's purchasing power. Aitken was no novice filmmaker, having worked with both D. W. Griffith and Charlie Chaplin. The contract stipulated that Villa would allow no other film companies on his battlefields and that he would try to conduct his battles during daylight hours to accommodate the ease of filming. It even stipulated that Villa's soldiers would restage battles when no satisfactory footage had been secured in the actual encounter.

On January 7, 1914, the *New York Times* reported:

Pancho Villa, General in Command of the Constitutional Army in Northern Mexico will in future carry on his warfare against President Huerta as a full partner in a moving picture venture with Harry E. Aitken. The business of Gen. Villa will be to provide moving picture thrillers in any way that is consistent with his plan to depose and drive Huerta out of Mexico, and the business of Mr. Aitken, the other partner, will be to distribute the resulting films throughout the peaceable sections of Mexico and to the United States and Canada. To make sure that the business venture will be a success, Mr. Aitken dispatched to Gen. Villa's camp last Saturday a squad of four moving picture men with apparatus designed especially to take pictures on battlefields. Another squad of four men with machines of the latest design is being assembled in San Antonio, Texas, and they will go to the front tomorrow. It is the hope of Mr. Aitken to have moving pictures from the field of Villa's operations here by Saturday and to show them to motion picture audiences, following them up with a fresh supply every week until Huerta falls.

Despite the profit opportunities, Aitken had some self-doubts about partnering with a man many thought to be a murderous bandit. To the reporter who wrote the above story, Aitken said:

How on earth did the Times *hear about that? I did not want the story to get out yet. But it is true. I am the partner of Gen. Villa. And it has been worrying me a lot all day. How would you feel to be partner of a man engaged in killing people, and do you suspect that the fact moving picture machines are in the range to immortalize an act of daring or of cruel brutality with have any effect on the warfare itself? I have been thinking a lot of things since I made this contract.*

Regardless of his concerns, within a month of signing the contract with Villa, Aitken was advertising "Mutual Movies of the Mexican War Made by Executive Contract with Gen. Villa and the Rebel Army." The ads continued, "The public is clamoring for a sight of the pictures—which are more exciting and sensational than any other pictures of actual happenings that have ever been shown before."

Ultimately, the motion pictures (especially the documentaries made along the border) were more useful than just for the entertainment of a clamoring public and profits for Aitken. After the United States entered World War I, the films were used in recruiting efforts.

The day that Villa decided to attack Columbus, New Mexico—across the border and firmly on American soil—no correspondents or filmmakers accompanied him and his army. The attack on American soil ended his "Robin Hood" reputation north of the border and resulted in American news and movie correspondents no longer accompanying the Villistas. The attack in New Mexico also ended Villa's visits to El Paso for ice cream.

Months before Columbus, Villa's popularity had already waned with his brutal tactics and his lack of success in fighting against the Mexican

Federals. He continued to blame the Americans for assisting Carranza in his defeat and began raiding ranches and small villages across the border in the United States as well as assaulting American citizens living and working in Mexico. Some of this killing and looting was based purely on anger and revenge, but Villa had another motivation. He thought that if he could push the American army into pursuing him into Mexico, the people would revolt against the incursion and the standing government to help rebuild his army.

The deadliest incident of Villa's scheme occurred on January 10, 1916, near Santa Isabel, Chihuahua, when a detachment of Villa's soldiers stopped and then boarded a train. They lined up eighteen American engineers, all of whom carried safe conduct passes from the Carranza government and were on their way to reopen mines owned by the Cusihuiriachic Mining Company. Villa had all of them shot except one who was allowed to escape.

That's when Villa turned to the even bigger target of Columbus and the adjacent Camp Furlong in New Mexico, located about two and a half miles north of the border town of Palomas. Although he never explained the exact purpose of this offensive, there were likely three reasons behind his decision. First, Villa believed (correctly) that an invasion of U.S. soil, the first since the British invaded during the War of 1812, would force the Americans to pursue him into Mexico and reinvigorate the revolution. Second, the businesses of Columbus would provide much-needed ammunition and other supplies. Finally, there was a simple motive of revenge against the Ravel brothers, Columbus store owners who had previously sold faulty ammunition to his army.

Other theories surfaced for the attack on the New Mexican town, including one that German agents paid Villa to make the raid in hopes that it would draw the United States into a war with Mexico and keep it out of the conflict in Europe. Another story claimed that Villa intended to kidnap Mary Slocum, wife of the Camp Furlong commander, Colonel Herbert Slocum, who had recently become very wealthy as the heir to the estate of financier and railroad magnate Russell Sage. Allegedly, Villa intended to hold Mrs. Slocum for ransom.

Early in the morning on March 9, Villa crossed the border at Palomas with about five hundred men. He divided them into two columns, with one advancing toward Camp Furlong and the other into Columbus itself. Villa's spies had mistakenly informed him that there were few soldiers at the camp when, in fact, there were more than three hundred cavalry and infantry soldiers with French Hotchkiss M-1909 machine guns. Many of their officers had just returned by train from playing in a polo match at Fort Bliss the day before opposite Lieutenant George Patton, who wrote to his father about the match, admitting that the visitors had "severely beaten" his team.

At 4:10 a.m. an attentive sentry fired at the approaching Mexicans, alerting the camp and town. A civilian telephone operator on the night shift immediately informed officials in El Paso, who relayed the information to Washington, D.C., marking a first in direct communications from a battlefield during an ongoing fight.

Second Lieutenant John P. Lucas awoke in his off-post quarters, grabbed his pistol, ran barefoot to the camp, opened the armory, and began issuing machine guns to his troops. The machine gunners fired on the Mexicans in the streets while others, including cooks arriving in their kitchens to prepare breakfast, fought back against the invaders with shotguns they kept to kill small game for the mess, as well as with knives and boiling water. The actions of Lucas (a West Point class of 1911 graduate) and his soldiers turned back the Mexicans from the camp with few American casualties.

Villa's second column found more success in their attack against Columbus itself. As the fight began, a Villista bullet stopped the clock at the railroad depot at 4:12 a.m. At the town's Commercial Hotel, raiders killed four residents and then looted and set fire to the Ravel brothers' store. They then turned to burning other buildings and shooting additional civilians. The damage would have been much worse except for the actions of the Camp Furlong Officer of the Day, First Lieutenant James P. Castleman. Aware that most of the officers lived away from the camp in Columbus, he assumed command of Troop F, armed the men with M-1903 Springfield rifles, and took their fight into downtown Columbus. Confronted by armed soldiers instead of unprepared civilians, the Mexicans retreated south.

Villa did not directly participate in the actual raid, instead observing the fight from a hilltop southwest of town surrounded by his personal bodyguards. These *Dorados* (Spanish for "goldens") were Villa's closest allies and family members from his native state of Durango. Most were officers and wore a half-dollar bronze insignia on their hats inscribed "Constitutionalist Army."

Squadron commander Major Frank Tompkins took charge of cavalry troops F and H and pursued the raiders. The Mexicans attempted a delaying action along the border, but Tompkins's cavalrymen broke their line in a rapid charge. He then pursued the fleeing raiders into Mexico for fifteen miles before he turned back because of tiring horses and depleted ammunition.

The casualty lists for both sides vary from source to source; however, the best estimate is that nine U.S. soldiers died in the fight while another seven were wounded. Eleven civilians were murdered and two wounded. Villa's casualties are estimated to be about eighty dead with that many more wounded.

By any tactical military measure, Villa's raid on Columbus was a failure. Not only had he received incorrect information from his spies, but he was also unprepared for how quickly the U.S. soldiers could react and pursue. Riding for their lives, Villa and his men discarded much of the plunder they had stolen in Columbus during their rapid retreat back into Mexico.

By any strategic measure, however, Villa's raid was wildly successful. Villa got exactly what he wanted. He had baited the United States into illegally entering Mexico and becoming entangled in Mexican affairs. The American press and public clamored for revenge, pressuring the president to respond. The day after the attack, President Wilson informed his cabinet that an "adequate force" would be dispatched into Mexico to find and punish Villa and his army.

Wilson, not one to go to war impulsively, decided to send an expedition of U.S. soldiers to solve two of his most pressing issues: to staunch the raids from Mexico into the United States before the border situation got out of hand, and to assess the state of the military's readiness to face what was beginning to appear as the inevitable commitment to the war in Europe.

Americans were incensed with the invasion of their soil and murder of citizens and supported the pursuit of Villa. Most shared the feeling of a veteran Indian fighter, retired general Nelson A. Miles, who, according to a March 10, 1916, *New York Times* article, said at a dinner speech in the city, "Villa and his bandits should be exterminated and the quicker that he and his followers are lined up in front of a wall and shot the better off will be Mexico and the United States."

Army officials quickly appointed "Black Jack" Pershing to command the Punitive Expedition (as the incursion into Mexico would be called) because of his past successes and because he was already stationed at Fort Bliss. On March 10, Pershing received specific preliminary instructions from General Frederick Funston from the Southern Department at San Antonio, including the lists of units to be under his command. Orders stated:

> *Secretary of War has designated you to command expedition into Mexico to capture Villa and his bandits. There will be two columns, one to enter from Columbus and one from Hachita, via Culberson's Ranch. Hachita column will consist of Seventh Cavalry, Tenth Cavalry (less two troops) and one battery horse artillery. Columbus column will consist of Thirteenth Cavalry (less one troop), a regiment from the east, one battery of horse artillery, one company of engineers, and First Aero Squadron with eight aeroplanes. Reinforced brigade of Sixth Infantry, First Battalion Fourth Field Artillery, and auxiliary troops will follow Columbus column. Two companies of Engineers will be ordered to Fort Bliss awaiting further orders. Necessary signal corps will be ordered from here. Will furnish you War Department instructions later.*

On March 11, the Southern Department forwarded the promised instructions with the added information, including, "As commander of the expeditionary force, the Department Commander leaves you free to make such assignment of the troops under your command as you think best in order to accomplish the purpose in hand."

Also included in the message was Washington's authorization for the expedition via War Department Order No. 883 to the Southern Department commander:

You will promptly organize an adequate military force of troops under the command of Brigadier General Pershing and will direct him to proceed promptly across the border in pursuit of the Mexican band which attacked the town of Columbus and the troops there on the morning of the 9th instant. These troops will be withdrawn to American territory as soon as the de facto government in Mexico is able to relieve them of this work period. In the event the work of these troops will be regarded as finished as soon as Villa band or bands are known to be broken up. In carrying out these instructions you are authorized to employ whatever guides and interpreters necessary and you are given general authority to employ such transportation including motor transportation, with necessary civilian personal as may be required. You are instructed to make all possible use of aeroplanes at San Antonio for observation.

Later that day, the War Department further advised, "The Secretary of War approved your general plan [of the two-column advance] except that it must not be based upon the assumption of any railroad in Mexico being opened and guarded by US troops. Your plan must assume that troops will be supplied directly from the border to whatever extent necessary and that the use of the railroad is contingent upon its being kept open by the de facto government and permission of that government for us to use."

CHAPTER SEVEN

March 1916

On March 12, 1916, Patton wrote his father, "Well at last we are about to go over the line [Mexican border]."

Patton continued the letter with insights that showed he had a good understanding of what would likely follow: "If we can induce him [Villa] to fight it will be all right but if he breaks up [his army into small units to fight a guerilla war] it will be bad, especially if we have Carranza [Federal troops] on our rear."

Patton abruptly interrupted his writing when he received bad news. He continued, "Since writing the foregoing I have discovered that we [Eighth Cavalry] are not going but will sit here and watch the rest go past us."

But, of course, Patton was not content to sit out the adventure. On learning that his unit was not to be a part of the Punitive Expedition force, he approached members of his regimental chain of command and officers of the Expeditionary force, requesting to join the operation. When he found no support, he went directly to Pershing to seek permission to join the ranks. Patton wanted to go as a cavalryman; however, he was willing to become the commander's aide-de-camp or work with newspaper correspondents who were to accompany the Expedition into Mexico, if only he could be included.

In a 1924 essay titled "Personal Glimpses of General Pershing," Patton detailed his quest: "Determined to participate, I got permission to speak to the General and asked him to take me to Mexico in any capacity. He replied, 'Everyone wants to go; why should I favor you?'"

"'Because,' I answered, 'I want to go more than anyone else.' This modest reply failed to get any response except a curt 'That will do.'"

The essay continued, "Undiscouraged I went home and packed my bedding roll and saddle. At 5 o'clock next morning the telephone rang and on answering it the General's voice inquired, 'Lieut. Patton, how long will it take you to get ready?' When he heard that I was ready he exclaimed 'I'll be G.---D.---. You are appointed Aide.'"

Pershing already had his authorized two aides—First Lieutenant James L. Collins and Second Lieutenant Martin C. Shallenberger. Collins, Pershing's aide in the Philippines, was remaining at Fort Bliss, however, until he recovered from an illness. Patton was to assume his duties until Collins was able to join the Expedition in Mexico. Ecstatic to have secured a place for himself, Patton's only disappointment was in learning the news that the sabers he had designed would not be carried by the cavalry on the Expedition. While he could not know at the time the significance the weapon choice foreshadowed, Patton had a front-row seat to one of the first signs of major changes that would transform his beloved military. The army, as well as Patton, was already focusing on developments on motor cars and trucks, airplanes, and rapid-fire machine guns of the future. Sabers, other than ceremonial, were becoming a weapon of the past.

In addition to the absence of Collins, there were other reasons why Pershing took on Patton as an aide. Patton wrote in his 1924 essay, "It was three years before I learned from him why he took me. It seems that in '98 Lieut. Pershing was an instructor at West Point. The policy was that no instructors should go to war. Lieut. Pershing used every normal means to secure an exception and finally went A.W.O.L. to Washington where, by a line of talk similar to the one I employed on him in 1916, he secured the detail to Cuba."

Patton mentioned neither in his essay nor in his other writings one other factor that might have played a role in his becoming the general's aide: Pershing's relationship with Nita Patton was rapidly progressing, and he might very well have been seeking her approval by appointing her brother as his aide.

While Patton was in his mad pursuit of permission to accompany Pershing, diplomatic actions were ongoing between the governments of the United States and Mexico. The Americans claimed the authority to conduct the Expedition under provisions of an 1882 agreement between the two countries that allowed each other's troops to cross the border if in "hot pursuit." Although these provisions referred to pursuit of Native American bands and had not been used for two decades, the agreement had never been officially rescinded. President Carranza ultimately conceded to reciprocal crossings, but only if "the raid effected at Columbus should unfortunately be repeated at any other point on the border."

President Wilson and the War Department ignored Carranza's condition, interpreting the Mexican authorization for "hot pursuit" to still be in effect although Villa's trail south was growing colder with each passing day. Pershing managed to secure a telegram from General Álvaro Obregón, the army commander in Northern Mexico, which served to sanction the presence of U.S. soldiers to the Mexican soldiers and civilians. The issues of how many U.S. soldiers were authorized to be there and how far they could penetrate into Mexico, however, remained far from settled.

After his notification from Pershing that he was to join him as an aide, Patton added a blank notebook to his field pack. On the first page he wrote, "Diary kept by George S. Patton, Jr., while on duty with Headquarters, Punitive Expedition into Mexico." He understood the influence and importance of his first combat and wanted to record as much of his observations as possible. For the next eight months he recorded, usually late at night at the end of a day's operations, what he had seen and accomplished. Although he skipped a day occasionally because of the intensity of operations or simply because little or nothing occurred, his record of the Expedition proved so complete and insightful that Pershing asked for a copy to assist in his post-Expedition writings. Patton's diary entries that follow are from the final edited copy he provided the general—with explanations in brackets, minor punctuation corrections, and the occasional elimination of an unneeded phrase.

Diary: March 13

General Pershing called me up at 8:30 a.m. to say that I could go with him as Acting Aide, but that I would have to be relieved later,

*as Lieutenant Collins was to be appointed. I loaded the Headquarters'
horses at 12:15. The general was in his office until 5:30 p.m.*

*At 5:40 General Pershing, Major Hines and myself rode to Camp
Cotton in an automobile. Lieutenant Shallenberger went ahead to
decoy the newspaper men away so they would not bother the General,
and we could board the train unseen.*

*I got the general a little lunch on the train from Captain Allen
Greer's company. We reached Columbus, New Mexico, at 10:30 p.m.,
leaving the train a mile from town. Colonel Cabell and Major Ryan
reported to the General. The horses were not detrained until 5:00 a.m.*

Major John J. Hines, West Point class of 1891, had fought in Cuba
and the Philippines before joining the expedition as its adjutant. Major
James A. Ryan of the Thirteenth Cavalry Regiment acted as the Expedition's intelligence officer. He was well qualified for the position, as he
was fluent in Spanish and had been on the West Point faculty for three
years as a professor of modern languages. Lieutenant Colonel DeRosey
C. Cabell, Expedition chief of staff, was a West Point graduate and a
veteran of the Indian Wars, the Spanish-American War, the China Relief
Expedition, and the Philippine Insurrection. Captain Allen J. Greer of
the Sixteenth Infantry had earned the Medal of Honor in the Philippines. In addition to Pershing as a role model, Patton was surrounded by
veteran officers from whom he could learn and gain experience.

The railroad into Columbus allowed for the rapid assembly of units
for the Expeditionary force. Camp Cotton, a temporary tent installation
with wooden stables located adjacent to Fort Bliss, had been established
in 1914 to receive National Guardsmen deploying to the border. Located
between Cotton Street, from which it got its name, and the Rio Grande,
the camp served as an assembly area for many units headed to Columbus.

Diary: March 14

*General Pershing worked all day organizing the Expedition, receiv-
ing reports, and dodging newspaper men. I secured some arms for Mr.
Stevenson of the Palomas Land and Cattle Company.*

A man we called "The Poison Doctor" came and told us we would all be poisoned with cyanide unless we took him.

General Pershing and myself rode around camp at 5:00 p.m., all was in pretty good order, the men were all on top of a little hill, looking toward Palomas, where they thought they saw Mexicans.

By the time Pershing and Patton arrived at Columbus, most of the five thousand men who were to compose the Expedition were already assembled there. Along with the soldiers was a vast array of characters, including "The Poison Doctor," who sought to accompany the Expedition, as well as Americans such as Stevenson, who signed on as a guide and interpreter. Others came to seek employment as automotive drivers and mechanics while many others—bored cowboys, city dwellers, former gunmen and lawmen, and those seeking adventure—showed up in Columbus to accept any position offered, for this Expedition was the greatest event of the time. Still more people arrived in the small town to establish saloons and brothels to take the soldiers' pay.

Also on hand were members of the Indian tribe known as the Apache—who were actually more than a half-dozen clans in the American Southwest that were culturally related—ready to be hired as scouts. While the tribal clans fought other tribes as well as among themselves for territory, influence, and affinity for warfare, the Anglo-Americans had enlisted Apache as scouts in the war against the Navajo in 1863 and the Yavapai in 1870. The U.S. Army had also employed as many as two hundred Apache scouts in their pursuit and final capture of fellow Apache Geronimo in 1886.

When the Punitive Expedition crossed into Mexico, the Native American scouts numbered only twenty-four, but Pershing recruited additional Apache to bring the number up to thirty-nine. The Apache welcomed the opportunity to fight Mexicans of any political or geographical affiliation, as they had been hated enemies since before the arrival of Anglos. In addition to providing a job when employment opportunities for Native Americans were scarce, the opportunity to fight Mexicans allowed them to continue the "warrior traditions" of their clans.

Varying historical accounts claim that the Columbus assembly area was disorganized prior to the arrival of Pershing. This was not the case, according to notes in Patton's journal. He reported that when they arrived, "all was in pretty good order." This would surely have been true because Pershing always surrounded himself with excellent subordinates. In fact, five of his staff members and unit commanders would go on to become general officers.

In his March 12 letter to his father, Patton noted that the general demanded his subordinates be physically fit and that the Eighth Cavalry Regiment had not been selected for the Expedition because its commander was "too fat" to endure sustained field activities. The fact that its overweight commander had prevented the Eighth Cavalry from joining the Expedition caused Patton to resent and distrust obese officers for the rest of his time in uniform.

In his 1924 essay on Pershing, Patton wrote, "Under the supervision of the General every unit, every horse and every man was fit; weaklings had gone; baggage was still at the minimum and discipline was perfect. When I speak of supervision I do not mean the nebulous US staff control so frequently connected with work. . . . General Pershing knew to the minutest detail each of the subjects in which he demanded practice and by his physical presence and personal example insured himself that they were correctly carried out."

Prior to the unit's move to Columbus, Patton had observed Pershing only in a garrison environment. Now he saw and absorbed the general's command and organizational abilities in the field. Carlo D'Este, in his masterful *Patton: A Genius for War*, wrote:

> *Pershing's influence on young Patton cannot be overemphasized. He was the very model of a military commander, whose ideas of duty and discipline meshed perfectly with Patton's own perceptions. Pershing would not brook disorder or sloppiness of mind or person or billet, and he was a superb organizer of troops. He even possessed the same short-fused temper as Patton. In his memoir of Pershing, Patton praised his professionalism. In Pershing he had found the perfect example of a*

senior commander, whom he later successfully emulated, refining to his own lofty standards what he had learned.

Diary: March 15

All officers' baggage was reduced to fifty pounds and Colonel Berry, Inspector General, inspected them to see that this was carried out.

I bought ten day's rations for Division Headquarters, which consisted of General Pershing; Colonel DeR. C. Cabell, 10th Cavalry, Chief of Staff; Major Hines, Adjutant General; Major Ryan, 10th Cavalry, Intelligence Officer; Captain Burtt, 20th Infantry, Assistant Chief of Staff; and myself. We had three wall tents, two conical tents, and three wagons. Lieutenant Stringfellow, 13th Cavalry, was detailed in charge of the wagons with ten men.

At 11:30 a.m., General Pershing told me to take two Ford cars and go to Las Cienegas and pick up the telefunken [radio] set there and take it to Culberson's Ranch. At this ranch I would find Colonel Dodd to whom I took orders to be ready to cross the line when General Pershing reached there. I started at 12:05 p.m. and reached Las Cienegas at 4:30, having traveled one hundred miles. No artillery team was on hand at Las Cienegas, as per orders, and so I took a four-mule team from Captain Benjamin Tillman, 18th Infantry, who was in command of two companies there. After starting the wireless set, I went ahead to report to Colonel Dodd.

I reached Culberson's Ranch at 7:00 p.m. and at 9:00 p.m., as the General had not appeared, I suggested to Colonel Dodd that he wire and see if the General had started. We could not get them so we sent a car.

During this time, General Pershing had crossed into Mexico, and gone a little way beyond the gate, and then returned and motored in a Dodge car over the same road which I had followed toward Culberson's Ranch.

Colonel Lucien G. Berry, a member of the West Point class of 1886, was an artillery officer. Captain Wilson B. Burtt, an infantry officer who served in Cuba immediately after his graduation from West Point in 1899, joined the Expedition after two years as an observer of the German army in France. Second Lieutenant Horace Stringfellow Jr., who graduated in the West Point class of 1915 with fellow cadets Dwight Eisenhower and Omar Bradley, had participated in the fight against Villa and his bandits at Columbus. Colonel George A. Dodd, West Point class of 1876, had campaigned against the Sioux, Cheyenne, and Apache in the Indian Wars; fought alongside Theodore Roosevelt and the Rough Riders in Cuba; and served in the Philippines before joining the Expedition as the commander of the Second Cavalry Brigade.

Telefunken was the generic term for all wireless communications equipment, named by a Berlin company established in 1903 that developed some of the first radio communications devices. The wireless systems employed by the Expedition were rudimentary and unreliable but demonstrated their future worth to Patton with their instant communications that far exceeded the speed of horse, automobile, or even air messengers.

Patton's duties as Pershing's aide were many and varied in that he basically performed whatever task the general desired. In addition to carrying messages, as he did to Colonel Dodd, Patton organized the daily activities of the headquarters, coordinated visits by the general to subordinate units, took notes at meetings, drafted letters and messages, and arranged for the delivery of supplies.

Diary: March 16

At 12:15 a.m., Mr. Stevenson arrived with orders for Colonel Dodd to start, leaving one troop as escort for the General. I had gotten eight horses from Battery B, Sixth Field Artillery for the use of the General and his staff.

Colonel Dodd started with the Seventh and Tenth Cavalry at 1:15 a.m. General Pershing and Major Ryan, with scouts Tracy and Houghton and some others, arrived at 2:00 a.m. We started, escorted by Troop D, Seventh Cavalry, Captain Boyd and Lieutenant W. H. Smith, at 2:45 a.m. We crossed the line at 3:16 a.m., reaching Car-

reso, a distance of twenty miles, at 7:00 a.m. As none of us had slept over eight hours since the night of the 12th, we were very sleepy.

General Pershing had the wireless set put up and tried to get into communications with Columbus, but failed. We ate some bacon and slept a little, starting again at 12:02 for Ojitos, at which place we arrived at 6:30 p.m., having covered a distance of 52 miles since leaving Culberson's Ranch.

Here at Ojitos there was plenty of water, and some Mexicans cooked us a good dinner. The General loaned me a saddle blanket to replace one that someone stole from me while we were eating. I stole another one for him.

We set up the wireless again and tried to get into communications but failed.

It was very cold. We killed five cows and distributed the meat.

Beyond the misspellings of some towns, Patton's diary entries contain few errors. In the turmoil and long hours of the initial march into Mexico, he misidentified Smith as a lieutenant rather than his actual rank of captain. Also, there is no Captain Boyd on the Expedition's roster of the Seventh Cavalry. He probably was referring to Captain Charles H. Boice. In any case, Patton's encounter with the two officers was brief, and he makes no further mention of either of them.

Patton's admission to stealing a blanket for his general shows that he was adapting to the real army rather than adhering to the unwritten West Point code—one that had permeated conduct since the Academy's founding in 1802 but became official only in 1947—that required "a cadet will not lie, cheat or steal." Life on the Hudson, however, was far from the reality and hardships of the real army.

Pershing certainly understood and accepted the actions of his subordinate. When his Black soldiers of the Tenth Cavalry had not received sufficient supplies in Cuba, Pershing had taken matters into his own hands and appropriated wagons, mules, and horses without proper requisitions and taken whatever food, clothing, and blankets he could find. Colonel Theodore Baldwin, a Civil War veteran and commander of the Tenth, wrote in a letter to Pershing on November 30, 1898, "You did some tall rustling."

Diary: March 17

The column started at 7:45 a.m. The cavalry and pack trains by trail and the artillery by road. We halted eight miles out at a very fine lake where we watered. We then continued at a walk over very bad trails, finally reaching Tres Alamos, just north of Colonia Dublan, having gone fifty-eight miles. The camp where the Seventh Cavalry halted at 6:30 p.m. was not large enough, so the General had to take the Tenth Cavalry to the river, about one mile further east.

During the afternoon, the General got the names of all the men in the 10th Cavalry and Sixth Field Artillery, who could use the heliograph, and of all locomotive engineers. There were three in the Tenth Cavalry.

Before we reached camp, Major Ryan and Ted Houghton [civilian guide] went ahead to Casas Grandes to get information.

In the late afternoon my horse fell and broke my flashlight. I found some hay in the camp so all the horses had a good feed. We lost two mules and eight horses in making this trip.

Pershing had selected Colonia Dublán as his forward headquarters and as the point where the eastern and western columns would merge. The village—established in 1885 by Mormon polygamist families who left the United States so they could continue to practice their beliefs— had become a thriving farming community in northern Chihuahua. Pershing also made the village his logistic supply center, where the Expedition received ammunition, food, clothing, fodder for the horses, and petroleum products for the automobiles and trucks that arrived by horse- and mule-drawn wagons, motorized trucks, and trains from a newly established depot in Columbus that received shipments by rail from El Paso.

Pershing was furthermore seeking to solve tactical problems. First, he recognized the problems with his rudimentary radios and sought other means of communication, such as the heliograph system—signals produced by flashes of sunlight reflected by a large mirror—which allowed the transmission of Morse code. Another problem Pershing was looking to resolve was controlling the rail lines, which was why he was identifying experienced locomotive engineers within his command.

Pershing had a keen understanding of the importance of knowing the whereabouts and intentions of his enemy, but he had no information section assigned to the Expedition. Therefore, he had to organize his own by detaching Major Ryan from the Thirteenth Cavalry, who had accompanied Pershing more often than any other officer other than his aides, to make him the intelligence chief. Ryan, fluent in Spanish and a former language professor at West Point, was well suited for the job. He chose Lieutenant Nicholas W. Campanole of the Sixth Infantry, a native of New Mexico who spoke both Spanish and Japanese, as his assistant. Several other officers served in the section at times during the Expedition.

Patton worked closely with Ryan and his team in developing a system of spies, scouts, and guides loosely in accordance with the tenets established by the 1885 Military Information Division even though the War Department would not formalize the Military Intelligence branch until 1962.

Diary: March 18

Moved the entire camp to the new camp at the river [Casas Grandes]. We set up the wireless and got in touch with Columbus. General Pershing and Major Ryan went to the railroad at New Casas Grandes in a Mormon vehicle to get information. I went there looking for them and saw the Carranza soldiers. They were a poor lot, about half in uniform, colonels and majors were young fellows not over twenty. The captains were older.

At the railroad station the General got important information of the Villistas. He arranged for the Seventh and Tenth Cavalry to continue south the next day. They intended to use the Mexican Northwestern Railway. We had dinner over at the Mormon Bishop's. It was a very excellent meal.

General Pershing planned the campaign under a large tree near the river. We had only one flashlight with which to see the map. Wagner and Fox, civilian guides, seemed very useful.

The Punitive Expedition faced far more opposition in Northern Mexico than simply Villa and his band. They had to contend with the harsh desert landscape, lack of water, long supply lines, and Mexican farmers and villagers, who, like civilians in most war zones, simply wanted to be left alone to raise their crops and take care of their families. However, if they found themselves amid the conflict, they readily sided with the forces of Villa or Carranza over the invaders from north of the border. Then, too, Carranza's Federal army and government proved to be more an opponent than an ally.

Patton's observation of the incongruent ages of the Carranza's army officers reflected the impact of the recent revolution. Carranza did not trust the officers of the old army and replaced the senior-ranking men with young supporters. Thus, captains of the old army were older than the new majors and colonels of the new.

Pershing did have the advantage of telegraph lines stretching from Dublán to Columbus. Like the wireless, however, they were not consistently reliable because the lines were easily cut.

Diary: March 19

Seventh Cavalry moved out at 3:00 a.m. with five hundred best men and horses. Moved the headquarters to a group of large trees across river. The Tenth Cavalry with five hundred best men and horses left by train at 2:45 p.m. Just after they left someone set fire to a large pile of hay near the stockyards.

Lieutenants Collins and Shallenberger arrived at 10:00 with four automobiles, one Buick, one Dodge, and two Fords.

The General placed one of the correspondents in arrest for sending a message without authority. Sent orders by wireless that night for Aero Squadron to start that night for Dublan.

Pershing's original plan was to trap Villa between the two columns marching south from Columbus on the east and Culberson's Ranch on the west. However, when he and the west column reached Dublán, Pershing learned that Villa, who had already passed through the village, was about sixty miles to the south. The general ordered the Seventh and Tenth Cavalry, under the overall command of Colonel Dodd—still in the saddle, leading his cavalrymen at the age of sixty-three—to continue their advance, not waiting for the arrival of the eastern column.

In hopes of quickly closing on Villa's column as well as providing a chance for their horses to rest, Pershing had elements of the Tenth Cavalry board a southbound train. However, reality trumped strategy when the locomotive and cars, in deplorable condition, had to be repaired before they could depart. Once in motion, the train experienced water and wood shortages that slowed the locomotive, which in the best of times had insufficient power to pull the loaded freight and passenger cars. After the Expedition unloaded some of the troops and horses, the train continued forward only to derail several cars, injuring a dozen cavalrymen.

This futile effort would be the only time during the Expedition that Pershing attempted to move one of his units by rail, which was just as well, for Carranza soon afterward ordered the Mexican rail network off limits to the Americans. In the meantime, a disgusted commander of the Tenth Cavalry finally gave up on the train, unloaded his troops, and continued south on horseback.

According to the original arrangement with Pershing, in which the general gave him permission to join the Expedition, Patton was to return to Fort Bliss when Collins rejoined the unit. However, after only five days as the general's aide, Patton had made such an impression and been so helpful that Pershing did not order him to leave when Collins caught up with the headquarters. Instead, Pershing reorganized the duties of his now trio of aides. Collins resumed his responsibilities of taking care of the general's personal needs, correspondence, and schedule. Shallenberger supervised the headquarters personnel. Patton took charge of the civilian guides and military scouts and acted as an assistant to the Expedition's intelligence officer.

All three brands of automobiles that arrived at Dublán experienced maintenance and tire problems, but the Dodge proved to be the best suited for the Mexican terrain. The all-steel construction of the vehicle—with its three-speed transmission, electric starter, and 35-horsepower engine—came with the company's promise of "dependability." Although according to the *Oxford English Dictionary* the word *dependability* originated in 1901 as a synonym for *reliability*, the Dodge Company claimed it coined the term for its 1916 automobile advertising campaign.

Within his new scope of duties, Patton devised a censorship policy for outgoing mail from members of the Expedition to maintain security. Officers could dispatch uncensored mail on an honor system by signing the envelope acknowledging they had complied with all the rules. Letters by enlisted men had to be read and approved by their commanding officer to ensure they contained no intelligence that might be useful if intercepted by the enemy.

Four directives made up the censorship policy. First, the writer was to give no location details other than "somewhere in Mexico." Second and third were that discussion of future plans or any information concerning weapons or logistics had to be excluded. Finally, Patton, well aware of the ingenuity of the American soldier, included that no codes or symbols were permitted.

The censorship policy extended to accompanying journalists and civilians, specifically overzealous news correspondents more interested in headlines and "scoops" than in secrecy and security. From time immemorial, reporters have presented a double-edged sword for military commanders; positive reports increased morale of those back home and encouraged politicians to support the troops while printed classified information put the operation at risk. Pershing welcomed the support, but he was well aware that any information printed in U.S. papers would likely reach Villa. Therefore, he censored their dispatches and, as Patton wrote, punished those who sent "messages without authority."

Diary: March 20

The aeroplanes got in about 9:00 a.m. having missed the camp in the dark, one had gone to Pierson and wrecked in landing, one got lost in Ascension, and Lieutenant [Thomas S.] Bowen's machine was wrecked late that day while moving it to a place near the camp. All the pilots found it difficult to land on account of the high altitude which was four thousand feet.

The First Aero Squadron—composed of eleven officers, eighty-two enlisted men, one civilian technician, one automobile, six motorcycles, twelve motor trucks, and eight Curtis JN-3 biplanes disassembled in crates—arrived in Columbus by rail on March 15. Except for the airplanes assigned to the aviation school in San Diego, the eight biplanes made up the entire aerial fleet of the U.S. Army. Their deployment to the border and within Mexico was the first use of airplanes in active combat.

Their mission was to maintain aero communications between Columbus, Casas Grandes, El Valle, Dublán, and Namiquipa. The squadron was likewise tasked with the responsibility of locating the enemy and informing the ground forces of their observations.

The squadron's deployment to Mexico also marked the first time a U.S. unit relied entirely on motorized transportation. Trucks, rather than horses and wagons, moved the aero squadron's men, equipment, supplies, and fuel. The trucks, acquired early in 1915 from the Thomas B. Jeffery Company in Wisconsin, were sixteen-and-a-half-ton, four-wheel-drive vehicles. Members of the squadron modified one of the trucks into a mobile machine shop for repairs in the field.

Patton had gained a great appreciation for motor cars prior to the Expedition, and the arrival of the combustion engine–driven "Jenny" planes fueled his curiosity about these machines even more. Although these front-runners of American aerial military might were hampered by maintenance problems and low power, Patton immediately recognized their value in providing reconnaissance of large areas and rapid transport of messages. He was also aware that airplanes were playing an increasing role in the broadening war in Europe and that they were likely to be an important part of future warfare.

Both Pershing and Patton learned their first lesson about airplanes on the initial day of their deployment into Mexico: the aircraft had difficulties navigating at night.

Diary: March 21

The Second and Third Squadrons of the Thirteenth Cavalry and their wagon trains got in at 11:00 p.m.

Diary: March 22

The First Squadron of the Thirteenth Cavalry, under Major [Elmer] Lindsley started south. Colonel Dodd went to El Valle in auto to see if he could not stir up some information. I went to the station in an ambulance and got General Garvia and his two aides. The General was dressed in an O.D. blouse cut like the French. He had dinner with General Pershing and scratched himself all the time. In taking the General back, the driver was very poor and nearly upset several times. It was pitch dark. I found that the General talked French well and had been a professor at the University of Vera Cruz before the war.

Major Tompkins with two troops and a machinegun troop of the Thirteenth Cavalry started south, late in the afternoon of the twenty-second.

Diary: March 23

The First Squadron of the Eleventh Cavalry under Colonel Allen arrived in camp. Their horses were all remounts and in very poor shape. The headquarters arrived with camp tents and bedding rolls. Aeroplanes went to look for the Seventh Cavalry but failed to locate it. I volunteered to hunt for the Seventh Cavalry in an automobile and General Pershing said he would go also, so I got ready but at the last minute decided not to do it. There was a heavy windstorm that night.

Once the units of the Eastern Column arrived at Dublán, Pershing continued to seek information of Villa's location. General Gabriel Garvia had provided little intelligence, his visit mostly useless other than giving Patton an opportunity to practice the French he had so much difficulty mastering while a cadet at West Point.

Frank Tompkins, as a major in the Thirteenth Cavalry, had pursued Villa into Mexico after the raid on Columbus and been recommended for the Medal of Honor for his actions. Awarded the Distinguished Service Cross (DSC) instead, Tompkins accompanied the Punitive Expedition and participated in many of its actions, including the battle with Carranza's cavalry at Parral. His DSC citation stated:

> *The Distinguished Service Cross is presented to Frank Tompkins, Major, US Army, for extraordinary heroism in action at Columbus, New Mexico, March 9, 1916. Major Tompkins requested and received authority to pursue a superior force of bandits into Mexico. Although wounded early in the pursuit, he carried on a running fight with the bandits for several miles, inflicting heavy losses upon them and stopped the pursuit only when men and horses were exhausted and ammunition was reduced to a few rounds per man.*

Tompkins, born in Washington, D.C., was the son and grandson of West Point graduates. He turned down an appointment to the Academy, however, to join the U.S. Army in 1891, only to earn a commission three months later. Before Mexico, he had fought with distinction in Cuba and the Philippines.

Colonel Henry T. Allen graduated from West Point in 1882 and led explorations of Alaska before fighting in Cuba and the Philippines. In addition to his accomplishments in the field, Allen had served as military attaché to Russia and Germany and as observer of the Japanese army in Korea.

Lice and fleas were irritants to soldiers on both sides during the Expedition. Patton's note that the Mexican general had "scratched himself all the time" shows the vermin had no respect for rank. Patton's comment on the weather is typical of the diaries kept by soldiers of all generations: infantrymen write about how much their feet hurt; cavalrymen mention the condition of their horses. Both complain about the heat, cold, wind, and other weather conditions.

Aware that speed was the best solution to catching Villa, Pershing reorganized the units arriving in Dublán from the east into four mobile units he called "flying columns." These units were to operate semi-independently with little guidance from his headquarters as they gathered their own intelligence on locating Villa. Although supplies were available in Dublán, there were no means for getting them to the rapidly advancing columns. As a result, the flying columns butchered and ate cattle for their meat and purchased other food from the locals. This would be the last operation in U.S. Army history where its soldiers "lived off the land."

Diary: March 24

Major Ryan and myself were wakened by the General who told us to get ready to go to Namiquipa with him by automobile. We had four automobiles, one Studebaker, one Dodge, and two Fords; one guide and four guards. We started at 9:00 a.m. and reached El Valle at 1:00 p.m. Here we found Major Tompkins with his two troops and the machine gun troop. The General decided to go on to Cruces with Major Tompkins' two troops as escort, after going six miles met Lieutenant [William C. F.] Nicholson who had come with a message from Colonel Dodd, who was in the mountains east of Cruces. This message told the General what he wanted to know. General Pershing wrote Colonel Dodd a strong order telling him to use all possible vigor in the pursuit of Villa. We sent Major Tompkins on and returned to El Valle.

It was very cold and there was a great deal of wind. Lieutenant Lucas gave us dinner in a dug out. General Pershing had only one blanket and tried to sleep in the automobile. Major Ryan, Lieutenant Lucas, and myself slept on some oats.

More automobiles were reaching the Expedition from Columbus, and Pershing did not hesitate to use them instead of horses to visit his forward units. The encounter with Tompkins and Lucas must have offered the opportunity to Patton to discuss with them the fight in Columbus and the initial pursuit of the raiders into Mexico.

Pershing's official report of the Expedition details the perceived location day by day of Villa's force from the time they departed Columbus in a hail of bullets. His intelligence on Villa's whereabouts, however, was always a day or more behind. He noted in his report, "The country was extremely dry, and that it was next to impossible to follow a trail of any kind."

Diary: March 25

The first train load of forage and provisions reached El Valle this afternoon with twelve White trucks under command of Lieutenant Wilburn, Twelfth Cavalry.

Later we talked with the Mexicans of El Valle. Here the people were all supposed to be in favor of Villa, yet when General Pershing offered to buy some supplies from them for real money, they seemed quite friendly. One of them said that on the night of March 23rd, forty men had deserted the Federal troops at El Valle and gone over to Villa, some of our scouts reported a trail supposed to have been made by the deserters running up the river. They lost it when it headed southwest.

Villa had been in El Valle the night of the nineteenth of March and had taken thirty-seven men and one woman by force. Some of the men had already deserted him. We expected two aeroplanes to report to us, but found that they had turned back to Casas Grandes.

The General was quite angry over their nonappearance.

Major Howze reported from Dublan about 10:00 a.m. He had two hundred and forty of the best men and horses of the Eleventh Cavalry with him. General Pershing and Major Howze talked over the operations and General Pershing gave Major Howze his final orders.

Lieutenant Collins was accompanying Major Howze. We started back to Dublan at 2:00 p.m., reaching there at 6:00. On the way we passed two companies of the Sixteenth Infantry in wagons, going to the advance base at El Valle. Also we picked up Lieutenant Christie who had broken his plane in landing and he had been out in the open prairie for two days and nights without any blanket and without anything to eat. He was very cold.

The identification of "Lieutenant Wilburn of the Twelfth Cavalry" is likely a shared error on the part of Patton and his diary typist. Patton is possibly referring to Lieutenant Arthur E. Wilbourn, West Point class of 1908, of the Thirteenth Cavalry. The Twelfth Cavalry did not serve with the Expedition.

Although Patton noted in his diary that the Mexicans seemed "friendly" when offered money for supplies, Pershing wrote in his report, "Practically every Mexican so far encountered had questioned our right to be in Mexico and claimed there was no authority for our presence." Despite these anti-American sentiments, Patton also observed that most Mexicans did not desire to fight either on the side of Villa or with the Federals, apparently switching sides whenever prudent.

While primarily a cavalry operation, the Expedition also included infantry regiments such as the Sixteenth. Due to their lack of mobility, they were deployed to defend supply trains and depots as well as head-quarters like the one at Dublán. Although the term dated to the Mexican War of 1845–1846, the "doughboy" nickname for the infantrymen became popular during the Expedition and would become even more prevalent in the upcoming World War I. Although there are several theories about the origins of "doughboys," the most common consensus is that infantrymen in Mexico were so called because they were constantly covered with chalky dust from marching through the dry terrain, giving the soldiers the appearance of unbaked dough, or they might have had that moniker because of the mud bricks of the area, known as adobe, which translates into "doughboy."

Frustration with the failures of the aero squadron was mounting. Patton marveled at Lieutenant Arthur R. Christie's successful escape from capture after crashing his plane. However, there is some conflict with Patton's account of the airman. In its official report, the First Aero Squadron stated that Lieutenant Christie had been forced to land because of a storm described by squadron commander Captain B. D. Foulois, the U.S. Army's first aviator, who had himself learned to fly from the Wright Brothers. Foulois contended, "The dust in the air was so thick that the snow was actually brown by the time it hit the ground." The report further records that after being grounded for two days, Christie was able to fly his plane back to Casas Grandes. It is likely that the aviator who evaded capture was Lieutenant Edgar S.

Gorrell, whose story more resembles the one in Patton's journal than does Christie's.

Regardless of which pilot was involved, this was the first instance when an American aviator evaded capture from behind enemy lines to return to safety. Patton later would encounter and seek out many more successful evaders during World War II when he frequently met with American airmen who found their way to the safety of his Third Army after being shot down over France or Germany. The official purpose of these meetings, like that one in Mexico, was to gather intelligence about what the airmen had seen behind the lines. Unofficially, Patton always relished good stories and liked to hear about airmen's adventures evading their pursuers.

The pilots assigned to the Expedition also had their frustrations in Mexico. In a plan for the support of future operations that Foulois submitted to Pershing on March 30, the aero commander detailed the difficulties faced by his pilots, stating, "All officer pilots with the squadron during its active service in Mexico were constantly exposed to personal risk and physical suffering. Due to the inadequate weight carrying capacity of the airplanes, it was impossible to carry even sufficient food, water, or clothing on many reconnaissance flights. During their flights the pilots were frequently caught in snow, rain, and hailstorms which because of their inadequate clothing, invariably caused excessive suffering."

"In several instances," Foulois's paper continued, "the pilots were compelled to make forced landings in desert and hostile country, 50 to 70 miles from the nearest troops. In every case, the airplanes were abandoned or destroyed and the pilots, after experiencing all possible suffering due to the lack of food and water, would finally work their way on foot, through alkali deserts and mountains, to friendly troops, usually arriving exhausted as a result of these hardships."

Diary: March 26

The General worked on the organization of the Expedition all day. He formed a pack train out of the combat train of the Fourth Field Artillery. We got Mr. Merril to act as guide of the train which was

*to go down along the river. Bishop Call helped me to find the guides
and told me that several soldiers had been to the Mormon church the
previous day.*

It was not at all unusual for Pershing to be reorganizing his forces
early in the campaign to meet new obstacles and challenges. He, like
every military commander who preceded him, understood even the best-
made plans changed when the first shot was fired.

Patton, who later became known far more for his profanity than
his prayers, was a deeply religious man who regularly attended church
services and saw to it that they were available to the troops. Although
a member of the Episcopal Church, Patton studied the Koran and the
texts of other religions while also professing to believe in reincarnation.
He wrote and often said that God was probably indifferent to the way
he was approached.

War either brings a soldier closer to his God or pushes him away with
the thought that no deity could allow such carnage. In Patton's case, his
time in Mexico and on later battlefields deepened his faith and practice.
By the time he led the Third Army in World War II, he was keeping a
Bible on his desk and read it daily. He not only attended church services
weekly but also memorized the Episcopal service.

Diary: March 27

*Lieutenant E. S. Hughes of the Fourth Field Artillery Pack Train
started south. General Pershing was preparing to go south and put
some more vim into things. I worked on a Buick all day to get ready
to start the next morning at five. Finally had to abandon it and take
the Studebaker and two Fords and a Dodge.*

Everett Hughes, West Point class of 1908, and Patton formed a friendship in Mexico that endured into World War II. Hughes gained the rank
of major general and became Chief of the U.S. Army Ordnance Corps.

Pershing believed in the importance of the commanding general
being on the front lines to be seen by the troops and to encourage (put

some "vim") into his subordinate leaders. Patton adopted this philosophy to the point that, later in World War II, he even took up guide positions at forward crossroads to see and to be seen.

Among other things that Patton was learning on the Expedition was that motorized vehicles required enormous amounts of maintenance to remain on the road. These lessons prepared him for the same type of mechanical challenges he would face when he commanded tanks and personnel carriers in the two world wars.

Diary: March 28

General Pershing, Major Ryan, Lieutenant Patton, cooks Booker and Lanckton, and Major Ryan's striker, with four cars started for El Valle at 3:30 p.m. Two cars with newspaper men accompanied us. These men were Dunne of the New York Tribune, *Gibbons of the* Chicago Tribune, *Elser of the* New York Times, *and Blakesley of the Associated Press. We had no tents or baggage, the tires on the cars were very old and we had a great many punctures and had to wait for the correspondents. We reached El Valle at 9:30 p.m. We passed the engineers working on the road en route.*

The Corporal Frank Lanckton that Patton refers to on this day was far more than a "cook." He had been Pershing's primary orderly since the Philippines, serving with the general at the Presidio in California before accompanying him to Texas and Mexico. He would remain at Pershing's side through World War I. Lanckton occasionally had problems with alcohol and bounced from corporal to sergeant and back again several times. Despite his problems, he remained a favorite of Pershing as well as of Pershing's son, Warren.

Patton interacted well with the newspaper correspondents, who were familiar with him from his exploits in the Olympic Games. He recognized the importance of good press, both for the Expedition and for himself, while also being wary of just what they observed and reported. It was during this time that a photographer from the Underwood and Underwood Company of New York took a photograph of Pershing with his primary staff that appeared in the April 12, 1916, edition of the *San Francisco Chronicle* as well as other newspapers.

The picture caption read, "First Pictures from the Front Passed by Army Censor." The photo featured the soldiers in their field khaki uniforms, boots with leggings, and campaign hats. Patton is the only one in the photograph wearing a tie—a standard he would later vigorously enforce throughout his commands. As Patton had taken on the duties of "censor," it is likely that he also was the person cited who approved the picture for release.

As Patton indicated in his entry, the Expedition arrived in Mexico to find only rudimentary trails sufficient for horses and donkey carts rather than automobiles, trucks, and military wagons. The Second Engineer Battalion spent their stay during the Expedition improving the existing trails and building new roads to enhance the transportation of men and supplies—particularly the route south from Columbus to Dublán.

Diary: March 29

Sent an aeroplane back to Casas Grandes and waited for its return. It got back at 9:30. While waiting I told the General of the arrival of Lieutenant [William W. Jr.] West, who had come over from Major Lindsey's column [Thirteenth Cavalry] and he told General Pershing of the conditions west of the mountains.

We started to Namiquipa at 11:00 a.m. Elser and Blakesley stayed at El Valle as their machine had broken a rear axle. I had to drive the car as the Mormon boy was no good. The roads were very bad and we had two punctures. We reached Namiquipa at dark.

Diary: March 30

Left camp at Namiquipa at 10:00 a.m., following Major Howze whom we passed just north of San Geronimo ranch. We drove on nearly to Bachineva, where we saw two Mexicans plowing in a field. When we questioned them, they seemed very frightened, and told us Colonel Dodd had left the day before.

The General tried to get one of them to take a message to him, but the man replied saying Villa would get him. He also told us that he would be shot, and as we would not be able to reach Colonel Dodd, we decided to return to San Geronimo. We met Colonel Howze and turned him back to San Geronimo also. At the ranch at San Geronimo we found much corn in the warehouse.

While Major Ryan was talking to the japs who ran the ranch, Lieutenant Collins came up with a report from Colonel Dodd, that he, Colonel Dodd had defeated Villa at Guerrero the day before, and that Villa was in the mountains south of us. General Pershing at once made plans to surround and comb the mountains. Major Howze was to enter from the east and lead northwest, while Major Tompkins from the southwest near Providencia would move east.

While he was writing the order, Private Gregg came up on a motorcycle and said that he had been fired upon near Bachineva and had turned back. I took the auto to Namiquipa with orders for Major Tompkins to move to Providencia. I reached there at 8:30. I had permission to accompany Major Tompkins.

Found Blakesley and Elser at Namiquipa and sent them back to San Geronimo in the automobile.

Major Tompkins took five days rations and two days grain and started for Providencia.

Mexico was the first Latin American country to recognize Japanese sovereignty after the end of that country's isolation policy in 1888. In 1897, Mexico began to receive immigrants from Japan, who worked mostly as farm workers and as miners. Efforts by the Japanese to establish coffee plantations failed, and their population had never exceeded more than five hundred before the arrival of the Punitive Expedition.

Patton's use of the word *japs* is not unusual. He often expressed anti-Asian, anti-Black, and anti-Semitic attitudes. Like many of his time, Patton looked on all minorities as inferior to Whites—and as untrustworthy. Even among his fellow Whites, Patton, a product of his position of wealth and family social order, felt superior. Regardless of his prejudices, he remained able to work effectively with all races and ranks.

The success of Colonel Dodd at Guerrero provided the first good news of the Expedition. On March 27, Villa and his band had successfully attacked a Federal garrison and occupied the town. In his "Punitive Expedition Report," Pershing wrote, "Dodd heard that Villa had been severely wounded in a fight with the Carrancistas at Guerrero on the 27th, and was then at Guerrero with 500 or 600 men. He promptly decided to act, and started toward Guerrero that afternoon, continuing by a night march toward Guerrero with a view to reaching Villa's camp at daylight."

In a message dated March 29, Dodd reported to Pershing, "At between six and seven o'clock this morning we struck Villa's command consisting of about 500 men in the town of Guerrero. Villa, who is suffering from a broken leg and lame hip from gunshot wounds received in a previous engagement, was not present, and I understand was carried away in a buggy sometime yesterday. The number known to be killed was 30, and in the connection it must be remembered that four-fifths of the Villistas are Yaquis and carry off their dead. Undoubtedly a much larger number than this was killed. We captured Villa's two machine guns, a number of horses, saddles, and arms. Our casualties were four enlisted men wounded, none of these seriously. A large number of Carrancista prisoners, who were kept for execution it is understood, were liberated or made their escape. In order to reach this point the command marched 17 hours out of 24 covering 55 miles and then kept up the fight for five hours. With Villa probably permanently disabled, Lopez seriously wounded, and Hernandez dead and the blow administered this morning, the Villista party would seem to be pretty well disintegrated."

Pershing forwarded the report up his chain of command and on March 31 received a message from the Southern Department at San Antonio. It stated, "Following just received from Washington. 'Secretary of War desires you to convey to General Pershing, Colonel Dodd, and command, his hearty congratulations of exploit.'"

Pershing, of course, welcomed the praise, but he understood success had not yet been achieved—and for good reason. Villa, hidden deep in the mountains and cared for by close family, would recover and resume operations. With his excellent foresight, Pershing had his chief of staff issue a directive stating, "All officers and enlisted men of the command are cautioned against a feeling of overconfidence as to the final result to be achieved by this Expedition. The Commanding General appreciates most highly the work already performed by this command and considers it exceptional in many respects to anything hitherto recorded in the annals of the army. All members of the command are urged to put forth renewed energy both as individuals and as organizations in the endeavor to accomplish successfully the mission entrusted to the Expedition by our people."

What Pershing could not have known at the time was that the fight at Guerrero would be the closest the Expedition would come to capturing or killing the bandit leader.

Diary: March 31

Major Tompkins reached Providencia at 7:00 a.m. I had a discussion with Major Tompkins for the way he interpreted the order did not correspond with the plan. I told him I would take responsibility for moving in the way I thought the order intended we should go.

We searched the mountains very thoroughly and all dwellings. In one of them we found several cases of very bad smallpox. Towards the afternoon it got very cold and hailed, rained, and snowed, and finally sleeted. All the men suffered. We reached San Geronimo at 7:30 having ridden at a walk for sixteen hours with only one hour's rest. It was still very cold.

Patton's discussion with Tompkins about his orders is remarkable in that he, as a lieutenant, had the confidence to challenge a senior, veteran officer. It also demonstrates that he had gained the respect of the field commanders in that Tompkins listened to him.

CHAPTER EIGHT

April 1916

Diary: April 1

Weather moderated at 10:00 a.m. The General sent me to Namiquipa with dispatches in car, giving as complete an account as possible of General Dodd's fight at Guerrero. I reached Namiquipa about noon.

During my absence the General and Major Ryan left San Geronimo at 1:00 p.m. and joined Colonel Dodd at Providencia, then they went to Bachineva and were lost for a time on the way, but finally reached the town.

I went to look for them at 9:00 p.m. but found nothing, and got lost myself in the hills. It was a very cold night.

The Expedition operated with only rudimentary maps at best—or none at all at worst—of their areas of operation in Mexico. Given the timeless saying within the enlisted ranks that "the most dangerous thing in the world is a lieutenant with a map and compass," Patton likely admitted to becoming lost only because Pershing had suffered the same difficulties himself that day, for he was aware that an officer's navigation abilities are crucial to mission accomplishment and subordinates' respect. His comments about the extreme weather further reinforced the difficulties and challenges faced by field soldiers.

Diary: April 2

Got word from General Pershing by motorcycle orderly at 10:00 a.m. Lieutenant Collins was in camp with me at the time, having returned from Major Howze's forces, which were then near Providencia. General Pershing and Major Ryan got back from San Geronimo at 3:00 p.m.

We received news at 6:00 p.m. that the Tenth Cavalry had had a skirmish with Villa, and that night Mr. Gibbons of the New York Tribune *secured an orchestra of Mexicans, who played for us from 7:00 to 8:30. General Pershing gave them some money.*

Taking time out to listen to music was unusual. Most of the time the living conditions for Pershing's headquarters mirrored the same challenges that faced his soldiers. In his "Personal Glimpses of General Pershing," written in 1924, Patton recalled, "From March to the end of May he [Pershing] slept on the ground without a tent, doubling up with one of his Aides for the additional warmth secured by the two blankets, but no frost or snow prevented his daily shave so that by personal example he prevented the morale destroying growth of facial herbage which hard campaigns so frequently produce."

A hint of sarcasm can be read into Patton's comment about "moral destroying growth of facial herbage," but he later adopted the general's grooming standards as his own. He continued in the "Glimpses," stating, "During our first stay at Dublan the General made frequent motor trips to our advancing detachments 30 to 50 miles in the front and never carried anything except one blanket and his toilet articles."

According to Patton, Pershing's mobile headquarters was bleak and vulnerable. He wrote, "When we moved forward to a place called San Geronimo Ranch, the Punitive Expedition Headquarters consisted of the General, Colonel J. Ryan, myself, a stenographer, a cook, three drivers, and four soldiers. For days at a time there were no other troops within miles. The office consisted of a box in front of the Dodge car which now carried the General and whose headlight formed his only reading lamp."

Pershing's willingness to forgo creature comforts served as a model of soldiering to Patton, and the junior leader adopted the same concept of an austere headquarters during the Second World War. Indeed, that desert minimalist formation was the impetus for the way Patton organized the enormous Third Army so that he could effectively command the force. He divided his army into two separate code-named organizations. Lucky Rear contained the larger, more stable echelon, while Patton mostly commanded from the much smaller Lucky Forward, located closer to the front lines.

While Patton gleaned the lessons offered through the Expedition experience, all members of the mission did not share his positive attitude, quipping with disgust about the pursuit of Villa, "We have him surrounded, but only on one side." No matter how rapidly the cavalry moved, they were nearly always a day's ride or more behind their quarry. Even Patton wrote that it was almost looking "for a needle in a haystack."

One small needle in the haystack was discovered by elements of the Tenth Cavalry on April 1. A chance encounter between the regiment's Second Squadron and a group of 150 Villistas commanded by Colonel Francisco Beltran occurred in the mountains near Agua Caliente, which resulted in a running gun battle that stretched over a distance of seven miles. The Americans killed two Mexicans while suffering no casualties themselves. This action was particularly significant because Major Charles Young, one of the few Black officers in the U.S. Army, led the charge.

Diary: April 3

General Pershing stayed in camp. Two troops of Major Howze's squadron got in, followed later by the others. They came from Bachineva. I left in an automobile at 1:00 p.m. to take a message to Colonel Dodd at Santo Tomas. Had six punctures and failed to find Colonel Dodd. I reached camp about 11:00 p.m.

Diary: April 4

General Pershing sent forage and provisions to Major Tompkins at Bachineva. Major Howze started south with pack trains and four troops. General Pershing personally inspected the conditions of the horses before dispatching the column. I started at 6:30 with an automobile to take additional information to Major Howze. I secured two horses at Providencia and rode from six to twelve p.m. through the mountains in order to find Major Howze. It was very cold but I finally located him by the reflection of his camp fire on the clouds.

Pershing's personal inspection of the column's horses taught Patton yet another lesson, indelibly imprinting on him the importance of the commander's personal attention to detail and the breadth of responsibility.

Diary: April 5

I returned to Providencia in company of two Mexican vaqueros, who had been Colonel Howze's guides, as far as Frijole Canyon the night before.

On reaching San Geronimo, I found that Colonel Allen's squadron had already gotten in. General Pershing ordered Headquarters moved to Namiquipa and arranged for further movements of troops to the south.

Despite the lack of definite intelligence, Major Tompkins convinced Pershing that Villa, even with his wounds, had likely retreated about 150 miles farther south of Guerrero near the border with the state of Durango to a site the Mexican outlaw had used as a base before the Revolution. Pershing concurred and ordered three parallel columns to march south, positioning elements of the Tenth Cavalry to the east and center and part of the Eleventh Cavalry in the west.

Diary: April 6

Lieutenant [Herbert A.] Dargue and Captain Foulois flew to Cusi, locating Colonel Brown. On the fifth Dargue made another flight, locating Major Tompkins.

That afternoon a Mexican came out to the camp and offered to give us a drink. He said he was a very unfortunate man, being a

Pacifico, first the Villa people came and hit him on one cheek and then the Carrancistas came and hit him on the other, and that he was very sad.

Lieutenant Herbert A. Dargue was commissioned into the Coast Artillery on his graduation from West Point in 1911. Two years later, he transferred to the new Air Corps and, prior to joining the First Aero Squadron, had been the only aviation-rated officer assigned to the Philippines. Colonel William C. Brown, West Point class of 1877 and a veteran of the Indian Wars before assuming command of the African American Tenth Cavalry Regiment in 1914, earned the affection of his Black soldiers in their initial sweep into Mexico when he purchased food for them with his own money after the regiment outdistanced its supply lines.

The Mexican populace was tired of the fighting and being caught between Federalists and Revolutionaries by the time the Expedition arrived on scene. One of the results of their despair was that many migrated across the border into the United States, reversing a quarter-century pattern of only a trickle being northbound while significant numbers fled south from Texas after the state gained its independence from Mexico in 1836 and then joined the United States in 1845. Over the next decade about twenty thousand Mexicans a year sought refuge in the United States, settling mainly in San Antonio and along its corridor to Austin.

In addition to making his diary entry, Patton wrote to his father on April 6 about his adventures two days earlier, giving more detail: "I had a most exciting ride the other night [April 4]. I went 26 miles through the mountains at night with two men. We expected to be jumped and once hid from some six horse wagons whom we thought were Mexicans. I did not know where the troops I was hunting were but I finally found them by the reflection of their fires on a cloud. On the way back I saw a flock of wild turkeys but could not shoot at them as I did not want to advertise my presence."

Patton continued, "I crossed the Continental Divide at about 8,000 feet and it was very cold. But hot by day. I have never been so dirty in my life but hope to get a bath someday. The General is fine and a great soldier full of energy. I think he likes me almost too much for I have volunteered to take several messages which he has refused to let me do for fear of my getting hurt."

He signed off, saying, "I am very well and most interested."

Diary: April 7

Captain Foulois and Lieutenant Dargue, and Captain Dodd and Lieutenant Carberry flew to Chihuahua. The Rurales shot at them, and Captain Foulois was put in jail.

I took rations to the Seventh Cavalry at Frijole Pass.

Lieutenant Joseph E. Carberry, West Point class of 1910, was one of the army's original aviators. It was Foulois, who greatly expanded the incident at Chihuahua in his appendix to Perishing's official report of the Expedition, who dominated the incident. He stated that his mission was to secure permission from Mexican authorities for the Expedition to use the Mexican rail system to move supplies southward. As Patton noted, the Federalist shot at Foulois's aircraft and arrested him after he landed outside the city.

According to Foulois's third-person report, "En route to the jail Capt. Foulois succeeded in getting word to an American bystander, requesting that he notify the American Consul of his arrival in the city and that the Consul take necessary steps for the protection of all aviators and machines that had arrived in the city."

After some delay, the Mexicans freed Foulois, and he delivered Pershing's dispatch to the consul. While the consul negotiated for use of the railroad, Foulois returned to his aircraft, gathered his other pilots, and, despite thrown stones and other efforts to sabotage their planes, they flew to American positions.

Diary: April 8

Captain Foulois, Dargue, Dodd, and Carberry returned with news from Consul Letcher who told General Pershing he could ship some supplies to the American troops along the Mexican Railway to San Antonio, Mexico.

General Pershing, Major Ryan, Major Brown of the Engineers and myself, left for San Antonio at noon, with all the staff in an automobile truck. We reached camp at dark and found Colonel Allen with one squadron of the Eleventh Cavalry.

Marion H. Letcher, a graduate of the University of Alabama, was the American consul in Chihuahua and a career civilian State Department diplomat.

Diary: April 9

Sent out aeroplane to scout. Colonel Allen took one troop and left about 10:00 a.m.

General Pershing, Major Ryan, myself, and [guide] Mr. Solomon Roker went to Cusi. At this place the General got on the wire and conferred with Consul Letcher.

Diary: April 10

Three aeroplanes scouted seven hundred square miles but failed to locate either our own men or the enemy.

Despite the lack of success in locating troops on these missions—as well as their frequent maintenance problems—Patton saw the potential of the airplanes in communications, reconnaissance, and possibility mapping. This belief stayed with him and influenced his written recommendations for the use of tanks in the World War I St. Mihiel Offensive in September 1918, when he suggested that at least "one low flying airplane accompany the advance." In World War II, Patton employed small "spotter" planes to survey the front in his Third Army's rapid advance across Europe.

Diary: April 11

Colonel [DeRosey C.] Cabell, Captains [Leon B.] Kromer [Eleventh Cavalry Regiment], [William O.] Reed [Sixth Cavalry Regiment], and [William E. W.] McKinlay [Eleventh Cavalry Regiment], and Lieutenant Campanole arrived with five Dodge cars about 9:00 a.m.

General Pershing, Major Ryan, Captains Kromer and Reed, and myself with six Dodge cars, and our baggage on a truck, left San Antonio for Satevo at 10:00 a.m. We had with us twenty-two rifles [soldiers]. At Santa Ysabel we found the road impossible so made a detour reaching Satevo at 9:00 p.m.

On the way, [we passed] an outpost of General Cavasas' men fifteen miles north of Satevo. On reaching Satevo we found two aeroplanes about three miles from town. The aviators not knowing whether we would arrive, were hiding in the bushes nearby and were very glad to see us.

The trucks of the aero squadron, with eighteen Sixth Infantry-men as guards, got in at 10:45. They were fired on eighteen miles out. About one hundred and fifty shots were exchanged, one man got a bullet through his hat. Lieutenant [Michael F.] Davis, commanding the Sixth Infantry guards, was driving one of the Dodge cars when the firing commenced, and he lost his head and ran into the rear of a truck, broke the radiator and the car had to be abandoned.

We thought it probable that the men who did the firing were some of the bandits under a person called General Tarrango.

Captains Kromer, Reed, and McKinlay were detailed from their regiments to augment the austere Expedition staff.

Pershing continued to move his headquarters farther south to be closer to the cavalry units pursuing Villa and his band. They advanced rapidly in pursuit in hopes of not only finding the bandit but also cutting off his retreat to his home state of Durango, where he had even more local support.

More and more cars and trucks were being delivered to Columbus by rail and then driven south to join the Expedition. The mention of a lieutenant driving one of the Dodges—and not doing so well—demonstrated a major adjustment the military would have to make in the future: the Expedition had more vehicles than it had qualified operators. Patton was among the forward thinkers who recognized that teaching troops to drive and to repair vehicles would need to be integral parts of training soldiers. Likewise, future military training would have to train troops to pilot planes and mechanics to specialize in keeping them in the air.

The Expedition provided lessons for future aviators as well as for motorized vehicle drivers. In the early years of World War II, shot-down airmen attempted to escape to Spain, Switzerland, or other neutral havens to evade the Nazis. After Patton's Third Army and other ground units began their push out of the Normandy beachhead toward Paris and Germany, many downed aviators, like their First Aero Squadron predecessors near Satevo, Mexico, simply hid and waited for the advancing Allies.

Diary: April 12

Captain Reed and Lieutenant Winters with fifteen men and two trucks left to investigate the shooting and salvage the cars. Lieutenant [Carleton G.] Chapman made a flight south but found nothing. Lieutenant Carberry reached camp in a plane.

Captain Reed returned with car and motorcycle, both of which had been burned. We used parts of the car for extra parts.

Colonel Allen, with two troops of the Eleventh Cavalry, came into camp at six p.m.

Unlike the cavalry, where a lame or dead horse could no longer contribute, Patton noted that disabled automobiles could be stripped of usable parts to keep others on the road. With the long supply line of spare parts stretching back to Columbus, a used part off a disabled vehicle worked just as well. This practice, known as "cannibalization," would one day play a major role in Patton's Third Army and its ability to dash across Europe.

Patton learned another important lesson on this date. In "Personal Glimpses" of 1924, he wrote that, though not yet fully informed about the fight at Parral, Pershing decided to move farther south to be closer to the advancing cavalry columns. The command convoy consisted of three open cars with fifteen men. He wrote, "The country we traversed consisted of 90 miles of unmapped and semi-hostile mountain and desert."

Shortly after nightfall, the headlights of the lead car illuminated an armed Mexican standing in the roadway with "a veritable army" lurking in the nearby bushes. As Pershing's escorts took up defensive positions around their general, Patton related, "With halting Spanish and beating heart, I rushed forward to solve the problem, always most difficult, as to the friendliness or hostility of the Mexicans. I had just prejudiced my hope of eternal salvation by a valuable description of ourselves as the advance guard of an automobile regiment when the General appeared at my side and frustrated my efforts at deception by declaring himself to be General Pershing, and demanding 'Why the hell these people dared to stop him.'"

Patton continued his story, relating that for a few moments he had a vision of a total massacre, "but the commanding presence of the General and his utter disregard of danger over-awed the Mexicans and we went on, though personally it was more than a mile before I ceased feeling bullets entering my back. Two hours later a convoy of three trucks with airplane spare parts and gas was attacked by these same Mexicans."

In conclusion, Patton noted, "The incident respires the statement attributed to Caesar that 'Fortune favors the bold.'"

Diary: April 13

Captain Foulois returned with news from Consul Letcher at Chihuahua, he also brought a rumor of the attack on our troops at Parral, which was supposed to be Colonel Brown's men. General Pershing sent Captain Reed in four automobiles to go out and investigate. They left at 11:00 a.m. We sent Captain Foulois to Chihuahua with two automobiles to take a letter of remonstrance to the Commanding Officer there. Captain Foulois got back at 10:00 p.m.

No further news of the troops at Parral or of the report attack.

The "letter of remonstrance" contained Pershing's list of grievances about the lack of Mexican assistance and occasions of direct opposition by the Federal troop in the Expedition's pursuit of Villa. His ire would become all that much more stoked when he learned what had occurred at Parral.

Sparsity of information about the fight at Parral emphasized the lack of communications within the Expedition despite the presence of radios, telegraph, aircraft, and motor messengers. It would take another full day before Pershing received details about the significant engagement.

The attack at Parral further diminished Patton's opinion of the Mexicans. In a letter on this date to Beatrice, he wrote, "They are much lower than the Indians."

Diary: April 14

Captain Reed got in at 7:30 a.m. with full report. It was clear that Major Tompkins had been attacked by Carranza troops. Full report of the circumstances was handed the newspaper men. We all left camp at 10:00 in eight autos. We had twenty rifles [soldiers] and went to San Antonio via Palomas.

At Palomas General Pershing got Consul Letcher on the phone and from him had word from Howze, dated the 13th day of April, at Parral.

The General sent word through Consul Letcher to General Funston, also to Major Howze. We passed Santa Ysabel just at dark and one of the Fords broke down. We were rather nervous for fear one of the many bands of Mexicans should fire on us. We reached San Antonio, a distance of ninety-one miles at 12:40. We took gas and oil here and left at 1:15 a.m.

Reed's report revealed that it had been Tompkins rather than Brown who had been attacked, and the attack had been by conducted by Carranza troops rather than those of Villa. Tompkins, accompanied by about one hundred men of the Thirteenth Cavalry, had encountered about two hundred Carrancistas led by General José Cavazos, who informed Tompkins that Villa was dead and warned him not to proceed south because there was the danger of angry civilians attacking the

American column as well as Federal forces. Tompkins, not accepting that Villa was dead, rode around Cavazos's positions and proceeded south in accordance with his own orders.

On April 10, the same cavalry troop surprised a group of Villistas in the act of robbing a small factory in Valle de Zaragoza. They gave chase, collected the goods the bandits had discarded in their retreat, and returned the items to the factory owner. Tompkins then made camp outside Parral. That evening, Captain Antonio Mesa of the town's Federal garrison approached the officer and offered to notify his own commander about the arrival of the U.S. cavalrymen and to assist them in acquiring supplies and a campground.

When Tompkins entered Parral, the local commander claimed to know nothing about what Mesa said and warned the Americans not to continue south because the angry local civilians—upset by rumors of Villa's death and their opposition to the Expedition—might be dangerous. Tompkins dismissed the warning, informing the commander that he would depart the next day after securing supplies. As they spoke, a crowd gathered in the plaza shouting "Viva Villa!" and "Viva Mexico!" Tompkins reported that a German agent, hoping to create additional difficulties between the United States and Mexico, incited the protest.

Carrancista guides led the Americans to a camp site outside of town, but Tompkins realized it was surrounded by high ground and impossible to defend. While the command was moving to a better position, they began receiving fire from civilians, who were emboldened by the more than five hundred Federal troops who had arrived. Tompkins began an orderly withdrawal with a rear guard covering the retreat when the Carrancistas joined the civilians in firing at the cavalrymen. Although wounded in the shoulder, Tompkins continued to trade space for time as his column slowly retreated under the cover of rear-guard action.

When Tompkins reached defendable ground, he turned his command to engage the pursuing Mexicans. Within minutes, forty-five Carrancistas fell to the cavalrymen's rifles. The rest turned back to Parral. The Americans continued to Santa Cruz with their own casualties—two dead and six wounded. There they were joined on April 12 by Colonel

Brown and the Tenth Cavalry, who had responded to courier messages for assistance from Tompkins.

Carrancista officers sent word to Brown that the Americans must immediately move north. In defiance, Brown answered that he would not move one step north "until I have orders from my commanding general."

Much of Pershing's account to his superiors about the incident at Parral appeared in his "Punitive Expedition Report." He wrote, "The unprovoked and outrageous attack at Parral, April 12th, on Major Tompkins' command by the civil population aided by the Carrancista forces under their own field officers, was the culmination of a long series of petty acts of hostility which grew in number and viciousness as our columns moved south."

Pershing delivered a narrative that closely followed that of Tompkins. He concluded, "Major Tompkins fired only after he was attacked and did everything possible to avoid a fight. After he was persistently pursued several miles he very properly deployed a troop at a time and inflicted severe damage upon his pursuers, killing 42 according to authentic reports of the fight received through native sources."

Diary: April 16

Drove until 7:30 when we reached new camp at Namiquipa. General Pershing came here in order to be on the land wire in communication with Columbus, on account of the many faults we had discovered in using the wireless and aeroplanes as means of communications.

Although General Pershing had not slept for two nights, he worked all day.

Lieutenant Campanole was fired upon in the evening while returning from Namiquipa on a motorcycle.

The wire to Columbus was cut as usual.

Diary: April 17

A very bad windy day. Colonel Cabell and Captain Burt arrived. General Pershing wrote several important telegrams as a result of the

information he received from Colonel Cabell and about the operations
at Parral and about Major Howze's fight in the Bellgasa Valley.

In order to secure communications with New Mexico, Texas, and Washington, D.C., Pershing moved his headquarters from near Santa Cruz to Namiquipa, where he could send wireless messages via the relay at Casas Grandes. Despite the usual difficulty with the telegraph, he eventually got his messages through. Pershing explained to his superiors that the Expedition faced "obstruction, changing more and more to open hostility the farther south we progressed." He recommended "the immediate capture of the city and state of Chihuahua and the seizure of all railroads therein."

Members of the army staff in Washington concurred with their Expedition commander, some going as far as to request a full-scale invasion to pacify Mexico. At the minimum, they recommended the call-up of several thousand National Guardsmen to protect the border against future raids.

President Wilson turned down both requests. Given the likelihood of the United States soon having to enter the war in Europe, Wilson had no desire to have more troops bogged down in Mexico, chasing an elusive bandit and facing increased opposition from the Federal troops. Instead, he dispatched diplomats and generals to negotiate with the Carranza government.

Diary: April 18

Still waiting orders to do something on account of the Parral incident.
A wire cutter was killed north of El Valle.
There is a persistent rumor that Villa is dead, and the body found south of Cusi. Lieutenant Shallenberger and Captain Reed went to Cusi to investigate on April 19th.

The rumor of Villa's death was, of course, incorrect. Villa remained hidden in the mountains recovering from his wound while relishing the news about the increased tension between the Americans and the Carrancistas. His army, now led by subordinate generals, remained in the field operating in small groups.

Diary: April 19

Campanole left at 3:00 a.m. to search for Villa men reported at Namiquipa. He returned about 6:00 a.m. with three men and two rifles. One man was the son of President Munios of Namiquipa.

Colonel Cabell decided to go toward Parral with five autos. Major Ryan with one auto and one truck started toward Santo Tomas.

Diary: April 20

Carberry and Chapman flew from Columbus, they left at 5:00 a.m. and arrived at 8:30. At 10:00 a.m. we received word of the death of a relative of General [Luis] Herrera in the Parral fight.

President Munios of Namiquipa informed Captain Reed of the death of several people of importance in the Parral fight.

This was a very fine day and no wind.

This flight of the two airplanes was the final mission of the original First Aero Squadron. In his appendix to Pershing's "Punitive Expedition Report," Captain Foulois wrote, "April 20, 1916. Orders received to return to Columbus, New Mexico to secure new aeroplanes. Of the eight aeroplanes taken into Mexico on March 19, 1916, but two were still in commission on the date. These two aeroplanes were in such condition as to be unsafe for further field service. They were therefore flown to Columbus, this date, and ultimately condemned and destroyed."

Foulois concluded his report with a summary of his unit's performance:

The Squadron Commander invites attention to the fact that the 1st Aero Squadron, S.C., is the first organization of its kind that has ever been used in active field service in the history of the United States Army. This command took the field with aeroplanes of very low military efficiency, and with less than 50% of its authorized truck transportation. Due to the lack of aeroplanes with greater carrying capacity, all flying officers were continuously called upon to take extraordinary risks in every reconnaissance flight made while on duty in Mexico. All officers thoroughly appreciated the fact that the failure of their aeroplane motors, while flying through mountains, canyons, and over rugged mountains, would invariably result in death. They also appreciated the fact that in a forced landing even if safely made, there was every possible risk of being taken prisoner by an enemy, whose ideas of the laws of war are on a par with an uncivilized race of savages.

Patton rarely used humor or irony in his journal entries, and a century later it is impossible to determine whether he meant it was "a very fine day" because of the weather or as a result of the death of "several people of importance in the Parral fight."

Diary: April 21

I inspected the horses at the rest stations for the general; found most of them in very poor shape. This was largely due to the failure to get long forage [straw and green fodder, as distinguished from hay, oats, etc.], which at this time was unavailable.

Diary: April 22

A truck train of Jeffery Motor Trucks arrived from Colonia Dublan. The rest of the Eleventh Cavalry and two squadrons of the Fifth Cavalry arrived in camp at 10:00 a.m. The horses were in bad shape. Major Ryan retuned from Santa Tomas.

Airplanes were not the only part of the Expedition that was wearing out. Six weeks of continuous operations had both horses and men near exhaustion. In addition to dispatching Patton to inspect the horses at the rest stations, the general issued his personal instructions on the care of the mounts.

In his original journal, Patton recorded, "I wrote a memo for Gen. on feeding of horses." In a revised version, he recorded, "General Pershing published a memorandum regulating the feeding of the horses." Patton was learning that the subordinate never takes credit away from the superior.

Diary: April 23

The Fifth and Eleventh Cavalry left for camp at Lake Itascate. Truck train from Columbus arrived with mail.

Colonel Cabell returned from near Parral with Lieutenant Collins who had been with Major Howze. He also brought with him the report that a truck guard of the Twenty-fourth Infantry had killed a Mexican near Santa Ysabel.

I rented a seven passenger Buick touring car from the Tailor [Taylor] Brothers, at the rate of twenty-five dollars per day.

While the pursuit of Villa was a cavalry operation, the security for motorized supply columns and headquarters fell to the infantry—in this case, the Black Twenty-Fourth. In the deserts of Mexico, Patton learned about the vulnerabilities of mechanized vehicles to attack by ground or horse-mounted troops if they were not diligently guarded.

The Taylor Brothers shipped cattle to U.S. markets, operated a tannery, and operated other businesses in the Mormon community. None of the *Patton Papers* make clear why he rented a car or provided a rationale for paying the exorbitant rate equal to $600.

Diary: April 24

General Pershing went to San Geronimo and returned this afternoon. I took five trucks to the Seventh Cavalry camp at Neuarachic Pass. Here I learned that Baca was reported to have been killed at Santo Tomas. I went there with three soldiers and Scout Baker in a light truck. I saw the Presidente and he said that Baca was shot the night of April 22nd by his orders and had been buried. I returned to Namiquipa and reported the fact of Baca's death to General Pershing.

General Manuel Baca had been one of Villa's primary subordinates in the raid on Columbus and in their retreat from the advancing Expedition. Villa bestowed rank generously, at times having as many generals and colonels as captains and lieutenants in his army. Generals often led only one hundred men or so. Baca's end, even though brought on by the Federals, was welcome news. Another of the Columbus raiders now lay on the "wrong side of the grass" in a Mexican cemetery.

Diary: April 25

General Pershing assembled the correspondents and told them that the orders for the withdrawal of the Expedition had been revoked.

Patton's journal entry would have been more accurate had he written that Pershing had assured the news correspondents that the Expedition had no plans to withdraw from Mexico. Post-Parral negotiations between the U.S. and Mexican governments had been proposed on April 22 and would begin on April 28. Pershing, like everyone else, had no idea what these negotiations would determine. All he could do was wait, but he used his time wisely in planning for future operations if it was decided the Expedition would continue.

In a letter to his father on this date, Patton expressed his feelings about President Wilson's decisions about the Expedition: "Wilson ought to take iron or something to stiffen his back." Patton also offered his opinion that the Expedition had benefited the image of the army in the eyes of the American public, stating, "We have helped the army and especially the cavalry by this trip."

Diary: April 26

Captain [William D.] Forsythe of the Third Squadron of the Fifth Cavalry got into camp.

Captain Reed and I went to Namiquipa to arrest Calanderio Cervantes, but after we got near the house we found that we could not approach it without being seen, and so we returned to camp.

The sleeping bag, which had been ordered for General Pershing, arrived today.

The Fifth Cavalry Regiment had recently joined the Expedition. Colonel Cervantes, a participant in the raid on Columbus, was one of Villa's most trusted subordinates. Patton left no record on how they had determined his whereabouts or why he did not take a larger force to arrest him.

In Mexico, Patton was learning the importance of details regarding not only military matters but also the aide's responsibility for making the general as comfortable as possible. The arrival of a sleeping bag for the cold desert nights merited sufficient importance to gain an entry in the diary on par with pursuit of a major bandit.

According to Pershing's "Punitive Expedition Report," Lieutenant Shallenberger left his position of aide on this date to become the assistant to the Expedition's adjutant, in all likelihood due to Pershing no longer needing three assistants. It certainly was no reflection of any shortcomings on the part of Shallenberger, who would continue to perform some duties for the general and later accompany him to Europe as an aide when the United States entered the war in Europe.

Diary: April 27

A very bad wind storm raged all morning. In the afternoon General Pershing and myself went for a ride about the camp and to inspect the forage. We found that while on the plains it was very poor, on the hillsides it was very good.

Diary: April 28

This was a very windy, dusty day. The wind blew so hard that two of the big storage tents went down. Major Ryan was ordered to rejoin his regiment.

On this same date in a letter to his father, Patton enumerated more of his opinion of what should occur in Mexico while also elaborating on the boredom of camp life. He wrote that current operations were not sufficient, declaring, "Intervention in this country would be the most futile thing in the world. We must take it or leave it. If we leave it, ruin total and complete will follow. Intervention would simply mean a continuation of this despotic system. If we take the country we could settle it and these people would be happier and better off."

In the same letter, Patton further wrote, "We have been very idle ever since reaching here and it is most tiresome sitting out on a bluff over a river in the sun and dust. We can't go to town because they shoot at us now and then and the General does not want to start anything unless he can finish it."

Patton added that the surrounding countryside was excellent game country with deer, bear, turkey, and ducks. However, he concluded, there were also "wild Mexicans so if you go out hunting you are very apt to be hunted."

Lieutenant Campanole, replacing Major Ryan, who had returned to his regiment, became the Expedition's intelligence officer. In the process of learning how to use scouts and spies, how to tap Mexican telegraph lines, and how to analyze human intelligence, Patton had developed a close personal and professional relationship with the major.

Diary: April 29

Colonel Dodd and Colonel Erwin came from Providencia to Namiquipa to confer with General Pershing.

Colonel James B. Erwin, West Point class of 1880, commanded the Seventh Cavalry Regiment. A veteran of the Indian Wars and the Philippine Insurrection, he had, as a captain, served as the military commander of Yellowstone National Park in 1887.

Dodd and Erwin were at Pershing's headquarters to be briefed on the reorganization of the Expedition and future plans. Negotiation between U.S. and Mexican officials had broken down when the Americans, promising to withdraw from Mexico, refused to establish an exact date. Although the talks ended on a somewhat friendly note with agreement to meet again soon, Pershing knew that standstill meant that any operations farther southward would be met with opposition from both the Villistas and the Carrancistas.

Thus, Pershing once again modified his offensive plans and called the meeting with his staff. Knowing that Villa was at least wounded—and possibly dead—and that his army was still operating only in small, scattered bands, Pershing decided now to focus on northern Chihuahua. He divided the area of operations into five districts with a cavalry regiment in charge of each—San Francisco de Borja, Eleventh Cavalry; Satevo, Fifth Cavalry; Bustillos, Thirteenth Cavalry; Guerrero, Seventh Cavalry; Namiquipa, Tenth Cavalry. This concentration on specific areas would allow the regiments to become more familiar with the terrain, develop relationships with the locals, and cultivate intelligence resources.

General Pershing made the new organization official by issuing General Orders No. 28 from "Headquarters Punitive Expedition, US Army, In the Field, Namiquipa, Mexico, April 29, 1916." Paragraph 1 of the order stated, "As a result of the arduous and persistent pursuit of Villa by various columns of this command, his forces have suffered losses of approximately one hundred killed with unknown number wounded, and have broken into smaller bands and scattered to different regions of the State of Chihuahua and elsewhere. The situation has changed to the extent that our troops no longer pursue a cohesive force of considerable size, but by surprise with small, swiftly moving detachments, they must hunt down isolated bands, now under subordinate leaders and operating over widely separated portions of the country. For this purpose the territory to be covered for the present is accordingly divided into districts and apportioned to organizations available for such duty."

Pershing recognized, and Patton learned, that decisions in the midst of operations could best be made by commanders on the ground rather than by those in protected headquarters. In paragraph 2 of the order, Pershing directed, "Each district commander will act on his own initiative on any information that seems likely to lead to the capture of any participants in the Columbus raid, and will keep the Commanding General and, as far as practical, the Brigade Commander, advised of all movements in his district."

Diary: April 30

General Pershing, Colonel Cabell, Captain Kromer, and Lieutenant Collins left at 2:20 p.m. for San Antonio, Mexico. General Pershing permitted me to join a column of the Thirteenth Cavalry and see a little service.

I left at 2:45 with one man and two horses, arrived at San Geronimo, a distance of seventeen miles. Captain [William C.] Gardenhire of the Tenth Cavalry gave me supper and breakfast.

General Pershing and his party reached Lake Itascate at 4:20, and inspected the camp of the Fifth, Eleventh, and Thirteenth Cavalry. They left at 8:30 and reached San Antonio at 11:30 p.m.

Most of Patton's duties to this date had been providing personal care for Pershing, delivering messages, and assisting in running the Expedition headquarters. He had had little time to participate in actual field operations; the opportunity to spend a day in the saddle with the Thirteenth Cavalry to "see a little service" merited an entry in his diary.

CHAPTER NINE

May 1916

Diary: May 1

The regiments at San Antonio, all the Sixth Infantry, six troops and the machine gun troop of the Tenth Cavalry, arrived from the south. Also, Colonel Allen and Colonel Howze and the second squadron of the Eleventh Cavalry, Major Tompkins with two troops of the Thirteenth Cavalry.

On this day also, the General went over the subject of guides, and dispensed with the services of those whose services were no longer useful.

In addition to all his other responsibilities, Pershing had to oversee the budget of the Expedition that between March 17, 1916, and February 10, 1917, totaled $3,287,649.82—the equivalent of nearly $80 million today. Now that his forces were no longer moving south into new territory—instead, they were establishing areas of operations on grounds familiar to the cavalrymen—civilian guides were no longer needed and their salaries could be redirected.

Diary: May 2

Captain Reed and Lieutenant Campanole arrived from Namiquipa at 7:00 p.m. Satisfactory news came over the wire of General [Hugh L.] Scott's conference.

General Scott, the army chief of staff and latest negotiator with Mexican officials, confirmed that the Expedition was not going to be withdrawn.

In his early diary entries, Patton was always factual and fairly self-uncensored, generally describing what he saw in unabashed detail, for he was not one to second-guess himself. This was, in part, why General Pershing would later request a copy of Patton's Expedition diary, and why Patton would deliver the copied pages virtually unchanged—except for the May 2 entry.

In the version for Pershing, Patton left out a significant story covered in the original in which Patton wrote that he, Lieutenant Innis P. Swift of the Thirteenth Cavalry, and Mormon guide Lemuel Spilsbury went to a ranch six miles north of San Miguel in an attempt to capture Julian (Julio) Cardenas, a member of Villa's personal staff at Columbus. Cardenas was not at the ranch, but Patton was able to detain the bandit's wife and baby and his uncle. In his original diary, Patton wrote, "Tried to get information out of the uncle. Failed."

In a letter to Beatrice, Patton added to the account, writing, "Spilsbury and I hung Cardenas' uncle three times to make him talk. Finally he did, though he fainted a couple of times first." To his father, Patton wrote, "The uncle was a very brave man and nearly died before he would tell me anything."

In his original journal entry, Patton had violated the diarist's axiom of "never write anything that will get you put in jail or divorced." By the time Patton edited his diary for delivery to Pershing, he had become much more discreet in his writings and simply left out what can only be defined as torture of the unfortunate uncle that amounted to a war crime. It would be more than a half-century after the incident and a quarter-century after Patton's death before the incident would be revealed with the release of Patton's papers. Likewise, Lieutenant Swift, West Point class of 1904, who had served as an aide to Pershing in the Philippines, made no mention of the event in his papers.

Diary: May 3

Lieutenant Campanole left for Namiquipa with Colonel Brown and two Japanese guides.

General Pershing and Colonel Allen inspected the horses of the Eleventh Cavalry in the afternoon. Colonel Allen was at this time Acting Inspector General.

The Thirteenth Cavalry, less four troops, got in from the Lake. Colonel Wilder with part of the Fifth Cavalry also arrived.

The news that we were to raise an army of one hundred and eighty thousand men got in last night.

Colonel William E. Wilder, West Point class of 1877 and a Medal of Honor recipient for valor in the Indian Wars, commanded the Fifth Cavalry Regiment.

News about the army of 180,000 came from the announcement by President Wilson that he was activating the National Guards of Texas, Arizona, and New Mexico to secure the border from any further attacks. Shortly thereafter, he called to active status Guards units from all the remaining states and the District of Columbia for duty on the border. The total number of Guardsmen fell short of the original order for 180,000, but the number did ultimately total more than 140,000.

In addition to border security, the Guardsmen were to provide "a show of force" to prompt Mexican authorities to reconsider further aggression against the Expedition. More important, the call-up allowed substantial training for units that would form the nucleus of the more than four-million-man army mobilized for World War I.

Diary: May 4

General Pershing, Captain Reed, and Lieutenant Collins worked this morning over the rate of pay for the guides.

The news came of the Villista attack on Ojo Azules. Here they captured seventy-seven of a garrison of eighty Carranzistas.

Major Lopez of the Carranzista Army asked the General to send troops to Cusi against the Villistas. In pursuance of this Major Howze with two squadrons of the Eleventh Cavalry left at 8:30 p.m.

Diary: May 5

General Pershing ordered the first squadron of the Thirteenth Cavalry to El Rubio at 1:00 p.m. At 12:00 just as I was saddling my horse, Colonel Allen told me that I was ordered back to Headquarters. I went to the General and told him that he would think me lazy if I came back too soon. He told me, however, to come.

About 2:00 p.m. a man came in with the news of Colonel Howze's fight at Ojo Azules, where forty-two Mexicans were killed. General Pershing was much pleased.

Diary: May 6

The rest of the Thirteenth Cavalry started for El Rubio at 7:00 p.m. Their camp was dirty, so I caught them at Ojo Calientes, and one troop came back to clean up.

At 3:00 p.m. Lieutenant S. W. Williams of the Eleventh Cavalry, Adjutant of Major Howze, came in with a full report of the fight, and also Sergeant Chicken of the Apache Scouts gave the General a saber he had captured.

At 7:00 p.m. we had news of the serious illness of Major Moore and General Pershing sent Major Nauberg to operate.

Cusi was the shortened name used by Patton, Pershing, and most troops for the Mennonite silver mining town of Cusihuiriachic. In his report to Pershing, included in the general's "Expedition Report," Howze wrote:

We made an all night march to Ojo Azules, distance thirty-six miles. Reached here at 5:45 a.m., unfortunately one-half hour after daylight. We surprised Julio Acosta, Cruz Dominques, and Antonio Angel and jumped them. Had a running fight for two hours; drove their bands into the hills between here and Carichic. Killed 42 verified by officers, captured several and some 50 or 75 horses and mules. It is believed we killed Angel, although identification not complete. We rescued a Carrancista lieutenant and four soldiers just before they were to be shot. We followed the enemy consisting of about 140 until our horses were wholly exhausted, but the chase did not stop until the enemy left unhit had been broken up entirely. In fact, those who escaped did so as individuals. Our approach was discovered by the Villistas' herd guard which fired at our Indians [Apache scouts] and also alarmed the sleeping enemy which ran pell-mell, half dressed, firing at us in their flight. The remarkable part is, although the clothing of several of our men was hit, not a single man was wounded, thanks to the utter surprise and confusion of the enemy. We lost three or four horses. It is needless to say that the officers and men behaved as would be expected. I intend to rest here.

Sergeant Chicken of the Apache scouts provided a much more concise report of the battle. According to Chicken, "*Huli!* Damn fine fight."

Sergeant Chicken had acquired his name when the Americans could not readily pronounce his Apache name of *Eskehwadestah*. In addition to tracking Villa and his band, Chicken and his fellow Apache served as guides for hunting parties, including Patton's, that went in search of deer, antelope, and other game for sport and table.

Patton noted more about Chicken in his original diary than what appeared in his final version. He wrote that when Chicken reported, "he had a note from Maj. Howze saying that he [Chicken] had three prisoners and a sword. I asked Chicken where the prisoners were. He could not read so he was ignorant of the fact that I knew of the prisoners. He looked surprised when I asked him." According to the diary, Chicken smiled and said the prisoners got "heap sick all dead." Apparently, Patton asked no further questions. He was learning.

Pershing added his comments about Cusi in his "Expedition Report," stating, "Major Howze's action showed enterprise and good judgement and resulted in the destruction and disintegration of Acosta's band. Since that time Acosta has never been able to assemble more than 20 men, and he has kept his band and himself hidden in the mountains back of Guerrero where he is reported at the present time."

Major James T. Moore of the Sixteenth Infantry was evacuated to El Paso, where he died of peritonitis in the Fort Bliss hospital on May 14.

According to his obituary in the May 15 edition of the *New York Times*, the forty-nine-year-old Moore was a Connecticut native, a graduate of West Point, and a veteran of the wars in Cuba and the Philippines.

Diary: May 7

Colonel Allen, Lieutenant Campanole, and Major Tompkins went to Namiquipa, but the General remained in camp working on the details of the Quartermaster supply.

Pershing faced the constant challenge of securing food, clothing, and ammunition for his soldiers; grain and fodder for their horses; and fuel and spare parts for the motorized vehicles. The hundreds of miles of supply lines back to Columbus had to be maintained and protected. On arrival, supplies had to be secured and then properly dispersed.

In Mexico, Patton observed firsthand the importance and difficulties in supplying a rapidly moving army. He learned that the combat head of an army could not be continually attacking without a sufficient logistical tail—a problem that would later plague him in the Third Army's rapid advance across Europe.

Diary: May 8

Got news of the defeat of the two hundred and fifty thousand amendment to the Army Bill.
    Captain Kromer and I went for a ride.

With the Punitive Expedition in Mexico and the looming war in Europe, there was a "preparedness controversy" in the U.S. Congress. Debate led to the National Defense Act of 1916, which increased the numbers of National Guard units and defined the authority of War Department supervision. It authorized the creation of the Reserve Officers' Training Corps (ROTC), the creation of an aviation arm, and the immediate contracting in advance for gunpowder to ensure availability at the outbreak of war.

The original act also called for more than doubling the current army numbers to 250,000. This was lowered to 175,000 in the final bill.

In addition to keeping up with the political side of the military, Patton continued to associate with the "best and brightest." Captain Leon B. Kromer graduated from West Point in 1899 and returned to the Academy for a year as its head football coach after a tour with the Tenth Cavalry Regiment. He had served in the Philippine-American War before joining the Punitive Expedition as its assistant quartermaster officer. He was one of the earliest supporters of the horse cavalry transition to a mechanized force.

Diary: May 9

Nothing of importance happened until 2:00 p.m. when Lieutenant Collins and I translated code message about imminent break with Carranza.

Collins went in three autos to recall Major Howze. The Quartermaster of the Fifth Cavalry left at 5:00 p.m. to bring back that regiment.

Truck trains with hay came in in the evening.

Diary: May 10

The General arranged March Table and sent truck trains to take away the forage. I went to El Rubio with orders to get in touch with Major Ryan. I found him there. On return to camp everything was ready to move. We took down the tents at 8:00 p.m.

The Sixth Infantry and the Eleventh Cavalry marched north to San Diego del Monte.

Diary: May 11

We all got up at 5:00 a.m. General Pershing, Colonel Cabell, Captain Kromer, Captain Reed, Lieutenant Collins, and Lieutenant Campanole started north at 6:30 in autos to Lake Itascate. The General

arrived at 10:00 a.m. I rode with the Fifth Cavalry, started at 9:00.
Colonel Wilder took one hour to find camp.
 General Pershing got word at 8:00 p.m. to suspend movement
north.

Negotiations between U.S. and Mexican diplomats meeting in El Paso had once again broken down, with Mexico threatening to send a large army to interdict American supply lines and drive it out of the country. Pershing's superiors ordered him to withdraw his troops to Colonia Durbán.

The order, however, was rescinded two days later when it became evident that the Mexicans were making no effort to follow through on their threat. Patton himself did not have to detail the frustrations felt and difficulties caused by the order and the counterorder. Colonel Cabell, as chief of staff, did it for him, and Pershing included a summary of Cabell's evaluation of the order and its recension in his "Expedition Report." Cabell wrote:

May 9th, at San Antonio the Commanding General received an order
to at once withdraw all troops at least as far north as Namiquipa, and
to start at once.

 At this time troops were moving into the five districts and were
continually occupying many stations, along a line of more than 300
miles from Columbus and many of them far off the main route. Their
supply was difficult and every truck and wagon was engaged in it.

 After receiving his orders of the Commanding General, the order
involving the movement of some forty different units at many different
locations was gotten out in two hours and the backward movement of
all started that afternoon. The movement included the evacuation of
Advance Depot at San Antonio and a large part of that at Namiquipa.

 By the night of the 11th, the movement was well under way,
all trains loaded and moving north. The rear troops at Lake Itascate,
33 miles north of San Antonio and 61 miles north of Carretas, the
southernmost station occupied.

 At 9:00 p.m., May 11th, an order was received from Department
Headquarters to suspend the movement. This necessitated a complete

reversal of all plans, including the return of supplies south. The troops were easily stopped where they found themselves; but the reversal of the trains taking supplies north was a serious matter.

Owing to the long distances, the rough roads, the amount of gasoline used by truck trains and the fact that a truck must return to the shop for repairs at frequent intervals, this movement north, its stopping, and its reversal of truck trains resulted in an average loss equivalent to two weeks use of all truck trains. The final result being the necessary reduction to the reserve ration for a considerable period.

Diary: May 12

I went hunting with Lieutenant Scott, saw two deer. We reached the Lake at 3:30 p.m.

Patton sought hunting companions from all parts of the Expedition in order to learn about different aspects of the army. Lieutenant Harold D. Scott was a medical officer assigned the operations Field Hospital Number 3.

Diary: May 13

General Pershing inspected the camp at 10:30 a.m. In the afternoon I went to inspect a camp where the General desired to have the Eleventh Cavalry camp. I found the spring about a mile further up the canyon than reported. Captain Reed and Captain Campanole went to Namiquipa that night.

Despite all the activities and confusion of the past three days, routine—including hunting—quickly resumed. For Patton, however, his most eventful and influential day of the Expedition was about to take place.

Diary: May 14

General Pershing sent me with ten men of the Sixth Infantry in our auto and scouts [E. L.] Holmdahl and [W.] Lunt to buy some corn. I

was to pay for this corn at the rate of four pesos per hectare. I went to
a ranch at Coyote, Rubio, and Salsido, where I secured two hundred
and fifty hectares of corn.

Then I decided to go to the ranch at San Miguel and see if I could
not find Colonel Julio Cardenas. I found him there and killed him
and two of his men, a captain named Isadore Lopez and orderly Juan
Garza. We captured three saddles, two rifles, three pistols, two sabers,
and two belts.

The fight started at 12:30 p.m. and lasted until 12:45 p.m.
Lieutenant Patton killed Cardenas and Garza.

The San Miguel ranch was a part of the large Zuloaga family estate, and one of the Zuloaga daughters had married a cousin of former Mexico president Francisco Madero, whom Villa had supported in the early days of the Revolution. Because of his initial backing, Villa and his fellow band members were welcome at the ranch. Cardenas had been using it not only as a recruiting base but also as a home for his wife and children.

Patton wrote several versions of the fight at San Miguel, but they are essentially the same. In his copy of the diary provided to Pershing, he added the complete names of the three Mexican casualties as well as the handwritten note that read, "Lieutenant Patton killed Cardenas and Garza." In his 1928 report on Pershing, Patton expanded on the details regarding the movements and locations of the participants.

According to his own account, after searching the dead bandits' home, Patton had their bodies loaded on the fenders of his automobiles like deer from a hunt and returned to the Expedition headquarters.

Pershing and the press corps inspected the bodies and, after positive identification, the rapidly decaying bandits were buried. Although there is no other confirmation, years later Patton claimed that, in the hasty funeral as the sun was going down, the only eulogy was made by a veteran sergeant who said, "Ashes to ashes and dust to dust. If Villa won't bury you, Uncle Sam must."

On May 15, Pershing sent a telegram to Columbus for the release to the media. It stated, "Lieutenant Patton with small detachment was sent to Rubio, twenty miles east of here [Lake Itascate] yesterday to search for corn. Upon arrival at adjoining ranch he was fired upon by Julio Cardenas, Villista captain. Latter and two companions were killed by Patton's detachment which suffered no casualties."

Pershing was pleased with the action of his aide and the favorable publicity it brought to the campaign through newspaper stories about the fight. In his "Expedition Report," the general wrote, "The activities of Colonel Cardenas, an important member of Villa's staff, had stirred up Rubio and vicinity and our troops had made several unsuccessful attempts to capture him. On May 14th, Lieutenant G. S. Patton of my staff, with a small detachment was sent to that section in automobiles to purchase corn. Upon reaching San Miguel Ranch near Rubio, several Villistas ran out, firing upon the detachment as they went. Lieutenant Patton and one of our men opening fire in return, killing three of the Villistas, one of whom proved to be Colonel Cardenas."

Newspaper correspondents, both at Lake Itascate and in Columbus, rushed to cover the story of Patton's fight, as positive news from the Expedition front had been sparse of late. The killing of one of Villa's leaders by an Olympic athlete attracted the journalists' attention, and they exploited it for an eager American public. One example was Frank Elser of the *New York Times*, who interviewed Patton shortly after his return to Expedition headquarters. Elser's story, written on May 16, went by truck convoy to Columbus; from there, it was telegraphed to New York. Apparently, the journalist allowed Patton to read the article before dispatch, as the lieutenant wrote to Beatrice on May 17 that Elser "wrote a good article on me."

Elser's account appeared in the *Times* on May 23 under the headline "Cardenas' Family Saw Him Die at Bay—Shot Four Times, Villa Captain—Dramatic Fight at Ranch—Lieut. Patton and Ten Men Killed Three Bandits—Peons Kept Skinning a Beef." Within the story, Elser credited Patton with initiating a new kind of combat through the use of automobiles while presenting the lieutenant as a modest hero, quoting him as saying, "As Patton put it to me, Cardenas had nerve even if he was a Mexican."

Other newspapers, especially those near Patton's home in California and his wife's in Massachusetts, reprinted Elser's story as well as articles by their own correspondents. The *Pasadena Star* featured the story on page 1 with the headline "George S. Patton Shoots Villista Outlaw Captain—Pasadena Officer With General Patton in Mexico Engages in Lively Brush With Bandits." Once again, Patton was national news—and he liked it.

Most of the stories that made their way to print were reasonably accurate, but, with journalistic license, writers tended to emphasize the "shoot out at noon," although it actually began at 12:30, and to inflate claims about Patton's success in the 1912 Olympics. One newspaper reported, with no substantiation, that the Villistas were wearing pieces of uniforms and carrying blankets captured in the raid on Columbus. All accounts seem fascinated by the old man and boy who calmly continued their skinning of a steer in the midst of the battle. Some of the media reports also expressed concern that Cardenas was killed in front of his wife and child.

Over the years, Patton biographers and Border War historians have offered additional analysis. Patton, of course, had personal bias in telling the story in the best possible circumstances, and the news correspondents and other writers were interested in selling copies as much as recording accurate history.

One account, however, stands out. Major Frank Tompkins, as an officer in the Thirteenth Cavalry, participated in many of the Expedition's significant operations. After his retirement from the army, he wrote a history of the Punitive Expedition titled *Chasing Villa: The Last Campaign of the U.S. Cavalry*, which was published in 1934 by the Military Service Publishing Company. In the preface to the 1996 reprint edition by High-Lonesome Books, Louis R. Sadler wrote, "Tompkins' literary method was to splice his own narrative with numerous official reports and letters by other officers and soldiers. While the result is thorough and authentic, there is an uneven flow to the narrative. At the same time it should be noted that Tompkins managed to lay his hands on a substantial quantity of documents and primary material which even now are difficult to find in the National Archives."

The story of any battle, no matter how large or small, always has many versions. All are accurate from the standpoint of the individual offering the information. Battles are fought from the perspective of the individual in a theater of only a few yards. The observer in the midst of the fight sees a limited picture. Unlike the movie camera that can pan out to show the entire battlefield, the individual fighting for his life sees an area measured in only a few yards or even feet. Two soldiers, fighting side by side, may have different accounts of the same action—with both being accurate.

Tompkins's narrative of the Expedition is the best by a participant and, despite its weaknesses noted by Sadler, the most accurate and complete account of the operation. His narrative of Patton's fight with the three Mexicans is without bias or agenda and provides the most precise information about the fight. His research combined the narratives of the participants from his personal conversations with them in Mexico as well as the official reports. He is a soldier telling a soldier's story. Tompkins wrote:

> Early in May several troops of cavalry were sent out in an effort to locate and capture Julio Cardenas, who was called a general and was captain of the Dorados or bodyguard of Villa.
>
> Lieutenant G. S. Patton, Jr., acting Aide de Camp to General Pershing, was attached to one of these troops, Troop "H," 11th Cavalry, Captain Eben Swift commanding. This troop marched from Lake Itascate, east toward Rubio, then north to a small ranch called San Miguelito where Cardenas' wife and mother were said to live. Just before reaching this place, the troop met a detachment of the 16th Infantry which had come up from San Antonio, Mexico, on a similar errand, but instituted solely on the authority of the regimental commander. They told the troop commander that in the early morning they had surrounded the house in San Miguelito, but before the envelopment was completed several armed Mexicans galloped from the house and escaped to the hills to the west.
>
> Troop "H" continued its march and surrounded the house, but as was expected found nothing. The command camped there and shortly after midnight marched west, combing the hills and finding nothing.
>
> During the hours spent at the ranch Lieutenant Patton familiarized himself with the lay of the land, and the location of the gates in the corrals surrounding the house.

About a week later, on May 14th, the shortage of corn became acute, so General Pershing directed Lieutenant Patton to take three Dodge cars, one corporal, and six privates of the 16th Infantry, and an interpreter, Mr. W. [Heaton in some documents] Lunt, and buy corn from some haciendas lying to the east of Lake Itascate. The start was made from the camp at the lake. The first ranch visited was called Las Cayotes and the second Rubio. At each of these some corn was contracted for, but not as much as was needed, so the party went to a village called by the ubiquitous name of Las Cienegas [meaning "swamp" or "wetlands"]. Lieutenant Patton knew that an uncle of Cardenas lived at this village, so decided to surround it and combine business with pleasure, so to speak. This was done, but only corn was secured.

San Miguelito was some six or eight miles farther north, but something in the confusion of the uncle led Lieutenant Patton to suspect Cardenas might be home, so he decided to investigate. In doing this a certain amount of caution seemed advisable, as a recent report had credited Cardenas with having a band of some 20 men.

A hill about a mile from the house defiladed the road to that point, so before topping the rise the cars halted and the following plan was explained by Patton. The house, which was fairly large, with a battlemented roof, was to the east side of the road. It was built around a court with its single large door facing east. This was the only place from which a horseman could emerge, but there were some windows high on the west wall from which a man could drop.

In view of the fact that quite a number of the enemy might be encountered, it seemed wise to hold a majority of the party in a unit at a rallying point in case of necessity. It was therefore ordered that the leading car with Patton, Lunt, one soldier and the driver should pass the house and stop at the northwest corner. The soldier and the driver were to remain at the car and cover the west and north sides, while Patton and Lunt went around the north side to the front.

The second and third cars were to stop at the southwest corner, where six men were to remain covering the west and south sides, while two went around the south side to meet Patton in front of the east face.

The corporal was left with the group at the cars and all were to assemble there if a serious fire fight became necessary.

Due to his familiarity with the corrals and outbuildings gained in his former visit, Patton outstripped both Lunt and the soldiers and came to the east face well ahead of them. When he got there, he saw an old man and a boy skinning a steer in front of the gate. A moment later three horsemen emerged, armed with rifles and pistols and, on seeing Patton, wheeled and dashed toward the southeast corner, but on reaching it turned north again having seen the soldiers coming along the south face of the hacienda.

As orders in the Mexican Punitive Expedition prohibited firing until hostile identification was assured, Patton held his fire. When the Mexicans turned north they opened fire on Patton and Lunt who had joined him. Patton returned fire with his pistol and knocked down one man, who then crawled in through the gate. It may be well to state here that at the time of this action Patton was one of the crack pistol shots of the cavalry service.

Both sides stopped to reload. At this moment the soldiers rounded the southeast corner and opened fire along the east face of the house. As Patton and Lunt were in the line of fire, they stopped around the northeast corner where Patton reloaded his revolver. As he completed doing this, the two remaining Mexicans galloped by at a range of ten paces firing at Lunt and Patton, missing both, a sad exhibition of marksmanship. Patton returned the fire killing the horse of the nearest Mexican, which fell on the man. Impelled by notions of chivalry, Patton did not fire on the Mexican until he had freed himself of the horse and rose to fire, then Patton killed him with a shot under the left arm.

When the second Mexican fell, the third swerved to his right and galloped to the east. Patton then opened fire on him and was joined in by the two soldiers. Mr. Lunt, though he stayed beside the lieutenant was unarmed, so he could not fire. The third Mexican was killed. At this moment shooting was heard at the southwest corner where the corporal and three men were posted, and a man was seen running along the wall to the south. All fired at him and he, dropping behind the wall, returned the fire. Then he stopped shooting. Upon being

*approached he held up his left hand in an apparent token of surrender,
but when the soldiers were within five or six yards he suddenly drew
his pistol with his right hand and fired one shot, then he died. On
examination this man proved to have been hit but once, through the
left forearm and chest with the .45 pistol carried by Patton. He was
shot off his horse and was later identified as Cardenas.*

*The second man, also killed by Patton, was identified as Juan
Garza, a private. The third killed by the combined efforts of the lieutenant and the two soldiers was said to be a captain.*

*During all this fighting and flying bullets the old man and the
boy kept skinning the steer. It speaks well for the discipline of the soldiers that these two workers were not fired on.*

*Now that all external enemies were accounted for Patton decided
to climb to the roof of the building as he was uncertain as to whether
or not there were more enemies within. It would have been the height
of folly for the young commander to have ignored the possibility of
a hostile fire coming from the fortified roof. A dead tree was placed
against the wall and Patton was the first to mount. As he stepped on
the dirt roof, he went through to his arm pits but managed to wriggle
out before he could lose a leg from a machete blow. Two soldiers were
now placed on the roof so as to command the court. Mr. Lunt having
selected a rifle from one of the dead Mexicans accompanied Patton to
the front of the house. Placing the old man and the boy in front of
them, they forced the gate open and entered the court. To their great
relief nobody was found in the hacienda but women and children.*

*As it was necessary to identify the dead Mexicans, they were
lashed to the hoods of the three cars and the party started back. The
road led through the town of Rubio, known to be filled with Villa
sympathizers, so the telephone line from San Miguelito to Rubio was
cut. The passage through Rubio was made without a fight, though the
inhabitants were much excited by the sight of the dead. Camp was
reached without further incident.*

First combat, first blood, first kill. These are, of course, significant
markers in the development of a warrior. For Patton, the fight at the

hacienda tested the marksmanship skills he had acquired and challenged his mettle when he actually faced another man in mortal combat. That he returned unharmed with the bodies of his enemies lashed to the hoods of his automobiles was a warrior's triumph.

While he had brought with him marksmanship mastery through practice from boyhood, at West Point, and for the Olympics, Patton acquired his audacity and boldness from Pershing in Mexico. Elsner reported in his *New York Times* article that Patton referred to advice he had received from Dave Allison in Sierra Blanca that "to kill a fugitive's horse . . . was the surest way of stopping him."

As noted in Tompkins's report, Patton was most vulnerable in the fight when he had to stop and reload his .45 revolver. Carried with the hammer down on an empty chamber for safety, the pistol held but five bullets. Had he carried the army-issued M1911 .45 semi-automatic pistol, he would have had eight bullets in the magazine and could have easily reloaded by pushing the eject button to remove the empty magazine and inserting a loaded one. Nevertheless, Patton remained loyal to his ivory-handled revolver. Shortly after the incident, Patton began wearing two revolvers—for which he was called "two-gun Patton"—though this flamboyant touch was probably more for show than practical employment.

Although both Patton and Tompkins claim two kills for the lieutenant, some historians and biographers claim only one kill or even none. The Tompkins account, which verifies the two, however, remains the most detailed and trusted account. Patton himself obviously believed he felled the two bandits because he carved two notches in the left-side ivory grip of his revolver, which is on display today in the General George Patton Museum in Fort Knox, Kentucky.

Patton did not record his personal feeling about the fight in his diary, but he did write to his family. To Beatrice on May 14, he wrote about the fight, "I have always expected to be scared but was not nor was I excited. I was afraid they would get away. I never heard a bullet but some say you do not at such close range. I wondered a little at first that I was not hit, they were so close."

To his Aunt Nannie on May 17, Patton wrote more about the fight, stating, "I was in great luck to be in it, also not to get hit at all. Three of them shooting at me about 15 yards off. I kept wondering why they did not hit me. The guns seemed pointed right at me. I did not get mad as one is supposed to do but was worried for fear they would get away."

Patton expressed similar thoughts in a letter to his father on May 15: "I was much less scared than I thought I would be, in fact all that worried me was the fear they would get away."

As for killing his enemies, Patton felt the emotions of soldiers from battlefields of the past and future—he was happy to be alive. In the May 17 letter to Beatrice, he wrote, "You are probably wondering if my conscience hurts me for killing a man. It does not. I feel about it just as I did when I got my sword fish, surprised at my luck."

In the same letter, Patton expressed the humor soldiers often find in difficult situations. He wrote that everyone was teasing him about using his pistol rather than his saber. Patton concluded, "It simply goes to show that an officer should be able to use all arms, for being on foot I could not have used a saber. The General has been complementary telling some officers that I did more in a half a day than the 13th Cavalry did in a week. He calls me the 'Bandit.'"

The reaction of Patton's family to the fight was best summed up by his father-in-law, Frederick Ayer, in a letter on May 31, 1916: "I am trying to think of words to express my feelings and admiration of your courage and bravery, and our joy that you came away alive. Congratulations and the whole list of ordinary expressions used in such cases do not cover the case and I am obliged to give it up, and say 'It is good to be alive.'"

His sister, Nita Patton, expressed different concerns. In a letter to her mother from Fort Bliss, she wrote, "I am sick at the thought that he killed somebody. I wish he hadn't. It isn't noble in my eyes to shoot a poor ignorant creature that does not know why he is fighting. Of course Georgie was brave, and the man shot first, but I should think it was a disagreeable duty, well performed, not an act of wonderful courage. But Oh! Ma isn't it great that the man missed! I am so glad of that I like to forget the other. Everyone at the post is ringing up and all are thrilled over it. Don't think I am not proud of your son, I am; only I can't rejoice over a thing like that."

The attack at the Rubio hacienda was far more significant than merely bringing Patton more national media attention and Pershing's praise. It opened the curtain on a new staging of warfare. Being very astute, Patton instantly realized this fact, and on October 3, 1917, he sent a letter to the commander in chief of the AEF in France requesting consideration for command of the new "Tanks" service. Patton wrote, "I believe that I am the only American who has ever made an attack in a motor vehicle."

Although Patton seemed satisfied with the praise he received at the time for his actions at Rubio Ranch, the ever-strategizing lieutenant wanted to miss no opportunity to be recognized for his unique accomplishments. On September 24, 1920—three years later—he approached Pershing about ensuring that his first firefight in Mexico was recorded in the annals of history, writing, "I trust you will excuse the personal vanity which emboldens me to intrude this upon your valuable time. But as I am one of the few officers who has ever registered hits on a human target I am very anxious to have that fact on my record."

Patton then asked Pershing to place a statement in his official file about the fight with the bandits. He included a summary of his actions, claiming it came from his diary, though it actually was a combination of information he had sent to his father and wife at the time. Patton made no mention of the great number of officers who had "registered hits on a human target" in the recent world war. Perhaps he was referring to "registered hits on a human target" from an automobile. He concluded his letter stating, "I trust that after the Great War you will not consider me too childish in mentioning this matter to you."

Pershing approved the request and forwarded a part of his Mexico report to the adjutant general of the U.S. Army. This later formed the basis for the award of the Silver Star to Patton.

Diary: May 15

This day, we have been two months in Mexico. I stayed in camp all day. Three troops of the Fifth Cavalry went toward San Antonio and one troop of the Thirteenth to El Rubio to leave for Namiquipa.

Diary: May 16

Sixth Infantry and one battery of the Fourth Field Artillery started for San Geronimo at 6:00 a.m.

The General and Collins went to the Fifth Cavalry camp.

We all started for Namiquipa at 9:30 and passed the Sixth Infantry about 10:30 a.m. They looked very tired and very dusty. General Pershing stopped for an hour at San Geronimo and talked with Colonel Allaire. Eight companies of the Sixteenth Infantry were there under Colonel Allaire.

We reached Namiquipa at 1:30 p.m.

Patton remained surrounded by officers from whom he could learn. Colonel William H. Allaire, a West Point graduate from Arkansas, was a veteran of the war in the Philippines, a former U.S. military attaché in Vienna, and an officer in the Office of the Army Chief of Staff in Washington, D.C., before assuming command of the Sixteenth Infantry Regiment. He later commanded an infantry brigade in the First World War.

Diary: May 17

Bad wind all day. Colonel Allen got in late from San Geronimo where had spent all day making inspection.

Nothing happened of importance around the camp this date.

Colonel Henry T. Allen, a West Point graduate from Kentucky who led the Eleventh Cavalry, had great influence on Patton, for he brought a firsthand knowledge about military matters from around the world. As a lieutenant, Allen had participated in one of the earliest explorations of the Alaskan Territory and fought in both the Spanish-American and the Philippine Wars. He also had served as a military attaché to Russia and as an observer in the Russo–Japanese War. Promoted to major general, he commanded the Ninetieth Infantry Division in World War I. When he died in 1930, Pershing served as a pallbearer at his funeral.

Diary: May 18

Two squadrons of the Eleventh Cavalry started out for El Valle at 1:00 p.m. Captain Reed and Campanole went to Santa Ana to see Aldarete. Jose M. Espinosa reported to General Pershing that Candelario Cervantes had been in the town of Namiquipa the preceding night.

The Sixth Infantry arrived from San Geronimo about 9:30 a.m.

Diary: May 19

A terrible windstorm lasted all day. No one could do anything.

Diary: May 20

Lieutenant Eangle arrived at Namiquipa and was put in charge of the maps.

The diary entries immediately following the fight at the Rubio hacienda reflect the return to routine operations, with units and individuals coming and going from the headquarters. Being reduced to writing about inclement weather must have felt like a great comedown for the young Patton.

Diary: May 21

We started to reorganize the headquarters.

Diary: May 22

Lieutenant Shallenberger has charge of the headquarters office and orderlies. Lieutenant Collins of automobile section, and myself in charge of mounted section. There were twenty-seven men in the automobile section, six autos and one truck. Twenty-three privates and two corporals in the mounted section. Also three cooks for the officers and three for the men. We did not think this organization would work at the time, but later we found that it worked very well.

I went to San Geronimo to get four of the Thirteenth Cavalry for my section. I saw a Mexican with a gun ride off from the mountain and at first I decided to kill him, but later I thought he might possibly be innocent and I let him go. I believe however, I should have shot him.

As Patton was learning, combat operations called for constant readjustment in organization and assignments in order to successfully accomplish the mission. As the aide in charge of the mounted section, Patton was responsible for the security of the headquarters, which is probably why being indecisive about letting the armed Mexican go rather than shooting him so obviously troubled him.

Diary: May 23

Captain Reed got information of Cervantes and the General sent four troops to the northwest from Santa Ana, the troops of the Thirteenth Cavalry northeast from San Geronimo, one troop of the Fifth Cavalry from Cruces and one troop of the Eleventh Cavalry southwest from Cruces. All the troops to start so to be in position by midnight. We were very busy getting all the guides off for the different places, particularly the guides who would go to Santa Ana. As usual with them they had lost their horse or saddle at the last minute. The Mexican guides that Alderete had promised to furnish us at Santa Ana were all busy and could not come and act as guides.

Although Patton made no mention of it in his diary, he was promoted to the rank of first lieutenant on this date of May 23. His failure to pontificate about the promotion then was likely because he did not receive word about it for several more days, the long and not-all-that-reliable lines of communications being what they were. It is reasonable to assume that, when the promotion order arrived, Pershing pinned the silver bar on Patton's uniform to replace his gold insignia. Although Patton did not note anything about the promotion in his diary, he must have been proud and pleased—and well aware that no second lieutenant ever joined the general officer ranks without their initial promotion to first lieutenant.

Diary: May 24

All troops moved out as directed but succeeded in getting nothing. At 2:00 p.m. a Mexican came up saying Cervantes was in town. Captain Reed went to town in four autos and my detachment, Shallenberger took the Headquarters detachment, but all this excitement was caused by the Mexicans seeing the advance guard of the troop of the Fifth Cavalry, this troop having started back. It was funny that this troop was ordered back to attack Cervantes. In other words to chase itself.

At five p.m. got word that Cervantes and his lieutenant had been killed close to Cruces. Private Hill of the Machine Gun Company of the Seventeenth Infantry killed both.

Collins went up to Cruces with orders to bring the body to Namiquipa for further identification.

The May 24 entry is confusing in its dating and contents. Patton focuses much more on problems with guides and maneuvers of cavalry troops than the killing of Colonel Candelario Cervantes, which was a significant feat. And, for the first time since arriving in Mexico, Patton skipped a day of writing—either that or he combined the events of the 24th and 25th under the date of May 24. The death of Cervantes, by all other accounts, took place on May 25. He also incorrectly recorded that Private Hill had killed the Mexican bandit rather than the actual shooter, who was Private George D. Huelett. Perhaps Patton was distracted by fatigue and duties, or perhaps he merely recorded the first reports of the fight rather than waiting for a more accurate account. He also may have been disappointed by the fact that, despite the large number of cavalrymen looking for Cervantes, the bandit had been found and killed by a small detachment of infantrymen.

Pershing provided a much more detailed and accurate version in his "Punitive Expedition Report." His account is supported by the later writings of Tompkins. Pershing wrote that in mid-May,

Candelario Cervantes with 25 Villistas boldly returned to the vicinity of Namiquipa and began to prey upon the peaceful inhabitants. Detachments were kept constantly in the field in his pursuit, following

up all reports that appeared credible. On May 25th, a detachment under Lance Corporal Davis Marksbury, consisting of 8 men of the Machine Gun Platoon, 17th Infantry, 2 men of the Corps of Engineers, and one man of the Quartermaster Corps from Cruces, happened to be about six miles south of there, sketching roads and hunting cattle, when they were attacked by a party of nine Villistas, and Corporal Marksbury was killed and three men wounded. The Villistas lost two killed who, upon proper identification, turned out to be "Colonel" Candelario Cervantes and Jose Bencome. Special credit is due Private George D. Hulett, 17th Infantry for success in this small skirmish, who killed both these bandits as they rode firing at him. The killing of Candelario Cervantes was particularly fortunate as, next to Villa himself, he was the most able and the most desperate of Villa's band.

Diary: May 26

There was a meeting of the Equipment Board and I was asked to give my opinion of the equipment.

Espenoso came to see the General and also to get permission to capture three hundred and eighty rifles and eleven machine guns, out in some caves in El Oso Canyon. He succeeded in doing this May 26th.

Captain Campanole tried to secure these guns but did not go far enough up the Canyon and on the way back met Espenoso returning with the guns.

We started a new mess this day for the correspondents, as the General's mess was too large. This mess at this time had ten members.

We had a rumor that Obregon had called all officers, of whatever faction, to the colors in order to attack the Americans.

The Punitive Expedition served a far greater purpose than just the pursuit of Villa and the professional development of Patton and his fellow officers. It also offered a playing field to test new weapons, transportation and supply methods, communications, and tactics. The Cavalry Equipment Board was a part of the evaluation process and met for several days at Pershing's headquarters to interview soldiers and to directly inspect various items of war fighting gear.

Capture of the cache of rifles and machine guns provided an excellent indication of the Expedition's continued success. Villa and other bandits now had more weapons than men to carry them.

Patton's comment about forming a new mess for the correspondents is not surprising in that the dining tents had limited space, and Pershing would have preferred to have meal time as an opportunity for his staff to confidentially and informally discuss daily updates.

Álvaro Obregón had joined the Mexican Revolution as a leader in the state of Sonora before he joined Carranza, who appointed him supreme commander of all forces in Northwest Mexico. Obregón, an able and innovative field commander, integrated machine guns and barbed wire into his army. Despite the loss of his right arm in a battle with the Villistas, he remained in the field and later represented Carranza in the negotiations with American officials about the removal of the Expeditionary force from Mexico.

Rumors are as much a part of a soldier's life as long hours and bad food. Although there is no evidence that Obregón was calling for a coordinated attack against the Americans, Mexican authorities over the next weeks did increase their demands for the removal of the Expedition.

Diary: May 28

Major Howze and Major Lindsley arrived for Cavalry Equipment Board.

Patton made no entry for May 27 and only a brief note the following day. In the original version of his diary, Patton noted that he and Howze had a long argument over the type and use of the saber. The cavalry did not carry their sabers in Mexico, and sabers would never again be used for anything other than ceremonial purposes. Still, the weapon remained a favorite—if not in the field, at least in the minds—of many traditional cavalrymen.

Major Julian R. Lindsley of the Eleventh Cavalry Regiment, a West Point graduate and Georgia native, had served in the Boxer Rebellion in China and went on to command an infantry regiment in World

War I. He and Patton both participated in the St. Mihiel Offensive in September 1918.

Diary: May 29

Captain Reed secured the arms captured by Espenosa, these consisted of three hundred and fifty rifles and eleven machine guns.

General Pershing, Collins, correspondents Clements, Baehr, Blakesley, and Elser went to El Valle at 9:45 en route to Dublan.

The Sixth Infantry started to El Valle at 8:00 a.m. The Sixteenth Infantry arrived from San Geronimo at 10:00 a.m. Colonel Dodd came in at 9:15 a.m.

Pershing continued to move units to best protect his lines of communications and to pursue the bandits. Patton's ability to be at the general's side in this process enabled him to learn far more about tactics and logistics than he would have been able to absorb as a lieutenant in one of the cavalry regiments.

Diary: May 31

Cavalry Board met and called several witnesses. Captain Fechet's saddle was examined.

There is nothing in Patton's diary or other accounts as to why he made no entry on May 30. Perhaps boredom was taking hold.

Captain James E. Fechet, born into a military family at Fort Ringgold, Texas, served as an enlisted man in the Spanish-American War, where he was seriously wounded. Following his recovery, he applied for an officer's commission and then fought in the Philippine Revolution before accompanying the Punitive Expedition with the Seventh Cavalry Regiment. During World War I, he transferred to the Air Corps and advanced to the rank of major general as he served in aviation command and staff positions all the way to the end of the Second World War.

Mention of his saddle's inspection by the Cavalry Board is one of the random tidbits that history still holds hostage.

SAN GABRIEL,   CALIFORNIA.

"Georgie"

Corp.; Sergt.-Maj.; Adj.; Expert Rifle-
man; "A" for Record; Track Team;
Football Squad (4) (3) (2) (1).

Confusion reigned supreme. The barracks were
being shaken by a violent earthquake, and men came
tumbling out of their divisions in all stages of disha-
bille. Suddenly the Cadet Lieutenant and Adjutant
appeared in the area, faultlessly attired, as usual.
Walking with firm step across the area, he halted
executed a proper about face, and the stentorian tones
rang out, "Battalion Attention-n-n-n! Cadets will
refrain from being unduly shaken up. There will be
no yelling in the area. The earthquake will cease
immediately. By order-r-r-r of Lieutenant Colonel
Howze!"

There is only one blot on the otherwise spotless
'scutcheon of George's military career—the absence
from reveille that he got at Fort Wright. Two
broken arms bear witness to his zeal, as well as his

misfortune, on the foot-
ball field—but misfor-
tune could not run fast
enough to overtake him
on the track. We be-
lieve   that   George's
heart, despite its arm-
ored exterior, has a big
soft spot inside, and
have heard that Cupid
has penetrated with his
dart   where   explosive
"D" might fail.

West Point yearbook, Patton entry, 1909.

George S. Patton Jr. as a
West Point cadet, 1909.

George S. Patton Jr. and
Beatrice Banning Ayer
wedding, 1910.

Lieutenant George S. Patton in Mexico.

Punitive Expedition staff, Patton in center rear wearing a tie.

General John J. Pershing in Mexico.

General John J. Pershing in Mexico.

Pancho Villa and his staff at Hacienda de Bustillos, Chihuahua, c. 1915.

Pancho Villa in the field, c. 1915.

Columbus, New Mexico, after Villa's raid.

Thirteenth Cavalry and dead Villista after the Columbus raid.

Thirteenth Cavalry burning bodies of dead Villistas after the Columbus raid.

Camp Furlong, New Mexico, supply center.

Mule train supply column from Camp Furlong to Colonia Dublán.

Truck resupply convoy from Camp Furlong to Mexico.

Unloading supplies at Expedition headquarters at Colonia Dublán.

Lieutenants H. A. Dargue and E. S. Gorrell arriving in Casas Grandes, Mexico.

Lieutenant C. G. Chapman preparing for a scouting expedition at Casas Grandes.

Baking bread in a field kitchen near Namiquipa.

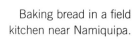

Field kitchen in Mexico.

Sixth Infantry Regiment near Namiquipa, Mexico.

Wireless radio near Casas Grandes.

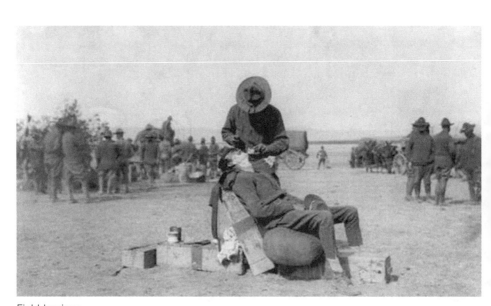

Field hygiene.

Blanket toss recreation.

Villista prisoners guarded by African American soldiers of the Twenty-Fourth Infantry Regiment.

Chinese peddlers at Casas Grandes.

Mexican refugees arriving at Columbus, New Mexico. Cavalry in distance.

CHAPTER TEN

June 1916

Diary: June 1

We received word in camp that there were some guns about sixteen miles northeast in El Oso Canyon. I started with Captain [Frederick G.] Turner, Troop M, Thirteenth Cavalry, Lieutenant [Clarence] Lininger, and [Hugh] Johnson and Campanole were also along. We reached the cave where the arms were concealed, at 10:00 p.m. and got ninety-four rifles and returned to camp reaching there at 5:25 a.m.

There continued to be more enemy weapons than enemy soldiers. The timeline recorded in Patton's diary nevertheless shows the stealth of capturing these weapons, as the operation occurred mostly during the hours of darkness.

Diary: June 2

Nothing to report, until 4th of June.

Diary: June 4

Colonel Dodd and Captain Reed went to El Valle.

Diary: June 5

Nothing.

Diary: June 6

*I went hunting with Carson and Bell, saw one deer.
Captain Reed and Major Ryan returned from El Valle.*

Diary: June 8

I went duck hunting with Captain Black.

Patton sought information and insights not only from cavalry and infantry officers but also from veterans of all branches, such as Captain Hanson B. Black, a senior Signal Corps officer assigned to the Expedition headquarters. Patton observed the use of radios and learned as much as he could about electronic communications.

The diary entries for this period disclose that Patton at times wrote about activities several days after they actually occurred. They also reveal the lack of activity. While Patton noted his time hunting, he also spent hours working on articles for the *Cavalry Journal*.

Daily field operations had slowed, but that did not mean the Expedition was finding any more acceptance by the people of Mexico or their government. In his "Expedition Report," Pershing wrote of this time period:

> *The relations between the United States and Mexico had become very tense and the Mexican people were much aroused in the belief that war was inevitable. De facto troops were being assembled at points on the railroads in the east and west, threatening our line of communications. The commanding general of the de facto troops in the district of Ahumada had issued instructions for his forces to hold themselves in readiness to operate against the Americans. A force of 10,000 men was reported in the vicinity of Ahumada, and a large number of troops had moved from the south of the city of Chihuahua. It was understood among the Mexican people that these troops, instead of being sent to pursue bandits, were actually for the purpose of driving the Americans out of Mexico. The commanding officer at Ahumada was in constant telegraph communications with the local commander at Casas*

Grandes, and the latter was advised that the troops at Ahumada were preparing to attack the American lines and directed him to cooperate.

The Mexican population held themselves entirely aloof from us, and the people who had been friendly became decidedly unfriendly. It was impossible to obtain the assistance of men who had hitherto been in our service as secret agents. The white population were alarmed and afraid to venture beyond our protection. Our small fleet of airships had been wrecked in the early days of the campaign and not one was available at this critical period. It therefore became necessary to rely upon the resources within the command to obtain information of the de facto troops. Frequent reconnaissance in all directions became imperative, in order to keep informed of any hostile movements of de facto bodies and be prepared to concentrate any at threatened point.

Diary: June 9

We moved our camp to a point two miles east of our first camp at Namiquipa. The move was made without any confusion and in very good order.

Diary: June 12

I went duck hunting with Captain Black. In the evening I got ready to go with Troop M of the Thirteenth Cavalry to look for Pedro Lujon at Tepehaunes.

Diary: June 13

Troop M Thirteenth Cavalry, Captain Turner and myself left camp at 7:30 a.m. We reached Santa Clara, twenty-six miles at 2:30 p.m. Saw several deer on the road. At Santa Clara we found Troop L, which reported having had a fight at the ranch with bandits the day before.

Diary: June 14

Left Santa Clara at 12:05 a.m. and reached Tepehuanes at 4:40 a.m. Surrounded the place and captured Pedro Lujan. We left there

at 12:00 noon and got to Santa Clara at 5:30 p.m. Just before we
left we received a message over the wire from the Carranza Com-
mander at El Rubio asking "what the ____" we were doing there
fighting the Mexicans.

The June 14 diary entry is revealing because Patton chose to use
dashes rather than spell out *hell*. Although infamous for his obscene
profanity around his troops in his field officer days, Patton in 1916 was
reluctant to record a curse word. His daughter Ruth Ellen later wrote,
"Georgie will go down through history as a man of vast profanity, but he
never used it around Ma [Beatrice]—it would not have occurred to him
to use strong language in her presence, or, for that matter, in the presence
of any lady."

Patton added a few more details about the capture of Lujan in a
letter to his father on June 15: "I planned the surprise and tried to work
up a fight. We surrounded the hacienda and a hill back of it with a dismounted line and the eight of us galloped up to the door but nothing
doing. They would not shoot. If they had we would have murdered them.
It had all the elements of good tactics but the shooting."

The reason for the lack of resistance on the part of Lujan was that
he was extremely ill and bed-ridden. Before being identified by his scars
and gold teeth, he professed to be a poor peon.

Although Patton did not seem overly pleased or excited about the
capture of Lujan, the news correspondents at Namiquipa were eager
to report news from the "front." George H. Clements of the *New York
Sun* wrote, "Pedro Lujan, a Villista lieutenant and one of the leaders of
the Columbus raid, was made captive by American troops yesterday at
Tepehaunes hacienda, 25 miles northeast of Namiquipa. Troop M, 13th
Cavalry, commanded by Capt. F. G. Turner, surrounded the hacienda
before sunrise."

Clements concluded, "Lujan is almost the last Villista leader uncap-
tured or alive."

Although the reporter claimed Lujan was "a leader of the Columbus raid" and a member of Villa's Dorados, his actual status among the

bandits is debatable; no further record exists of Lujan being captured in Mexico or sent to the United States as a prisoner.

Diary: June 15

Left Santa Clara at 8:00 a.m. and reached Namiquipa at 3:30 p.m.

Diary: June 16

I went through the mountains north of camp on an expedition of my own, looking for some rifles. I found caves which had been recently lived in but there were no guns. This day Captain Reed intended to make a round up at San Geronimo, but decided not to do so.

Diary: June 17

Three Carranza majors came to Namiquipa to force Espenosa to surrender to them the prisoners he had captured, all of whom were supposed to be Columbus raiders. Captain Reed, who had gone to Cruces, was called back in haste, he was much disturbed over the circumstances.

Diary: June 18

Captain Reed secured the prisoners without a fight but it was very close. We had one squadron mounted and two others ready to move at a moment's notice.

The rising tensions between the Expedition and the Carranza government were formalized by a series of telegrams. On June 16, a message from General J. B. Trevino, the Mexican in command of the state of Chihuahua, to Pershing declared:

I have orders from my government to prevent, by the use of arms, new evasions of my country by American forces and also to prevent the American forces that are in this state from moving to the south, east, or west of the places they now occupy. I communicate this to you for your knowledge for the reason that your forces will be attacked by the Mexican forces if these indications are not heeded.

Delivering a telegram, such as this one, to Pershing fell within the purview of Patton's duties. So, too, was assisting in preparing the reply, which said:

I am in receipt of your telegram advising me that your government had directed you to prevent any movement to the east, south, or west of the American forces now in Mexico and that should such movement take place the American forces will be attacked by Mexican forces. In reply you are informed that my government has placed no such restrictions upon the movement of American forces. I shall therefore use my own judgement as to when and in what direction I shall move my forces in pursuit of bandits. If under these circumstances the Mexican forces attack any of my columns the responsibility for the consequences will lie with the Mexican government.

In addition to the telegrams, Pershing and Mexican officials exchanged verbal messages. Pershing included the following in his "Expedition Report": "The local commanding officer of the de facto troops delivered me a verbal message on the same date to the effect that 'General Carranza had ordered that the American troops should not move in any direction except north.' In reply I asked him to telegraph his superiors that I declined to respect such instructions, saying, 'I do not take orders except from my own government.'"

Diary: June 19

The Sixteenth Infantry left at 6:00 a.m. for Cruces. We received news this night that the militia had been called out, or would be called out, on June 20th. I left with the mounted section of the Headquarters at Namiquipa at 8:15 a.m. and got to Cruces at 3:00 p.m.

The call-up of the National Guard was a continuation of the enlistment and deployment of 140,000 soldiers to the U.S.–Mexican border, an activity that was providing both a "show of force" to deter any Mexican army offensive against the Expedition and opportunities for training troops as a precursor to an inevitable world war.

Diary: June 21

Left Cruces at 9:15 a.m. and got to El Valle at 2:30 p.m. having stopped two hours for lunch.

Although operations at headquarters were so routine that Patton made no notation in his diary for June 22, important actions were taking place in the field that greatly influenced the future of the Expedition.

Diary: June 22

Made our camp on some cleared ground. Major Hines arrived about 1:30 p.m. We got news of the Tenth Cavalry fight at Carrizal.

Diary: June 23

Pitched the headquarters tents in the morning and got orders at noon to start for Dublan. We left camp at 2:30 p.m. and got to Ojo Laguna at 5:30, a distance of eighteen miles, and we camped there with detachment of the engineers. Here we got the first news of the death of Captain [Charles T.] Boyd and Lieutenant [Henry R.] Adair.

The battle at Carrizal, fought against Carranza forces rather than Villa's bandits, was the costliest action of the Expedition for the Americans. Although numbers vary in the many official and unofficial reports of the battle, those of Major Frank Tompkins are likely the most accurate. According to Tompkins, twelve Americans were killed, eleven wounded, and twenty-three captured. Boyd and Adair were among the dead, the only two officers killed in direct combat during the entire Expedition. Mexican casualties, according to their own accounts, totaled twelve officers dead, including their commanding general, Felix U. Gomez; thirty-three enlisted men were killed, and fifty-three wounded.

Although he makes little mention of the battle in his diary, Patton, in his role of aide and preparer of much of Pershing's correspondence, undoubtedly assisted in putting together the official report. In his "Expedition Report" that Pershing submitted, he included:

Among other reconnoitering detachments, Captain Boyd with Troop G, 10th Cavalry, was sent eastward in the direction of Ahumada to thoroughly scout the country and obtain information regarding the troops and movement [of the Carrancistas]. He was told that he could probably learn the facts at Santo Domingo or in that vicinity and was cautioned not to bring on a fight. Captain [Lewis J.] Morey with Troop M, 10th Cavalry, was sent from Ojo Federico upon the same mission and with practically the same caution.

Captain Boyd and Captain Morey met at Santo Domingo Ranch, about 60 miles east of Dublan, on the evening of June 20th. They obtained from the American foreman in charge, who had recently visited Ahumada, much reliable information concerning their mission without going to points garrisoned by the de facto troops. Captain Boyd, however, decided to enter Carrizal and continue from there to Ahumada with Captain Morey under his command.

Arriving in the vicinity of Carrizal on the morning of the 21st, he was met by the commanding general and other officers at the outskirts of the town and told that their orders would not permit him to go further to the east. Superior numbers of Mexican troops were in battle formation, both mounted and dismounted, at the edge of town, and all their preparations indicated that they would carry out their instructions and oppose Captain Boyd's progress by force. After some further discussion, Captain Boyd rode up within a short range of the Mexican position, dismounted his troops preparing to enter the town. At the moment of dismounting, he received a heavy fire from all parts of the Mexican lines. Captain Boyd's own men pushed forward with dash and carried the Mexican position, Lieutenant Adair leading. The memory of the splendid bravery of these two officers who lost their lives and of the men who personally followed them is cherished by this entire command.

In closing this brief report of Carrizal it should be emphasized that this expedition entered Mexico in pursuit of bandits, through the courtesy of the Mexican government, and, that the de facto military forces, in firing on our troops, committed a deliberate act of war. Also, in declaring through their military commander in Chihuahua, that the Americans forces were to be attacked in certain conditions, the Mexican government accentuated its own responsibility in the premises. In other words, the Mexican government itself was entirely responsible for the opposition offered to Captain Boyd's progress and, finally for the culminating act of open hostility to the United States[,] which started the fight at Carrizal.

Although there was evidence that Captain Boyd had initiated the fight, Pershing viewed the battle as an escalation of the conflict between the Expedition and the Mexican government. In his "Expedition Report," he continued:

When the fight at Carrizal was reported, orders were prepared and immediate steps were taken to assume the aggressive with all available troops of this command. Superior instructions indicated such action, and the situation seemed to demand it. Further concentration for prompt movement became imperative, if we were to be ready to meet without delay what appeared to be a crisis. The troops south of El Valle were ordered north by telegraph, truck trains were assembled for use that might be required of them, and the command as a whole was at once placed and held in action for quick action.

Mexicans (both Federals and rebel bandits) celebrated the defeat of the Tenth Cavalry at Carrizal, hailing General Gomez as a national hero while the Americans fumed. President Wilson ordered the seizure of all bridges across the Rio Grande and National Guard preparation for invasion into Mexico. In response, Carranza attempted to appease the Americans by freeing the Tenth Cavalry prisoners; however, as an affront to Pershing, he did not deliver them to Dublán, but rather transported them by rail to Juárez, where he released them to U.S. officials in El Paso on June 29.

Patton assisted in delivering orders for the consolidation of the Expedition forces at Dublán as part of his usual duties. Convinced that full-scale war between the United States and Mexico was on the horizon, he outlined the difficulties of such a conflict in a June 27 letter to his father-in-law in which he offered his opinion of the Mexican government and people as a whole:

> *I think that war is the best for two reasons. First it is inevitable hence the sooner the better. Second it will surely give us a better army for I doubt if over half of the militia muster in and even they will be too few.*
>
> *This is a big country and very difficult to operate in. There are no roads at all, just tracks over the plains and mountains. There is very little water and most of the cattle are dead so there will be no way to live off the land.*
>
> *It will not take many of us to beat the Mexicans in battle but it will take a lot to cover the lines [supply] so that those who fight may also eat.*
>
> *You have no idea of the utter degradation of the inhabitants. One must be a fool indeed to think that people half savage and wholly ignorant will ever form a republic. It is a joke. A despot is all they know or want. So when they lost Diez [Porfirio Díaz] they set up bandit kings who were worse tyrants than he ever dreamed of becoming.*

Patton concluded the letter on a more personal note: "I have written Beatrice that if we go to war she ought to go to you. It will last six months at the least. If I am wounded she could get to the border before I could and if I am killed—which I shan't be—she would be better at home."

American and Mexican officials began negotiations on the future of the Expedition that would last into the fall. Pershing consolidated his forces around Dublán, aggressively patrolling the area and pursuing Villa. President Wilson decided not to invade Mexico; neither country was eager to go to war. The Carranza government continued to demand the removal of the Expeditionary force, but the Americans thought that having Pershing remain in place would force the de facto government to pursue and disperse Villa and other bandit groups to end the threat of cross-border raids. While the high-level talks continued, with the fate of the Expedition a primary subject, Pershing, Patton, and the soldiers remained alert.

Diary: June 24

Left camp at 4:15 a.m., stopped at Charcos at noon. This was a very poor camp with but little water. Saw some Chinamen who seemed to be favorable to the Mexicans. I also recovered a mule at this place, that a Mexican had found, giving the Mexican ten dollars for the mule.

Despite Patton's suspicions of the "Chinamen," overall the Chinese in Mexico supported the Americans and the Expedition despite the fact that the U.S. government had enacted the Chinese Exclusion Act in 1882, ending further immigration on the pretext of preserving jobs for White Americans. This bill had driven a few hundred Chinese to Northern Mexico, where they intermarried with the native population and established general stores. But Mexico had not welcomed them either, targeting them for racially inspired violence—especially the successful ones. Many of the Chinese were killed, some crossed back illegally into the United States, a small number returned to China, and a few lowered their profiles and remained in Mexico—the latter group being the ones Patton encountered.

The Chinese were drawn to the Expedition as it advanced into Mexico because they could supplement the long and difficult supply lines by opening the mobile exchanges that sold "comfort supplies," including soap, fruit, candy, tobacco, and matches; the Chinese also cooked and did laundry for the soldiers. Everyone benefited.

Diary: June 25

Started at 4:55 a.m. and reached Dublan at 9:00 a.m. where we found the General and the rest of his staff.

Late in the afternoon we received word of the discovery of Captain Morey. Lieutenant Collins went for him in an automobile and brought him in, he was not much hurt.

Captain Lewis S. Morey and four of his troopers of the Tenth Cavalry had been unhorsed about two miles from the main Carrizal battle. They managed to avoid capture, and on June 25 Collins brought Morey to Dublán. As the senior surviving officer after the death of Captain Boyd, Morey was an eyewitness, and Pershing was eager for his report on the fight. As Patton recorded in his journal, the captain's wounds were not serious; however, he was evacuated to El Paso for treatment, where he visited the cavalrymen who had been prisoners of the Mexicans before their release.

Morey, a West Point graduate of 1900, was a veteran of the Philippine Insurrection and later served in World War I. The battle in Mexico was the most significant event in his career. When he died in 1947, the headline of his obituary in the *New York Times* stated, "Col. Lewis Morey, in Army 46 Years Hero of the Carrizal Skirmish with Mexican Troops in '16 Dies in Capital at 72."

Diary: June 26

I heard confidentially that Villa was still alive.

For all practical purposes, the Expedition concluded with the fight at Carrizal, even though the status of Villa remained a matter of continued debate since his hurried retreat from Columbus. By the end of June, consensus was that he was alive and hiding in the mountains, recovering from his wounds. Patton's "confidential source" was undoubtedly one of the Mormon guides or interpreters employed by the Expedition.

Diary: June 28

I went to the Mormon Lakes with some orders for the Seventh Cavalry. Movements of the truck trains to the border was suspended, owing to the reported presence of Carranza troops near the line of communications.

Diary: June 29

First Squadron of the Eleventh and all of the Seventh Cavalry got in from Mormon Lakes. Truck trains started south from Columbus. Nothing else to report, nothing else to report until July 4th.

Patton again skipped several days of writing in his diary. The consolidation of units at Dublán and the routine duties of the headquarters did not merit his making any record of the activities.

The future general, however, was never one to waste hours. Whenever possible, he went riding or hunting and continued his habit of reading. He also passed the time writing what even he admitted in a letter to Beatrice were "disgusting poems" and instructed her to "tear them up" after reading. Patton had begun writing poetry while a cadet at West Point and continued the rest of his life. His daughter Ruth Ellen later wrote that her father wrote verse primarily to cheer and inspire himself. In 1991, Patton's poetry was edited and published by Carmine A. Prioli as *Lines of Fire: The Poetry of General George S. Patton.* Fortunately for Patton, he never gave up his "day job," as his poetry never advanced beyond "disgusting."

CHAPTER ELEVEN

July 1916

Diary: July 4

Field Day, and also concert given by the Twenty-fourth Infantry band. Very amusing.

To celebrate Independence Day, Pershing gave the entire Expedition the day off to enjoy roasted whole calves, freshly gathered vegetables, and baked desserts. In addition to a good meal, the soldiers participated in mounted and unmounted sporting events with much good-spirited rivalry between the regimental individuals and teams. Then they enjoyed the performance of the Twenty-Fourth Infantry band, an African American regimental musical group known for their excellent musicians and their concert performances.

Diary: July 5

A very bad wind all day.

Diary: July 6

Captain Campanole and myself went to Old Casas Grandes and took some pictures. While we were there the Presidente of the town seemed to think we had no right to be there, and while we were talking with him, we could see men in various houses. We did not like this and left.

The weather and actions with the local officials continued to highlight diary entries. Temperatures rose to the high nineties in the daytime and dropped to the low sixties at night. Wind and dust prevailed. Potentially outnumbered and under orders from Pershing to avoid conflict with the locals, Patton prudently and hastily departed the town to return to Dublán. Just when to heed discretion when confronted with possible enemies was a difficult lesson for the aggressive Patton to learn. As for the weather being cold, hot, or wet—they required only endurance and adjusting to the harsh conditions.

Patton did not include in his diary—nor with General Pershing, at the time—his correspondence with R. F. McReynolds, a former army captain currently serving as the collector of internal revenue for the City of Los Angeles, who offered him a major's commission in a volunteer infantry regiment he was raising. Patton seriously considered the offer for a brief period because the idea of immediate advancement from lieutenant to major certainly had its appeal. However, he ultimately turned down the offer, even though he appreciated it. He was reluctant to leave the regular army, adamantly believing that a protracted war with Mexico would be fought primarily by cavalry rather than infantry. Patton also felt an obligation to remain with Pershing, who had been "good enough to bring me down here." Furthermore, he had hitched his career to a star, and he knew Pershing was the best mentor for future success.

Diary: July 8

General Pershing went for horse exercise with me in the morning, we rode eighteen miles, it rained in the afternoon. Lieutenant Shallenberger and I went to the telegraph station at New Casas Grandes to find out whether the train was coming in from Juarez with supplies for the American troops. The train arrived at 11:15 p.m. but had no supplies.

Diary: July 9

Some of the officers went to the Mormon Church in the afternoon.

Diary: July 10

A train of hay from Juarez over the Mexico Northwestern Railroad got in at 8:00 a.m. It rained in the afternoon.

Although the Mexicans still declared they would oppose any movement by the Expedition's cavalry, the government was continuing to allow supplies to be delivered, at least temporarily, from El Paso via their rail system. These resupplies included hay and fodder for more than four thousand horses and mules in the area, belonging to the cavalry, that had already overgrazed the local pastures and exhausted the Mexican ranchers' crops.

Diary: July 11

The train left for Juarez.

Diary: July 12

A train of nine cars of supplies came in at 8:00 a.m.

Original diary entries include almost daily reports during this period of killing rattlesnakes in camp and while exercising horses. Patton apparently did not deem this of sufficient importance or of any influence to the Expedition when he prepared his final edition for Pershing.

In a letter to his father on July 12, Patton wrote of his boredom and his feelings about the president:

We are rapidly going crazy from the lack of occupation and there is no help in sight. I would like to go to hell so that I might be able to shovel a few extra coals on that unspeakable Wilson. How you can support him is beyond me and if he is reelected the American people are worse than even I imagine.

Diary: July 13

I took the correspondents to Colonia Juarez and thence to Pierson in the afternoon. At Pierson there was a large number of wooden buildings, we were much surprised that the Villistas or some other bandits had not burned them down.

On the way back to camp we got stuck in the river and had to get out and push in order to get the car across.

Colonia Juárez, located a dozen miles southwest of Colonia Dublán, was another village established in the 1880s as a Mormon sanctuary. Known for its peach, apple, and cattle production, it shared nothing with its namesake city adjacent to El Paso. Patton rarely mentioned the impact of the Expedition on the civilian population. His reference to the buildings in nearby Pierson shows that he was aware of the destruction and hardships suffered by the locals.

By this point in the Expedition, both Patton and Pershing relied more on automobiles than horses for transportation. As noted in the July 8 entry, riding on horseback was now more for exercise and recreation than for the performance of actual duties. Patton was learning that while horses never had to be pushed out of streams, there were limitations to the kinds of terrain automobiles could successfully traverse.

Diary: July 14

Ted Houghton brought me a new carbine, it shot too high.

It rained in the afternoon. Two truck trains got in from Columbus reaching camp at 6:00 p.m.

Ted Houghton was one of the Expedition's civilian guides. Houghton obviously held Patton in high esteem, regardless of the lieutenant's criticism of the gift's accuracy.

Diary: July 15

One truck train got into camp.

Quite a heavy rainstorm. Mr. Blakesley of the Associated Press went north, we were all very sorry to lose him.

Howard W. Blakesley departed Mexico to assume the duties of editor at the Chicago Associated Press (AP) office. He was popular among the Expedition officers for both his companionship and, more important, his accurate, unbiased reporting of operations.

Diary: July 16

General Pershing went to Colonia Juarez. One truck train arrived.

Even at this point in the Expedition, Patton still mentioned the arrivals of truck trains that were responsible for delivering what supplies could not be brought in by rail. Mule- or horse-drawn wagons from the Columbus supply depot had served as the first supply vehicles when the troops spread out into Mexico only to be replaced over time by motorized transports. Jeffery (later the Nash Company) vehicles drawn from border security units on March 18 formed the first truck company organized in Columbus.

By mid-July, seventeen companies of trucks manufactured by the Jeffery, White, Packard Locomobile, and F.W.D. (Four Wheel Drive) companies were ferrying supplies from Columbus initially to Namiquipa and later to Colonia Dublán.

In good weather the round trip to Dublán could be accomplished in two weeks. When it rained, it took much longer. The trail south was little more than wagon ruts and did not merit, even with improvements by engineer units, its name of the Lincoln Junior Highway. Despite constant maintenance and improvements, it remained a difficult tract to traverse.

Any soldier with experience driving an automobile or truck was transferred from his cavalry or infantry unit and placed behind a wheel. Even then, only enough of these uniformed drivers were available to man about half of the trucks, forcing the Quartermaster Corps to hire civilian operators.

Captain Francis H. Pope, West Point class of 1897, was one of the first officers detailed to manage the trucks as a member of the Quartermaster Corps. Pope later recorded his observations about the period in an article titled "Motor Transport Experiences with the Mexican Punitive Expedition" that was included in Frank Tompkins's book.

In summing up the use of trucks, Pope wrote, "The Mexican Punitive Expedition was the first opportunity given the United States Army to handle motor transportation on a reasonably large scale, and the experience gained, although confined to comparatively few officers, was of inestimable value in our subsequent operations in the World War."

Patton closely monitored the activities and advancement of the truck companies as a matter not only of duty regarding supplies but also of professional interest in their potential. By the conclusion of the Expedition, 588 cargo trucks, 57 tankers, 12 truck-mounted machine shops, and 6 wreckers were in the inventory. Later, in World War II, he would once again find that long supply lines did more to slow his advance than anything done by the opposition.

Diary: July 17

Nothing happened until 10:30 a.m. when a train with General Gonzales and Colonel Chavis and seventy-five cavalrymen came into camp. Colonel Chavis had a consultation with General Pershing. He acted as interpreter for General Gonzales.

The purpose of this meeting was to ensure that the Mexican army and the Americans avoided further bloodshed. Pershing also used the opportunity to reassure Mexican citizens and officials in Namiquipa, who assisted the Expedition, that they would not be harmed or otherwise punished.

Diary: July 18

Nothing except that General Gonzales and his men returned, having found a broken bridge near Pierson.

In the evening a lot of newly made captains reported to the General on their way to the border to join new regiments. Among these were Captain [Innis P.] Swift, Captain [Charles P.] George, Captain

[Telesphor G.] Gottschalk, Captain [Herbert E.] Mann, Captain [Claude de Busse] Hunt, and about five others.

Promotion to the rank of captain in the regular army in 1916 took from eight to twelve years. Just as Patton used the lessons learned in Mexico for the remainder of his career, the lieutenants who earned captain bars while members of the Expedition took their expertise to other regiments to share their knowledge and experience.

Diary: July 19

General Pershing went as far as Corralitos to inspect roads running north. He was gone all day.

Jap spies returned and reported that Villa was still alive but injured and still using crutches.

Other than a few spy missions, as mentioned by Patton, the Japanese remained as neutral as possible, otherwise favoring the Mexican government or bandits when it ensured their continued safety. Interaction with, and support from, the Chinese was far greater than that of the Japanese.

Diary: July 20

Truck train Number Twenty got in from Columbus. It had started the sixteenth but the rain had delayed it.

Mr. Robert Bacon and Doctor Strong got in about 11:00 p.m. to visit General Pershing.

Diary: July 21

Mr. Bacon and Doctor Strong left in the afternoon. They went over the camp with the General in the morning.

Robert Low Bacon—Harvard graduate, U.S. congressman from New York, and son of the U.S. secretary of state and ambassador to France—

was also an officer in his state's National Guard. At the time of his visit with Pershing, he was serving with his unit in Texas. He did not make this visit in his capacity as a junior National Guard officer, but rather as a member of the U.S. Congress.

To his father, Patton wrote on July 20, "I now begin to think that we will be here till November. It is hard on everyone. The flies are getting bad too."

Diary: July 23

Jumped my mare and also Major Hines' gray horse. Discussed the saber with General Pershing, he does not think much of it.
It rained a little. I went to the Mormon church in the afternoon.

The days were becoming so routine, if not boring, that Patton made no mention of skipping a day in his journal. Despite its lack of use in Mexico, he remained a great proponent of the saber. After all, he had designed the current rendition and "wrote the book" on its deployment. But weapons, as well as transportation modes, were rapidly changing. The army had replaced the .30-40 Krag-Jorgensen rifle with the .30 Model 1903, known as the Springfield or 03 rifle. It proved far superior to the German-manufactured rifles and other long guns carried by the Mexican army, Villistas, and other bandits. The accuracy of the bolt-action Springfield was largely the reason why the casualty rate vastly favored the Americans in every encounter with the Mexicans. Its only drawback as a cavalry weapon was that it had to be sling-carried on the soldier's back while in the saddle.

The M-1911 .45 caliber semi-automatic pistol that had replaced the .38 revolvers added to the soldier's firepower. It also could be easily reloaded by a quick change of magazines rather than placing individual bullets in a revolver cylinder.

Advancement in weapons caused Pershing to doubt the future of the saber in modern warfare. Patton, however, remained reluctant to admit that the saber would have little or no role in the army's future.

Diary: July 24

This is Pioneer Day for the Mormons. General Pershing and staff went to Colonia Juarez today and witnessed some interesting ceremonies at the church. It consisted of the children singing and giving a play representing the Mormon Expedition across Utah. Afterwards, Alonzo Taylor gave us a dinner. He had two of his wives present at this dinner.

 One of Bishop Bentley's daughters seemed to attract the attention of Colonel Cabell and several other officers.

Pioneer Day celebrates the arrival in 1847 of Brigham Young and his Church of Jesus Christ of Latter-day Saints (LDS) followers from Nauvoo, Illinois, into the Salt Lake Valley. While Patton wrote, especially in his later diaries, critically of individuals and nationalities, he remained tolerant of all religions. He did not seem bothered by the Mormon practice of plural marriages or other beliefs, an attitude that reflected his earlier writing that said, "God was probably indifferent in the way he was approached."

Colonel Cabell and the other officers had now been away from their wives and families for months. There is no evidence, however, of their "attention" being anything more than mild flirtation.

Diary: July 25

General Pershing, Colonel Cabell, and Lieutenant Collins went to El Valle. Colonel [George O.] Cress, Captain [Wilson B.] Burtt, and Colonel [Lucian G.] Berry and three other officers went to Columbus.

 There was a prize fight in the evening and about fifteen hundred men were present.

Pershing's staff had the critical responsibility for coordinating and communicating with the Columbus depot for the success of the Expedition. At this time, Colonel Cress was acting inspector general, Burtt was assistant chief of staff, and Berry was the Expedition artillery commander.

They and the other officers would have used this visit to maintain relations with the Columbus supply depot. Their visit to New Mexico also undoubtedly doubled as a reward by Pershing for their good service.

In 1916, champion boxers were among the best-known and honored celebrities in the United States. The sport was so popular in part because it required little in the way of equipment to stage a competition. Where entertainment and other diversions were few and far between, boxing matches served as a huge diversion from the day-to-day routine, especially when soldiers could wholeheartedly support the pugilist who represented their regiments.

Patton admired the athleticism of the boxers. Even more, he appreciated their willingness to fight and desire to defeat their opponents.

Diary: July 27

Nothing to report.

Diary: July 28

Three truck trains arrived from Columbus. General Dodd arrived from El Valle. He had just made general and was on his way out having just been retired.

The Tenth Cavalry gave a dinner, celebrating the Fifth-eighth year of its organization. The dinner was preceded by some very interesting ceremonies, in which the Tenth Cavalry soldiers gave imitations of all the fights in which the regiment had been. This was staged by Major Young, who refused to sit down at the table on the pretext he was not feeling well.

Major Hines, in behalf of General Pershing [who was still in Columbus], gave a reception for General Dodd at Division Headquarters.

Despite his advancing age, Dodd had withstood the rigor of field operations and earned the praise of his men as well as Pershing. Dodd got to wear the single star of a brigadier general for only a few weeks on active duty before his mandatory retirement from the army at age sixty-four.

The famous Tenth U.S. Cavalry, formed at Fort Leavenworth, Kansas, on July 28, 1866, was an African American regiment, composed of Black enlisted men and White officers. The unit had served throughout the Western United States in the Indian Wars, was first to reach the top of San Juan Hill in Cuba, and then fought in the Philippine Insurrection. After returning to the United States, the Tenth made its headquarters at Fort Huachuca, Arizona, before becoming a part of the Expedition into Mexico.

Major Charles Young, only the third Black man to graduate from West Point, was one of the few African American officers in uniform during his more than thirty years in the army. Young proved himself a competent, brave leader, earning the respect of his men and his regiment's White officers. Claiming illness as an excuse not to sit with the White guests on the night of celebration referred to by Patton was Young's acknowledgment that many of the White officers had never sat at a table on an equal basis with a Black man.

Ironically, it was this Tenth Cavalry to which Patton was officially assigned during the Expedition. Although he never actually served with the regiment because he was detached to "special service" with Pershing's headquarters, Patton openly expressed the racial prejudices against Blacks common at the time. In Mexico, however, he saw firsthand that Black soldiers could and would fight—the primary characteristics he valued in warriors. This recognition was another lesson that remained with him for the rest of his career. In October 1944, Patton requested more tankers for his Third Army, and the War Department replied that the only unit available was the Black 761st Tank Battalion. Patton responded, "Who the hell asked for color? I asked for tankers." Patton, who also was the first American general to integrate Black soldiers into previously all-White infantry companies when casualties outnumbered replacements, addressed the 761st on their arrival:

Men, you are the first Negro tankers to ever fight in the American army. I have nothing but the best in my army. I don't care what color you are, so long as you go up there and kill the Kraut sonsofbitches. Everyone has their eyes on you, and is expecting great things of you.

*Most of all, your race is looking forward to your success. Don't let them
down, and, God damn you, don't let me down. They say it is patriotic
to die for your country. Well let's see how many patriots we can make
out of those German sonsofbitches.*

Diary: July 30

*Lieutenant Collins came up from El Valle to go to Columbus to get
General Bliss.*

Major General Tasker H. Bliss was the U.S. Army assistant chief
of staff who would become the chief of staff in September 1917. Bliss
had traveled to Columbus to inspect the facilities there and then to visit
Pershing and the Expedition headquarters in Dublán.

Patton expressed his envy in Collins's being selected to escort Bliss
to Columbus. In a letter to Beatrice on this date, he wrote, "I wish I were
going." He could not be too critical of his fellow aide as an escort, however, as Collins needed dental care available in Columbus for a bad tooth.

Diary: July 31

*Captain Johnson and myself went antelope hunting and I killed one.
My horse got away when I dismounted to fire and I had to walk home
while Johnson hunted up my horse[,] which he finally found.*

Patton continued to seek hunting companions from whom he could
learn more about aspects of the army other than the cavalry. Captain
Hugh S. Johnson was one such source. At age fifteen, Johnson had run
away from his family home in Kansas to join the Kansas militia. Before
he could be sworn in, his father came after him, promising he would
secure his son an appointment to West Point if he would return home
and finish high school. Using his political connections, the senior Johnson kept his word, and Johnson entered the Academy, from which he
would graduate in 1903 with Douglas MacArthur as a classmate.

Johnson had served in the Philippines, assisted in caring for victims
of the San Francisco earthquake of 1906, and acted as the army super-

intendent of Yosemite and Sequoia National Parks. In 1914, he received orders to attend law school and on graduation joined the Punitive Expedition in Mexico. He would later write that while in Mexico he studied "the whole body of constitutional, administrative, State and municipal law of both the United States and the Republic of Mexico," which "soaked me through with the theory and practice of Federal, State and municipal political structure in the United States."

After the Expedition, Johnson wrote the draft version of the congressional bill that established the Selective Service System. Disappointed that he did not get to serve in combat in the First World War, he left the army and, after a career in business, joined President Franklin Roosevelt's "brain trust" that established the New Deal. He then headed the National Recovery Administration and, later, the Works Projects Administration. In 1933, *Time* magazine honored him as "Man of the Year."

CHAPTER TWELVE

August 1916

Diary: August 2

Colonel Cress returned from Columbus.

Diary: August 3

I went antelope hunting with Johnson but got nothing. We found some old cliff dwellings in the mountains east of camp.
General Pershing and his staff returned.

The Mexican state of Chihuahua contains dozens of archeological sites of cliff dwellings, kivas, and other relics from the Mogollon and Hohokam cultures dating from 300 to 1500. This visit marked the continuation of Patton's interest in studying ancient ruins and battlefields, which he maintained in Europe and North Africa during the world wars. Patton made no claim to having visited the Mexican ruins in past lives as he did later at other archaeological sites during World War II.

Diary: August 4

The General, General Bliss, Major Connor, Major Nolan, and all the General Staff got in at 11:00 a.m. They went to El Valle with General Pershing at 1:30.

Diary: August 5

Both Generals returned to Dublan at 1:10 p.m. General Pershing told me that I could go to Columbus with General Bliss.

Diary: August 6

I started north with the General at 7:00 a.m. We had one Studebaker, one Ford, and two Dodges. We reached Columbus at 7:00 p.m. I saw General Bliss to his car.

Diary: August 7

Looked up property for Shallenberger, saw to the repair of the two Dodge cars. Went to El Paso at 11:55 a.m.

Once Patton delivered Bliss to Columbus and saw him off for duties that did not involve the Expedition, he took care of preparing the automobiles for the return to Dublán and running errands for his fellow aide and other members of the staff. He then caught the train to El Paso on official business to visit militia camps and, more important—at least to him—to reunite with his wife and children for a brief visit.

George and Beatrice had been apart now for more than four months, typical of officers and their families for all periods of army service. The Pattons, unlike most couples, had the advantage of sufficient wealth for Beatrice to travel and join her husband whenever the opportunity arose. Patton was not on leave while in El Paso, however; he still had official duties to perform.

Diary: August 8

I inspected the camps of the militia in order to report on their condition to General Pershing, also called on General Bell, and saw about having General Pershing's horses taken care of. Saw Colonel Holbrook of the Seventeenth Cavalry.

In addition to inspecting newly arrived militia units, he checked on the condition of Pershing's personal horse and the general's son's pony at the Fort Bliss stables. He made a formal visit to Brigadier General (later Major General) George Bell Jr., commander of the El Paso Military District, and then called on Colonel (later Major General) Willard A. Holbrook, commander of the newly formed Seventeenth Cavalry.

Diary: August 9

Looked up Pershing's property, and got two cases of White Rock, took train to Columbus at 2:55 after seeing about cars. I got a new Studebaker for the General.

Patton was checking on Pershing's vacant quarters in El Paso, unoccupied since his surviving son, Warren, had gone to live with his father's spinster sister May and her widowed sibling Elizabeth Pershing Butler in Lincoln, Nebraska, and his own departure for Mexico. Then he procured White Rock, the general's favorite mineral water. In Columbus, Patton also filled requests from his fellow staff members. From storage he secured a sack of saddle tact to take to Lieutenant Collins and from a local merchant purchased cigars for Major John L. Hines, the Expedition adjutant.

Diary: August 10

I started at 7:06 a.m. with eight guards, three Dodges and one Studebaker. Got into the mud at Vado Fusiles. A very heavy rain started at Corralitos. We had to push the cars for some distance, and got into camp at 8:30 p.m.

Patton's recording of exact times by the minute is a good indication that he intended to use his diary later as an official source, rather than keep it for his personal recollections—which accounts for his omission of his visit with his family. The fact that the small convoy had only eight guards reflects the overall security of the line of communication between Columbus and Dublán.

Diary: August 11

General Pershing went horseback riding. A truck train was reported stuck in the mud at Corralitos but it later got in at 3:00 p.m.

Diary: August 12

Another truck train arrived from the north, having been a long time on the road.

Diary: August 14

Lieutenant Shallenberger, Mr. Boyd, and myself went hunting on the Parajo mountain. We rode thirteen miles but saw nothing.
      Nothing further to report until August 18th.

Diary: August 18

Field Day
      I was one of the judges, and also won the shooting event. The shooting was very poor.

By August, the soldiers of the Expedition had settled into the routine of garrison duty in the Dublán compound. With patrolling limited to the immediate area, Pershing instituted rigorous training, including rifle marksmanship, machine gunnery, and combat maneuvers, to improve the readiness level of the units and to keep the troops occupied. The training had a more important mission as well. Both Pershing and Patton believed the officers and men of the Punitive Expedition would form the nucleus of the expanded army that would soon be committed to the world war. They approached the activity with the belief that sweat shed in the desert of Mexico would later result in less blood spilled on the European plains and forests. For the remainder of his career, Patton never allowed his soldiers idle time. If not fighting, he had them training for future battles.

Surrounded by a fence with guard posts, the Dublán compound was safe from the bandits and Federal troops but vulnerable to dust when dry and extremely muddy following rainstorms. In his book, Tompkins wrote:

The camp was most uncomfortable, due to the high winds, frequent dust storms, tropical heat of summer, freezing cold of winter, deep mud in the tropical downpours, and swarms of flies. The soldiers had no tents or other shelter except the shelter half each man carried with him. The men soon set to work to build adobe walls on which they placed their shelter halves as roofs. Considerable ingenuity was shown in making cots of poles, and other "furniture" for camp comfort.

Each troop, company, and battery built its own kitchen of adobe bricks, thus enabling the men to eat under shelter from dust or rain . . . mail and supplies were received regularly, so the troops were once more well fed and clothed.

Apache scouts and soldiers from the various units also formed hunting parties to add ducks, antelope, and venison to the daily fare. Because Pershing did not allow alcohol on the compound, local and other merchants established several cantinas along the edge of Colonia Dublán and other villages occupied by Expeditionary forces. The soldiers cleared areas not only for their boxing contest but also for baseball and football fields for competition among the regiments. A small motion picture theater showed nightly films, and its stage was also used for plays performed by the soldiers. Card games likewise helped pass any idle time. Regular field days were held for the enjoyment of participants and spectators alike. Patton's observation of poor shooting on August 18 led to increased marksmanship training.

Despite military inactivity, the Expedition maintained its discipline. Tompkins wrote, "Under these conditions the discipline should have suffered, but quite the contrary the men were cheerful, well behaved, and ready at all times to respond to any demand their General might make upon them. During their entire time in Mexico no one in the command was guilty of anything that could bring discredit upon the Expedition."

One item of soldier recreation mentioned by neither Tompkins in his book nor Patton in his diary was Pershing's authorization of a "sanitary village"—that is, the services of prostitutes to the soldiers. Some of Pershing's own officers encouraged him to close the village, but the general maintained that monitored houses of prostitution met the needs of the soldiers and, more important, lowered the rate of venereal disease.

Captain Julien E. Gaujot of the Eleventh Cavalry Regiment, who had earned his officer's commission in the West Virginia militia, supervised the village. A veteran of war in the Philippines, he had been convicted by a general courts martial of using the "water cure" on a Filipino insurgent, for which he was suspended three months and fined $50 for each month.

Gaujot had proven himself a brave soldier, earning the Medal of Honor for "extraordinary heroism in action on 13 April 1911, while serving with Troop K, 1st US Cavalry, in action at Aqua Prieta, Mexico. Captain Gaujot crossed the field of fire to obtain the permission of the rebel commander to receive the surrender of the surrounded forces of Mexican Federals and escort such forces, together with five Americans held as prisoners, to the American line."

Diary: August 19

General Pershing and myself with Barker and Boyd as guides went antelope hunting east of camp. The General got one shot at about four hundred yards.

We rode back in a car and the auto stuck in the sand and broke the propeller shaft and the General, Barker, and I started to walk. We traveled four miles in fifty minutes, the General setting the pace. The hardest walking I had ever done. Both Barker and myself were stiff for several days.

When I reached camp I found that one of my horses had been badly cut up in a barbed wire fence.

This instance demonstrated to Patton the importance of an officer, regardless of his age, maintaining his personal physical conditioning as well as his professional expertise.

The American antelope (more correctly called a pronghorn) stands 32 to 41 inches tall and weighs from 75 to 140 pounds—not an easy target at 400 yards. Pershing likely used an issue 03 Springfield to bring down the animal. Despite the accuracy of the rifle, this was still a shot remarkable enough to merit the attention of Patton and inclusion in his diary.

Cavalrymen considered walking an infantryman's skill and preferred to accomplish their movement on horseback. At fifty-six years of age, Pershing could still tire out his much younger subordinates and guide in the long walk. Patton not only took note of this instance in his diary but also began performing some kind of strength or endurance exercise daily, which he would continue for the rest of his life.

Diary: August 20

General Pershing and I started to go pistol shooting but it rained.

Diary: August 21

The General reviewed the entire command at 10:30. It took fifty minutes for it to pass at a walk.

Diary: August 22

Inspected the Seventh and the Eleventh Cavalry. The General and Collins inspected their appearance. Colonel Cabell and myself inspected the equipment and horses, the condition of the horses, and the shoeing. Colonel Cress and Captain Reed the personal equipment.

Diary: August 23

I inspected the Tenth Cavalry and Twenty-fourth Infantry; also Fourth Field Artillery and the camp in the afternoon.

Parades and inspections, along with field training, dominated the Expedition's activities for its time remaining in Mexico. While the artillery played little or no role in the fights with the bandits and government troops, Mexico provided an excellent opportunity for the artillerymen to hone the skills they would later employ in France. During this period, Pershing also instilled into Patton the importance and value of soldiers looking like soldiers and maintaining themselves, their equipment, and their animals in prime condition. Patton would later remark that a soldier who did not wear the proper uniform and maintain his gear could not be depended on to fight well.

Diary: August 24

General Pershing, Colonel Cress, Colonel Cabell, Colonel Glennan, Lieutenant Collins and I left at 10:30 for San Joaquin. We inspected the Third Battalion of the Seventeenth Infantry stationed there.

The fifty-four-year-old lieutenant colonel James D. Glennan acted as the Expedition's surgeon general after having been present at the Battle of Wounded Knee in 1890 and serving in the Philippines. Glennan went on to become the army's senior medical officer as a brigadier general; in his final years, he supervised the construction of the Walter Reed Hospital in Washington, D.C. His experience in South Dakota had given Glennan such a great respect for Native Americans that he became a serious collector of their artifacts. His collection, some of which he gathered in Mexico during the Expedition, was contributed to the Smithsonian after his death.

Glennan was but one more source in the education of Lieutenant Patton. From this senior officer, Patton learned about the importance of emphasis on the care and visitation of the ill and wounded. In his later years, Patton became well known for his calls on medical facilities to visit his wounded soldiers.

Diary: August 25

We inspected the headquarters Seventeenth Infantry in the morning. General Pershing went to inspect the old ruins. Captain Wright, Seventeenth Infantry, was excavating. It rained hard in the afternoon.

John W. Wright had volunteered for the army at the outbreak of the Spanish-American War and had advanced in rank to captain and adjutant of the Seventeenth Infantry during the pursuit of Villa in Mexico.

As a self-taught archaeologist, he discovered and excavated the ancient mounds at San Joaquin. Artifacts he recovered at the site are today in the collections of the Smithsonian Institute in Washington, D.C., and the Field Museum of Natural History in Chicago. Patton did not elaborate in his diary or letters, but with his interest in history and ruins, he must have spent some time with Wright at the digs.

Diary: August 26

We started to inspect the Thirteenth Cavalry but the San Joaquin River was too high and we had to stay in camp. All the staff except General Pershing went up the canyon on horseback this morning.

In the afternoon Collins and I climbed the high hill in the back of the camp and got a fine view.

Diary: August 27

Left camp at 8:30 a.m. and got to Angostura at 12:30, having left the machines about five miles out and taken horses brought over by Captain Merchant. We had to nearly swim the river in order to reach the camp.

We inspected the regiment at 1:30 p.m. It was very poor. Especially the wagon train. Very few of the men had underclothes. Nor had there been any attempt as far as we could find out made to secure any for them.

We left there at 4:00 p.m. and camped at Carbolinea for the night. This place was also called by the truck drivers "Naco."

Patton rarely misidentified the rank of his fellow officers in his diary. In this case, however, it should have been First Lieutenant rather than Captain Bekerley T. Merchant who provided the horses.

Soldiers of all eras and wars have come up with their own names for events and places—especially for those hard to pronounce, such as Carbolinea, and those that were particularly uncomfortable. *Naco* is Mexican Spanish slang for "low class" or "uncultured."

Diary: August 28

Left camp at 7:20 a.m. and reached El Valle at 9:10 a.m. We were met by Lieutenant Chamberlin. We rode over to El Valle, leaving the automobile west of the river, which had just broken down the Engineer's bridge.

The engineers under Captain Graves were working on the bridge as we passed. Here again it was almost necessary to swim the river. After reaching camp General Pershing held a review of the entire command and inspected until noon. Started the inspection again at 2:00 p.m. and inspected until 5:30 p.m.

The General sent in the wagon trains of the Sixteenth Infantry and Sixth Field Artillery as being too dirty for inspection back to camp.

All the officers called on the General at 7:30 p.m.

Lieutenant Harry D. Chamberlin, best known as the West Point class of 1910 football player who had picked up a fumble and returned the ball almost to the navy goal line to ensure victory in the 1908 match between the academies, had recently rejoined the Fifth Cavalry Regiment after his graduation from the Mounted Service School. Chamberlin would later become a member of the U.S. equestrian team in the 1920 Antwerp, Belgium, Olympic Games.

Captain Ernest Graves, a 1905 West Point graduate and also a football star, had helped build the first permanent facilities on Corregidor Island in the Philippines. Graves's son later described the duties of his father (nicknamed "Pot") during the Expedition:

Supply by truck was new, as was the construction of military roads to sustain truck traffic. Pot commanded the forward company, which in the course of constructing the road marched 250 miles on half rations into the barren wilderness of Mexico, with no vehicles except a mess wagon and a tool wagon, both drawn by mules. The roads were built and maintained with hand tools and a few mule-drawn scrapers. Pot's axiom then, so often repeated since, was "get the water off and the rock on."

Roads and bridges were not essential to cavalry operations, but those features were crucial for the resupply wagons and trucks. Properly maintained infrastructure became even more important in the First World War with the increase in motorized forces and the introduction of tanks and mechanized vehicles.

Although Patton made no further comment about Graves, the young engineer must have made an impression on both him and his boss, Pershing. When Pershing and Patton sailed for France in June 1917, Graves was a part of the small staff that accompanied the American Expedition Forces (AEF).

During his time in Mexico, Patton was maturing not only in his military skills but also in his diary notations. Now, he rarely recorded any evaluations of his fellow officers in his diary, withholding his opinions almost as a disciplinary form. He would not be so brief, or restrained, in his future journal entries. By the time he took command of the Third Army in World War II, Patton often emphasized his opinions of his subordinates, peers, and superiors alike. At times he praised their abilities and actions, but far more often he wrote about their lack of intelligence, leadership skills, and, for several, bravery.

Diary: August 29

The General inspected the camp of the above named wagon trains. I helped Colonel Cress condemn horses and inspect the hospital.

We started north at 10:30 a.m. We lunched on the road and inspected Company I of the Twenty-fourth Infantry at Charcos. It was in the most excellent condition. Before we reached Charcos we met a patrol of the Thirteenth Cavalry looking for two escaped prisoners. These were the two men who had held up a Chinaman and taken all the provisions out of his wagon. Just before reaching New Casas Grandes, the car in which I was riding with Colonel Cress and Colonel Glennan had a puncture so that we were about ten minutes behind the rest in reaching Dublan. As we neared it the whole sky became black and we absolutely could not see the town or the street. When we finally reached the town, the water in the streets was over a foot deep. In the gutters it was still deeper. In attempting to cross one of these it flooded our carburetor, and we were stuck. It was necessary for a truck to tow us in and I had to walk ahead in order to find the bridges. The water was running clear over the top of them.

The 6,500-man Punitive Expedition, composed primarily of professional soldiers, was well disciplined, and their crimes, both internal and external, were few. Patton's mention of the "two escaped prisoners" who had "held up a Chinaman" was one of the few instances when he mentioned misdeeds. According to the judge advocate's summary, included in Pershing's "Expedition Report," there were only nineteen offenses that required courts martial in the first four months of the operation. Of these, more than one-half were for strictly military offenses, such as sleeping on guard and disobeying orders.

Diary: August 30

General Pershing worked all day on Adjutant General and Judge Advocate papers.

Duties of a commanding general were much more than issuing orders and inspecting men in the field. Paperwork also competed for the commander's time. Patton learned from Pershing that there was a balance between the two types of demands. Field time remained the most important duty of the commander, Pershing insisted, and subordinates were to be trained to perform complete paperwork without the direct supervision of the superior. From Pershing, Patton learned to alternate days between field and desk time—a practice he followed for the remainder of his career.

Diary: August 31

General Pershing, Colonel Cabell, Colonel Cress, Lieutenant Collins, Lieutenant Patton, Mr. Adamson, the General's clerk, and Mr. Smith of the Hearst papers, Mr. Schovall of the Associated Press, and

Mr. Fox, the Underwood and Underwood photographer, started for Columbus at 10:00 a.m.

We reached Ojo Federico at 4:00 p.m. and inspected the first battalion of the Seventh Cavalry and Headquarters Tenth Cavalry. We suffered much that night with mosquitoes.

Pershing led the group to check supply facilities in Columbus on the pretext of inspecting units along the way. Just as important, or perhaps more so, the visit to the New Mexican town allowed Patton the opportunity to reunite with Beatrice and Pershing to see Nita, with whom his relationship was developing through correspondence.

The inclusion of the news correspondents also offered the opportunity for press coverage of the general's visit and a chance for the reporters to briefly "return to civilization." Most of the journalists, believing that "the story" was in the commander rather than in the operation, wanted to stay as close to Pershing as possible.

To enhance their stories, the correspondents had begun publishing news photographs provided by Underwood and Underwood, an innovative company established in 1881 that specialized in producing the latest craze in photography in 1916—the stereoviews, an optic trick by which two images of the same view sit side by side on a card and, when seen through a viewer, become one three-dimensional image in the eye of the beholder. By the time of the Expedition, this largest publisher of stereoviews in the world was selling more than ten million views a year.

CHAPTER THIRTEEN

September 1916

Diary: September 1

We left Ojo at 7:20 a.m. and after stopping along the road to examine the engineer work which was being done, we reached the Wind Mills.

The General wanted to have the reservoir there fixed so that it would hold water.

We reached Vado Fusiles at 3:00 p.m. and inspected one troop of the Tenth Cavalry and one company of the Seventh Infantry.

Left at 4:00 p.m. and reached Columbus at 5:10 p.m. A total distance of one hundred and seven miles.

While the soldiers could go for days without proper food, potable water was essential to their accomplishing daily activities. According to Pershing's "Expedition Report," "the number of sick in this command . . . has been about three percent, although often much below that figure." He reported that, according to his medical officer, much of the illness came from polluted water:

One would be safe in saying that all surface water, and shallow well water in Mexico is dangerous, for the Mexican peon is most careless as to the disposition of his excreta.

All organizations brought their Lyster bags [canvas containers that held 36 gallons] with them, and where these bags and the chloritization of the water was used very little sickness of intestinal type occurred. Unfortunately the chlorinated water is very objectionable to many persons, and after a few weeks use it was hard to keep the men on this water. Many of the men drink water from the streams and irrigation ditches and this infected water was undoubtedly the cause and starting point of later cases of diarrhea and dysentery.

The windmills noted by Patton provided pure, good-tasting water. Much of this water, however, was going to waste, as there was no reservoir to collect the liquid. Pershing, in his constant attention to detail, had the situation "fixed"—another lesson for Patton in "taking care of the troops and the army."

Patton's reference to the Seventh Infantry was in error, as this regiment did not serve in Mexico. Since he wrote "company" rather than "troop," it is apparent he was referring to an infantry unit—most likely the Seventeenth Infantry.

Diary: September 2

General Pershing, Lieutenant Colonel Farnsworth, and I inspected the tentative camps for the Expedition in case it were left at Columbus.

We also looked at the camp of the Second Massachusetts Infantry. In the afternoon General Pershing, my sister, Mrs. Patton, Colonel and Mrs. Farnsworth and myself went to Palomas for a ride.

General Pershing investigated the reasons for the slow issue of Quartermaster and Ordnance supplies.

In the evening the Mayor and the leading citizens of Deming called upon General Pershing. They were anxious to get the Expedition there and tried to persuade him that that was the best place in the world.

Patton made no mention of his reunion with Beatrice and referred to her only as Mrs. Patton in the copy of his diary that he submitted to Pershing. In his first diary edition, he identified her simply as *B.* The journal entries for the stay in Columbus focus on inspections of units and visits with local officials, but Patton made time for an extended visit with his wife, as did Pershing with Patton's sister, Nita.

Columbus had grown since the raid and now had ice cream parlors, saloons, restaurants, and other entertainment venues. As the March 24, 1916, edition of the *Columbus Courier* stated, "We are well advertised now."

Colonel Charles S. Farnsworth, West Point class of 1887, commanded the Columbus supply base that supported the Expedition. Farnsworth had served in Cuba, Alaska, and the Philippines, mostly supervising the building of fortifications before assuming his duties on the Mexican border. He would later command an infantry division in the First World War and establish and serve as the first commandant of the U.S. Army Infantry School at Fort Benning, Georgia. In that capacity, he reviewed several papers submitted by Patton on the tactics used in combining infantry and armor units.

Deming, the county seat of Luna County, which also contained the town of Columbus, was a thriving place that had just opened Camp Cody to its northwest for arriving army units. Many of the captured bandits from Villa's raid on Columbus were tried at Deming's courthouse.

Diary: September 3

General Pershing, Mrs. Patton, my sister, and Mrs. Collins and Lieutenant Collins and I went to Deming and saw General Granger Adams and a lot of Arkansas and Kentucky troops. We returned at 7:20 to dine with General Pershing.

General Adams supervised the assembly and training of National Guard units arriving at Deming's Camp Cody. The artillery officer commanded the First and Second Arkansas Infantry Regiments and the First, Second, and Third Infantry Regiments, as well as an ambulance company and a field hospital from Kentucky.

Diary: September 4

General Pershing worked over the supply question and looked over the remounts in the afternoon. Also General Pershing, Mrs. Collins and Mrs. Patton went in an automobile in the afternoon to look over the Aviation Field.

Pershing continued to conduct official business to justify his stay in Columbus. In his original diary, Patton wrote about the visit to the Aviation Field, saying, "I was sick and stayed home with B." No reason is known for its omission in the final diary.

Diary: September 5

General Pershing inspected all the troops at Columbus. Second Battalion of the Seventeenth Infantry, Second Mass. Infantry, Troop H Twelfth Cavalry, Signal Corps Detachment, and Truck Companies. The Second Mass. Infantry marched very well but their arms were very dirty, their being as many as eighty dirty rifles in a company of one hundred and twenty.

In the afternoon we inspected the camp and found many extra articles beyond Equipment C.

Patton obviously was feeling better the next day and accompanied Pershing in what were not precursory inspections. It is evident that they checked each soldier and his equipment by the notation of how many dirty rifles they found. Pershing, and later Patton, believed in units using what the army issued, not acquiring "extra articles."

Diary: September 6

Inspected the Aero Squadron in the morning and started out at 12:30. Lanckton and Booker and Burgie were absent so I drove the General's car.

We inspected the Engineers at Palomas and at Vado and Esquillia. We camped at this last place in a light rain.

The Engineer equipment was dirty and the camps not properly made. Many of them had hair which was too long.

Patton made no mention in his diary about once again leaving his wife behind while he returned to remote duty. According to their letters, they hated the separations but accepted them as professional soldier and spouse.

The two surviving JN-3s and their pilots and crews of the Aero Squadron had returned to Columbus in late April and remained there over the past months. There they had received four Curtiss N-8s. Foulois, promoted to major, immediately began testing the new aircraft only to quickly discover that the 90-horsepower N-8s were too underpowered and their landing gear too weak for operations in Mexico. Foulois disassembled the planes, packed them aboard rail cars, and shipped them to the Aviation School in San Diego to be used as trainers in the rapidly expanding aero force.

At the same time the N-8s were headed west, the Aero Squadron began receiving what eventually totaled twelve Curtiss R-2s. The 160-horsepower R-2 was much better suited for operations in Mexico, but the hastily built planes were far from being airworthy on arrival. Fuel tank leaks, faulty wiring, and lack of spare parts and tools kept the planes grounded for weeks. During the wait, Foulois's mechanics added automatic cameras, radios, Lewis machine guns, and bomb racks to the planes. The squadron also received numerous other airplane models and equipment for testing.

Once Foulois was satisfied with his squadron of R-2s, he flew to Dublán to meet with Pershing. With the area of operations now restricted, the Expedition no longer needed the reconnaissance and messaging capabilities of the planes. The two officers agreed that the main portion of the squadron would remain in Columbus while two planes would be stationed at the Dublán air strip. When Pershing reviewed his entire command on August 21, three planes flew over the parade—the first aerial review conducted by a U.S. air unit.

The First Aero Squadron remained in Columbus until the Expedition recrossed the border. By then, many of its veteran pilots had transferred to units for deployment to train for the inevitable war in Europe. Foulois, who later joined Pershing in France, would advance in rank to major general as the Chief of Air Service for the AEF and then Chief of the Air Corps.

Diary: September 7

Left camp at 7:15 and inspected the camp at Vado and the Engineers at Ojo Federico, where we ate lunch. We left at 1:00 p.m. Lieutenant

Colonel Cress inspected the camp at the Wind Mills and also at Car-rolitos and the Twenty Fourth Infantry camp there.

The General pushed on and reached camp at 4:30. Colonel Webb Hayes had accompanied us on this trip, he was a politician from Ohio, but a very nice man.

Although Patton identified Webb Cook Hayes, son of President Rutherford B. Hayes, as a "politician," he was far more than an office seeker. In 1887, the younger Hayes helped found the National Carbon Company, which eventually became National Carbide. As a part-time soldier in the Ohio National Guard, he had served in the Spanish-American War and in the Philippines, where he earned the Medal of Honor fighting on the island of Luzon. Before his visit to the Expedition in Mexico, Hayes had also participated in the Boxer Rebellion and acted as an observer in the Russo–Japanese War.

Patton was well aware of the importance of developing and main-taining good relations with elected officials—opportunities he would cultivate for the remainder of his life. Personally, however, he had no interest in politics. Many years later, on February 7, 1945, he wrote in his diary, "I have no more gift for politics than a cow has for fox hunting and am not interested in it. Also, I am sure it is very bad for a man's military reputation to be confounded with it. Personally, I have never voted and do not intend to."

While Patton disdained politics, his father felt differently. When the elder Patton was running in California as a Democrat against Republican Hiram Johnson for the U.S. Senate, his son had advice for him. With Johnson running as a staunch opponent of the United States entering the war in Europe, Patton advocated the offensive "attack, attack, attack" philosophy he had developed in Mexico. On September 7, Patton wrote to his father from Dublán:

I am sorry you have to fight Johnson but nevertheless feel sure of your ultimate success for you will have a big Republican backing.

Try and get them to come out for you and split the party. You ought to do it. Also, don't hesitate at rough stuff with Johnson. He will probably sling mud. If he does you sling rocks. In fact I would start it as you have more on him than he can have on you.

Go after his private life. This will get the Suffrage vote. Remember this is no practice game but the whole show the finals. You can go to bed for a month after November 7th but till then keep moving and never assume you have a vote. Go after each and every vote as if it were the only one you had. You must win. All your life had been in preparation for this so you must land it.

You are not polite enough to people in general. Treat each one as if he was an army officer you were friendly to on my account.

Get a lot of cigars and give them to people and ask about the children and crops.

It is perfectly possible to be for every policy under heaven to the man who is interested in that policy.

Diary: September 8

Colonel Hayes went north, nothing happened except that the El Paso Herald *reported a battle at El Valle, there was none.*

Diary: September 10

Major Hines, Lieutenant Patton, Mr. Boyd and Mr. Baker and some soldiers went hunting. We saw fifty antelope and four deer, but shot none. We spent the night in a deserted ranch where we all walked guard in turn. The rats ate up Major Hines' hat cord and some parts of the saddles.

Diary: September 11

Got up at 4:00 a.m. and hunted all day, Boyd and I killed two antelope. I missed a fine shot at a big one. We got home at 8:50 p.m. having gone over fifty miles. We killed eight rattlesnakes and four tarantulas on this trip.

Hunting provided a great pastime for Patton in Mexico and throughout his life—in both peace and war. He did not, however, indiscriminately kill birds and animals for the pleasure of the hunt, but rather for the general's table or for other mess facilities.

Apparently, Patton and his party were not aware that rats were a prime meal for rattlesnakes. Perhaps if they had let the reptiles live, they would not have had the problem with the rodents in their camp.

Diary: September 12

Captain Reed went to El Valle on business yesterday over the killing of one soldier and two Mexicans in a brawl.

Reed's investigation was in response to the article in the El Paso newspaper mentioned in Patton's diary entry of September 8. The incident proved not to be a battle, but rather a "brawl" between American and Mexican soldiers—likely fueled by alcohol—in one of the cantinas just outside the camp.

Diary: September 13

Major Hines, Major Lindsley, Captain Hoyt and myself went to the lake duck hunting. I killed two plover and the automobile got stuck in the mud.

Once again, Patton's hunting party was composed of officers who added to his military education. In addition to his military experience, Major Lindsley had organized the first West Point polo team. Captain Charles S. Holt offered insights from his experience as the commander of one of the truck train companies that delivered supplies from Columbus.

Diary: September 14

General Pershing and I went out to watch a problem, First Squadron of the Thirteenth Cavalry under Captain [John H.] Lewis. The men did not take cover properly. One of the aeroplanes made too fast a landing and broke the running gear and right lower wing. Captain [William O.] Reed returned home.

Captain Reed, attached from the Sixth Cavalry to the Expedition head-quarters on "Special Services with Expedition," was one of Patton's closest friends in Mexico. Patton included no explanation for his return home.

Patton did not make a diary entry for September 15 but did write Beatrice. He wrote that he wished his father was out of politics "so I could say what I think about Wilson." The young Patton still harbored resent-ment against the president for not allowing the Expedition to continue its offensive in Mexico and for hesitating to join the Allies in Europe.

Diary: September 16

Went duck hunting today and got seven. On the way back, met several Carrancistas and one of them fired right in front of us for the purpose of frightening us as far as we could see.

Diary: September 17

Colonel Beacom died at noon, from excessive blood pressure. We held services in the afternoon, all the officers were present.

The death of fifty-nine-year-old West Point graduate Colonel John H. Beacom, commander of the Sixth Infantry Regiment, was a reminder of the harshness of campaigning in Mexico. After the services in Dublán, Beacom's body was returned to his Wellsville, Ohio, home for burial. He was the highest-ranking member of the Expedition to die in Mexico.

Diary: September 18

Major Hines, Captain Kromer and I were going hunting but just before we started the General decided against our going on account of the danger of being picked up by some roving band of bandits.

In addition to absorbing supply skills from Captain Kromer, Patton appreciated that Kromer had been a member of the Academy's fencing team. Kromer went on to serve in World War I and become the chief of the U.S. Cavalry Branch.

In a letter to Beatrice on this date, Patton noted that the death of Major General Alpert L. Mills in Washington, D.C., would free up a two-star billet in the army and Pershing would likely get the rank. Patton wrote that Pershing "ought to be" promoted. He added that "he's all the time talking about Miss Anne. Nita may rank us yet."

Pershing did indeed receive the promotion to major general. Colonel T. Bentley Mott, a West Point classmate, sent a letter of congratulations from his military attaché post in Paris. Pershing, with the death of his family in the Presidio fire still heavy on his mind, wrote back on October 2, saying, "All the promotion in the world would make no difference now."

Nita Patton also responded to the announcement of the promotion. In a letter dated October 17, she wrote, "Dear Major General Pershing. Do you feel horribly dignified now, or can you still smile occasionally?"

Although Patton made no diary entry on September 20, he did write to his father that day encouraging him to continue the political fight and "stay to the end." He further advised his father to seek support from the president, while also writing, "My own views on Wilson are not fit to print so I will keep them to myself." Patton did, however, include his views on Mexico in the letter: "The Carranzistas fear to chase Villa for fear their men will desert. And they would. Intervention is useless. We must take the country and keep it."

Diary: September 21

General Pershing and I went out to watch some practice and rode up the canyon northeast of camp about ten miles.

Diary: September 23

Colonel Wilder came to camp to report on the shooting at El Valle. One soldier of the Fifth Cavalry was killed and one badly wounded and two Mexicans were killed.

Nothing else to report until October 2nd.

In a letter to Beatrice on September 24, Patton commented on his lack of diary entries, writing, "Nothing to report. Even the wind did not blow today." The next day he again wrote his wife, saying that Pershing had received his second star and that the staff had a reception for him "with lemonade for refreshment."

With his promotion to major general, Pershing was now authorized a third aide. Although Pershing at times referred to Patton as his aide, he never made the assignment official. Patton remained "on special service with the Expedition" and did not receive the aide's collar insignia. Perhaps Pershing was trying to add a bit of humility to the oftentimes overconfident lieutenant, or maybe he just overlooked making the appointment.

On September 27, Patton wrote his wife that training maneuvers had resumed and that he had been working on maps, "as I know the country around here better than anyone." He added that he and Lieutenant John Lucas were organizing polo teams and sent for balls and mallets, saying, "It will be something to do."

The next day he wrote his father again, expressing his loathing of Wilson: "He has not the soul of a louse nor the mind of a worm. Or the backbone of a jellyfish." He added that Wilson's claims about the preparedness of the military was "a lie" and that "we have no army and will never have until we have universal service [the draft]."

On September 29, Patton wrote his wife about the excitement he and Pershing felt on observing cavalry maneuvers that "shows that even in open country a charge will work." He added that Lieutenant Collins had again gone to Columbus to have a tooth repaired and concluded, "I wish I had one like it."

CHAPTER FOURTEEN

October 1916

In early October, Patton had much news to record in his journal. In a later correspondence with Beatrice during World War I, he wrote, "I had my usual annual accident" when his car crashed into a closed railroad gate and badly cut his head. His "annual accident" in Mexico was about to occur.

Diary: October 2

I was working on some musketry reports for General Pershing and I was burned by a lamp. I went to the hospital and Major [Frank C.] Baker [commander of Field Hospital No. 3] fixed me up.

General Pershing, Colonel Cabell, Major Hines and other officers came to see me that night, which I appreciated.

Diary: October 3

Major [William E.] Vose [medical officer of the Twenty-Fourth Infantry Regiment] dressed my face and all the officers again called. I remained in the hospital until October 9th, when on reporting to the General that I would not be fit for duty for at least three more weeks, he told me to take a sick leave, so I left on a Truck Train with Captain Graham and Doctor [Captain Taylor E.] Darby [of Field Hospital No. 7] at 10:30 a.m. They were very nice to me and we reached Columbus at 3:30 October 10th. From October 10th to November 10th, I was on leave.

Patton made no diary entries for the month he was on leave to recover from his burns. Before departing for Columbus, he wrote Beatrice on October 7 explaining the accident with bits of humor:

You are indeed fortunate in not being able to kiss me right now. My face looks like an old afterbirth of a Mexican cow on which had been smeared several very much decomposed eggs. I have a large and flatulent double chin and jowls like the typical Wall St. Magninate. Also both ears are red and inflamed and I have no hair nor eyebrows nor eye lashes. No, I have nothing catching. I simply set myself on fire with the above distressing results. All this happened on the second and I have been back in my own tent for the past two days. So don't get excited. Also it will leave no scar.

I came back from the movies and having some work to do I pumped up my lamp [likely the lamp he had purchased in El Paso the previous October] and lit it. It did not burn well so I started pumping again while it was lit. There was too much gasoline in it so when I stopped pumping a lot of gasoline flew out of the hole instead of air and caught fire. As it came it hit me in the face and got in my hair. I ran outside and put myself out. Then came back and put out the lamp and the tent. Then I reported to Gen. P. that I was burned and went to the hospital. The first persons I met were dentists who only announced that fact and told me to hunt for a surgeon. Then I found Maj. Dr. Baker who was very nice but everything he tried to get for my face was "just out" like a cheap hash house so at last he put Vaseline on it. It was hurting like hell by then. Gen. P. and all the staff and Mr. Lucas of the 13th came to see me that night and repeated their visits daily. The Gen. and Shallenberger and Collins coming two or three times each [day]. Marchant and West and Col. Tompkins and Mr. Blunt also came. I was much touched by their interest as I probably would not have visited them. Also my corporal and cook came over.

I really did not suffer too much the first night and got to sleep for short periods after about 2 a.m.

Next day they put a saturated solution of Bi Carbonate of Soda and wet it every half hour all day. It was fine. I slept all night. They repeated that the next day then yesterday they started bandaging with Zinc Oxide. And today took the bandage off but will put it back tonight so I will not stick to my pillow.

The first couple of days I had to eat through a tube but now can eat almost anything solid. I ate roast beef, potatoes, green peas, coffee, and pudding for lunch.

My eyes are not hurt at all and I can read which is a great comfort. The Dr. says I will be all pealed off in five more days. He says it was just like a very severe sunburn and will make no scars except on my right cheek a little one.

I wrote you this long letter to keep you from being worried. I also had a couple of pictures taken which I will send to you. I love you with all my heart and would have hated worst to have been blinded because I could not have seen you.

Beatrice met Patton in Columbus on October 10, and the two then journeyed to Lake Vineyard in California. Several Los Angeles newspapers noted his return and carried pictures of him with his bandaged head with headlines that read, "Rubio Hero Here" and "Pershing's Aide Returns."

Nita wrote Pershing on October 12 expressing her surprise when, on returning home the previous day from attending a lecture and working in her father's campaign office, she found that Patton and Beatrice had arrived: "I certainly gasped with surprise. Poor George, surely did get in a 'mix up' with that lamp. But he was lucky not to hurt his eyes. We are too happy to have him home again. He was pretty weary when he got here."

On October 29, Nita again wrote Pershing expressing her appreciation for the general's extension of her brother's sick leave and stating that she had had "a fun time" during their visit in Columbus and hoped to do it again. She concluded with references to her brother's propensity toward accidents and her belief that he was "certainly lucky to get off so well, it was a narrow escape. George can do more awful things to himself than anyone I know."

Patton's daughter Ruth Ellen, in her biography of her mother, wrote that Beatrice often changed his bandages, but this gesture "made her sick to her stomach, which embarrassed her terribly. She felt it was wrong to have such a reaction—not a bit like Florence Nightingale."

Patton thought he could be of no use in his father's campaign because, as he described it, "I look so funny in my present hairless state that I would frighten people away." The senior Patton insisted and took his son along on a tour of the Imperial Valley, introducing his son at various events and even touting him as "the Bandit Killer."

Early in his stay in California, Pershing wrote Patton on October 16 wishing him a quick recovery and offering good advice for his young aide's future. Well aware of how politics and public opinion had advanced his own career, he might possibly have also been urging his aide not to say anything about the president or about the Expedition that might impact his future. Pershing wrote:

> I hope you are rapidly recovering from your accident and that your personal appearance has improved. At the same time no doubt you are enjoying the visit with your family.
>
> Apropos of your discussions with your father on the Mexican situation, do not be too insistent upon your own personal views. You must remember that when we enter the army we do so with the full knowledge that our first duty is toward our government, entirely regardless of our own views under any given circumstances. We are at liberty to express our personal views only when called upon to do so or else confidentially to our friends, but always confidentially and with the complete understanding that they are in no sense to govern our actions.
>
> The real purpose of this letter is to tell you that, in addition to the new bridle which you were kind enough to present to me, I have purchased the Saumur [French home of the Butet saddle, considered the world's finest] saddle you ordered for Captain Johnson. I am now in the market to buy a horse in keeping with such an outfit. I wish you would keep your eye open for anything in that part of the country that might suit me.
>
> Everything is moving along here about the same as when you left. Please give my regards to Mrs. Patton and your sister and tell

Mrs. Patton I cannot thank her too much for the sleeping bag, which is now in constant use. But I must hold you to your promise to obtain for me the cost of the bag so that I may remit.

Pershing did not include in his letter that he had officially recognized Patton's performance at Rubio Ranch with a "mention in the dispatches" in a report to General Funston at San Antonio. He reported:

The activities of Colonel Cardenas, an important member of Villa's staff, had stirred up Rubio and vicinity and our troops had made several unsuccessful attempts to capture him. On May 14, Lieutenant G. S. Patton, 8th Cavalry, of my staff, with a small detachment was sent to that section in automobiles to purchase corn. Upon reaching San Miguel Ranch near Rubio, several Villistas ran out, firing on the detachment as they went. Lieutenant Patton and one of our men opened fire in return, killing three of the Villistas, one of whom proved to be Col. Cardenas.

Patton's burns healed slowly and were further treated by Dr. Lemoyne (Billy) Mills, an uncle by marriage, in Los Angeles. Both Patton and Mills wrote Pershing requesting an additional two weeks of sick leave for the burns to heal safely and properly. Pershing granted the requests and wrote Patton about his hopes for his father's victory in the coming election. He also wrote Dr. Mills expressing his appreciation for the care of "my aide." He concluded, "I am sure that he would not remain away one moment longer than his leave, unless he thought it necessary. I have already granted two weeks extension of his leave and hope this will suffice, as his services are important and I need him right along."

Patton's father, described as a "colorless campaigner," lost the senatorial election by a wide margin to the governor of California, Hiram Johnson. In his 1927 writings titled "My Father," Patton wrote:

In October 1916 I came home on sick leave to recover from a burn. Papa was in the midst of his senatorial campaign and campaign for Wilson. I accompanied him on a trip to the Imperial Valley and was with him at the California Club the night the returns came in defeat-ing him. He never flinched and took it with a smile. Papa's efforts carried California for Wilson and secured the latter's reelection. On the strength of this I tried to get Papa to push himself for the secretary of war, but he was too high souled to be a good advocate for himself and lost out. This was a calamity as he would have made a magnif-icent secretary. My love for Wilson was not heightened by his failure to reward the man to whom he owed so much.

There is no evidence that Patton's father's efforts in California car-ried the state for Wilson, nor that he would have made a "magnificent" secretary of war. If he had gained the cabinet position, it obviously would have benefited his son.

Chapter Fifteen

November 1916

Patton and Beatrice boarded an eastbound train on November 9. When they arrived in Columbus and discovered there were no truck trains scheduled for Dublán, the couple continued to El Paso. An indication of their private wealth is that they stayed in a hotel rather than in their quarters at Fort Bliss. The next day they took another train back to Columbus.

Diary: November 11

Traveled from Columbus to Dublan, November 11th and 12th. I reached camp at 2:30 p.m. Everyone was very glad to see me and Lieutenant Collins had Captain Reed's room fixed up very nicely for me.

Captain Reed's quarters had been vacant since his departure for home in mid-September. This upgrade to a captain's room was a welcome-back gesture to Patton. Also, his former quarters, damaged in the fire that burned his head, were not yet habitable. (There are some discrepancies in the dates of these occurrences from Patton's original diary to the edited one he later provided Pershing. This account follows the edited version.)

Diary: November 14

Stayed home all day on account of my ear, it was not well. I returned to General Pershing's mess.

I found that I was on the pistol board with Major Lindsey, Captain [Osmun, Jr.] Latrobe [Thirteenth Cavalry], also Lieutenants [Homer M.] Groninger [Fifth Cavalry] and [Horace M.] Hickam [Seventh Cavalry].

Lieutenant Hickam's name stands out in this entry as one of Patton's fellow officers who shared his appreciation for the use of airplanes in the military. After the Expedition concluded, Lieutenant Hickam transferred to the Air Corps and established the training for many American World War I pilots. He continued to train and lead aviation units in the years following the end of the Great War until he died in a crash landing at Fort Crockett, Texas, on November 5, 1934. Hickam Air Field in Hawaii is named in his honor.

Lieutenant Groninger later served on Pershing's AEF staff, advanced in rank to major general, and commanded several U.S. posts during World War II. Captain Latrobe advanced in rank to full colonel and became the military aide to President Calvin Coolidge.

On this date Patton also wrote a consoling letter to his father that reads more like advice from father to son than son to father:

After the fight you made there is certainly no one man entitled to the gratitude of Wilson than you and you ought to get something good but you will not get a thing unless you go after it at once as there are few places and many who think themselves deserving.

I was awfully sorry that Johnson beat you but it may all be for the best and will be if you get some post that is more important than senator.

It would be a crime for you to settle down and fold your hands after the fight you have made. And in fact it would not be just to the thousands who supported you. The only way you can show them that you were worthy of their support is to keep on and get something worthwhile. Besides if you stopped now you would get sick.

Patton concluded the letter with observations of the current conditions in Dublán. He wrote, "This place is as usual colder, but the flies are all dead."

Diary: November 15

Shot on the pistol board in the afternoon.

General Pershing told me to write an article on the instruction the troops received and also to get pictures.

Diary: November 16

Went out riding with the General in the morning, inspected the troops, sat on the pistol board in the afternoon and worked on my article in the evening.

Diary: November 17

Got my right ear out of the bandages.

After his return to Dublán, Patton occupied much of his time supervising training as well as discussing and experimenting with the M-1911 .45 semi-automatic pistol. During the late afternoons, he continued his reading of military history while also writing papers on cavalry operations and arms. In a letter to Beatrice on November 15, he wrote, "The General has asked me to write an article which he will be sponsor for the proper training of cavalry. Since there are a lot of supposed good cavalrymen here I am quite elated over it. He must think I have some brains after all."

Patton had already recorded his thoughts on reconnaissance operations in an unpublished paper titled "Notes on Some Faults of the Advance Guard of a Squadron of Cavalry." In the paper he emphasized that the Advance Guard, like the rest of the army, must always be aggressive, stressing offense rather than defense. He believed that information acquired should be rapidly delivered to the main attacking force and concluded that the more mobile cavalry should always remain on the offensive "and not poke along like infantry must until it bumps its nose."

The same day he wrote his wife that, with the cession of offensive operations, "Even Gen. P. thinks now that we may come out" of Mexico, concluding, "I hope we do so."

After more than six weeks, Patton's burns had finally sufficiently healed to have his bandages removed. In his original diary, he included a note that, despite having the bandages gone, he did not shoot with the pistol board because his doctor "thought ear too sensitive."

Diary: November 18

General Scriven of the Signal Corps flew down in an aeroplane. He was so stiff that when he tried to get out of the aeroplane he could not move and had to be lifted. At retreat he failed to come out and the General had to tell him that retreat was blowing before he would come.

Diary: November 19

General Scriven left by auto with Captain Dodd. We had a turkey dinner.

Brigadier General George P. Scriven certainly did not make a positive impression on Lieutenant Patton. In addition to his diary entry about the senior officer, he wrote to Beatrice on November 18, saying, "Gen. Scriven, chief signal officer, came down by aeroplane this morning and when he got here he was so scared he could not move and had to be lifted out of the machine. He has been reviving himself on whiskey all day."

Patton did not note that Scriven, at sixty-two years of age, was the veteran of more than forty years of service in the army and might have been stiff from riding in the small cockpit. He also did not credit Scriven with serving in Cuba and in the Boxer Rebellion with distinction, nor did Patton laud him for acting as the military attaché in Mexico, Italy, and Turkey. Appointed by President William Howard Taft as the seventh chief signal officer of the army, Scriven, West Point class of 1878, had been instrumental in the organization of the air service that came under his command.

The purpose of Scriven's visit to Dublán was to observe the airplanes in operation. He did not stay long, however, returning by car rather than plane to Columbus the day after his arrival in Mexico.

Captain Townsend F. Dodd of the First Aero Squadron accompanied Scriven on his drive north. Dodd, a graduate of the University of Illinois, was one of the first officers to receive his aviator wings. His outstanding service in the Expedition inspired Pershing to select him as his aviation officer on the AEF staff when they deployed to France months later. Dodd survived the war only to die in an air crash near Philadelphia during a transcontinental race on October 5, 1919.

Patton's diary entry mentioning "a turkey dinner" is supported by a document titled "Menu, General Pershing's Mess, Sunday, November 19, 1916." It lists the menu as "Oyster stew, celeries and ripe olives, roast turkey and dressing, cranberry sauce, banana fritters with cream sauce, mashed potatoes, string beans, lettuce with mayonnaise, apple pie and cheese, assorted fruit, coffee, tea, milk, distilled water."

The Expedition was not all hardship, as indicated by the elaborate menu items that were to be served to American soldiers and sailors stationed all around the world. This was following President Wilson's Presidential Proclamation No. 1352 declaring that Thanksgiving Day would be the last Thursday of November, which in 1916 fell on the 30th. Military cooks, who prided themselves for serving a Thanksgiving meal to rival anything found in homes or commercial venues, spared no efforts—even in the Mexico desert, and even though they prepared the meal on November 19.

The questions arise, of course, about why Pershing and the Punitive Expedition celebrated Thanksgiving on Sunday the 19th rather than Thursday the 30th. Neither Patton nor Pershing offers an explanation, but the reason was likely a simple matter of food preservation. The meal's ingredients had probably been delivered from Columbus early to ensure they would be there on time for the holiday. The early arrival of oysters and turkeys would need to be consumed immediately because of the outpost's lack of refrigeration. Pershing may have also had the meal served on Sunday, a day of rest for the army, to have an additional training day.

The soldiers not only ate well on Thanksgiving but also received adequate rations once the Expedition settled into semi-permanent camps around Dublán. Locally procured beef along with seasonal fruits and vegetables found their way to the mess tables to accompany ever-present pinto beans and coffee. When fresh local provisions were not available, the army cooks prepared meals from canned goods—most commonly "Corn Willy," made from canned corned beef mixed with butter and potatoes, and "Goldfish," made from canned salmon and breadcrumbs.

Unlike most soldier diaries, Patton rarely mentioned food other than holiday meals. Either he did not overly care about what he ate or, more likely, he simply did not think it important enough to include in his journals.

Diary: November 20

Went out early to show Colonel Winn of the Twenty-fourth Infantry where to go to start the problem.

After having placed him, I watched with my field glasses the deployment of the attacking force and later joined General Pershing. We were almost run over by two black tailed deer while watching the final attack. We got in at 6:00 p.m.

Bishop Bentley and Mr. Call, and Apostle Ivers had supper with us. Ivers, who is one of the twelve Mormon Apostles, is a very intelligent looking man. He funded the original colonies in Mexico. After supper he gave a talk to the soldiers over at the moving picture show.

After months of individual and squadron training, the regiments of the Expedition were now ready for larger operations. Colonel Frank L. Winn, a veteran of the Indians Wars, Cuba, and the Philippines, led the Black Twenty-Fourth Infantry in maneuvers with four cavalry regiments and a battery of artillery.

In a letter to Beatrice on this date, Patton elaborated on seeing the deer, complete with a brief history lesson. He wrote that, during the Civil War Battle of Chancellorsville, the first warning for the Union army of the flank march by General Thomas "Stonewall" Jackson came from the approach of deer and other wild animals driven out in front of the advancing Confederates. Patton compared his experience that day standing with Pershing awaiting the cavalry charge to that of the Union soldiers, writing that "two big deer, a buck and a doe, rushed by within twenty-five yards of where Gen. P. and I stood." He concluded, "It was the prettiest thing I ever saw in Mexico."

Mormon apostle Anthony W. Ivins (misspelled by Patton as Ivers) was the leader in establishing LDS colonies in Mexico. In his letter to Beatrice on November 21, Patton wrote:

> *Mr. Ivers, one of the twelve apostles of the Mormon Church, took dinner with us yesterday. He is a very interesting and educated man and is the one who led the migration to Mexico and founded the colony. He made a speech to the soldiers which was fine. It seems strange that such a smart man could be a leader in such a fool religion. But such is the case.*

Although tolerant of all religious beliefs, Patton found the LDS "a fool religion." Nevertheless, he was willing to give it additional study, though he did not change his mind. On December 5, he wrote Beatrice, "I have been reading the Book of Mormon and it is the darndest rot I have run into."

On November 21, Patton wrote his wife, "Tell Nita to send Gen. P. the *Lions of the Lord*; he would like it." Reading was a great pastime for Patton in his off-duty hours, and his personal wealth allowed him to order books through the mail as well as have Beatrice and other relatives forward him copies. He focused on military history and biographies, but, as shown in his November correspondence, he had an interest in a broad range of reading material.

Lions of the Lord, subtitled *A Tale of the Old West*, was written by Harry Leon Wilson in 1915. Although fiction, it provided excellent insights into LDS polygamy as well as the Mountain Meadows Massacre where Mormon militiamen and Native Americans attacked, robbed, and killed a wagon train of families from Arkansas bound for California in 1857.

Diary: November 21

General Murray and General Roger Williams of Kentucky, with their aides, Captain Pratt and Lieutenant Woods, came down by automobile. They made the trip in nine hours.

Diary: November 22

The visiting generals went home. We had a polo game in the afternoon.

General Roger D. Williams, the direct descendant of his name-sake who established the colony that eventually became the State of Rhode Island, commanded National Guard troops along the Rio Grande from Las Cruces, New Mexico to Fort Hancock, Texas.

Patton must surely have enjoyed meeting Williams, given his ancestry and the fact that the general owned hunting dog kennels in Kentucky, belonged to a number of hunt clubs across the eastern United States, and authored books on hunting fox, wolves, and big game. Theodore Roosevelt, in his 1893 book *The Wilderness Hunter*, wrote, "Roger D. Williams, more than any other American is entitled to speak upon hunting big game with horse and hound."

Diary: November 23

Nothing to report.

Diary: November 24

Tried advancing one hundred yards, firing the pistol fourteen times while at the run. Did not like the idea of allowing the men to halt to reload. Because it is believed that they would never advance again.

With the departure of the visitors, Patton returned to training. He was becoming firm in the belief that offense was the superior battlefield tactic and "attack, attack, attack" was the best way to achieve victory. Momentum in the assault remained key to victory, and Patton firmly thought that soldiers who stopped to reload were difficult to restart.

Unlike the previous cavalry Colt M-1892 .38 caliber revolver, which was difficult to reload on the move because of its six-round cylinder, the M-1911 .45 caliber semi-automatic pistol was fairly easy to reload because of its seven-shot magazine. In a one-hundred-yard advance, Patton could see the cavalrymen reload and deliver a total of fourteen rounds at the objective. Even so, Patton and others wanted to remain loyal to the old revolver despite the fact that the .45 proved itself over and over again in training and in combat. The .45 remained the primary sidearm of the Armed Forces of the United States for three-quarters of a century before finally being replaced by a M-9 Beretta 9 mm semi-automatic in 1985.

Diary: November 25

We got reports of the Army and Navy game by periods. Collected fifteen dollars to pay for the wire.
  We had the defense problems of the machine guns in the morning. General Swift reported at 1:00 p.m.

One of the oldest rival football series in the country evolved when the army and navy began their competition in 1890. Soldiers and sailors around the world, especially those officers who had graduated from the academies, sought any means possible to follow the games—or at least to learn the scores.

Patton's efforts on behalf of the soldiers at Dublán to receive updates on the score during the game via the telegraph from New York's Polo Grounds was but another example of his innovative thinking. He and his fellow West Pointers must have been very pleased with the result of the army victory over the midshipmen by a score of 15–7, a victory that completed a 9–0 record by West Point and earned the team the title of National Champions.

Machine guns had been used effectively by the Thirteenth Cavalry defenders of Columbus to repel Villa's raid. American observers had seen their effectiveness in the Russo–Japanese War and in the European conflict, but Pershing, Patton, and the entire U.S. Army were still developing the operational use and tactics of the weapon that would prove so deadly to both sides in the First World War.

Brigadier General Eben Swift arrived from Fort Bliss to replace Brigadier General Dodd, in command of the Expedition's Second Cavalry Brigade. Swift, class of 1876 at West Point, who by this time had more than forty years of service, was a veteran of the Indian Wars and

Cuba. He brought excellent organizational skills to the Expedition. In 1897, he had introduced the Five Paragraph Field Order—consisting of Situation, Mission, Concept of the Operation, Support, and Chain of Command—that is still in use by the U.S. Army today.

Diary: November 26

Chased coyotes on horseback with the Eleventh Cavalry in the morning. Discussed cavalry with General Pershing who seemed to think my ideas were alright.

The mark of a "good ropeman" among southwestern cowboys of the time was the ability to chase a coyote from horseback and capture the animal with a well-tossed lariat loop. Although Patton and his fellow cavalrymen were not adept with ropes, the swift and agile coyotes must have given them exciting runs across the Mexican desert.

In his original diary, Patton quoted Pershing's praise for him: "He said I was very broad cavalry man. Quite a compliment from him." However, in his revised rendition given to Pershing, Patton tamped down the compliment, making him appear more modest.

Patton was not so modest in a letter to Beatrice on the same date, writing, "Gen. P. and I were going over my article tonight and I mentioned the fact that though I was crazy over the saber I saw some good in the rifle too. He said, 'Why of course you are one of the broadest and best cavalrymen I know.' The more I see of the man the better my opinion of his brain becomes."

These two entries about chasing coyotes and a discussion with Pershing about cavalry are, oddly, the final entries in Patton's Punitive Expedition diary. In the revised version, provided to Pershing on April 23, 1917, Patton wrote, "I did not carry the diary beyond the Twenty-sixth of November; Lieutenant Collins was always present, and he had a complete record of events."

Patton never explained why he so abruptly ceased his diary entries, nor why the task fell to Collins, who had taken over keeping the journal for the Expedition during Patton's month-long sick leave to recover from his burns.

The records for the remainder of Patton's activities in Mexico come from the personal letters he continued to write to his wife and others, his writings for various publications, memories of Pershing he wrote a decade later, and a black-covered small journal in which he recorded thoughts for future articles and other observations.

On November 28, Patton wrote Beatrice that he was becoming more of an advocate for the use of the new .45 pistol in the cavalry charge. He said, "If this proves true it would be a great help against the lance for the saber alone is rather inferior to the lance."

The next day he wrote his wife, "Just one year ago I was sitting up at Sierra Blanca waiting for Senior Chico Conjo to attack me and here I am still at it. I certainly have not seen much of you since and miss you more all the time."

CHAPTER SIXTEEN

December 1916

In a letter to Beatrice on December 1, Patton detailed a disagreement he had with General Pershing over the content of an article he was writing:

I had a little spat with the Gen. about the saber. In his quotation on page ten he had written, "Perfect control of the horse and expert use of the pistol." I said by leaving out saber you imply it is useless. He said well I don't like it but don't want to start an argument. I said why not put in "and saber." He said no I can't do that. I immediately picked up the papers and said very good sir but went out slowly. Just as I left he called out "put in the saber." I did as it was what I had expected. Today he said, "Well you got your way didn't you." I said, "No sir, not at all," and we both laughed. I also got the pistol board to endorse the saber.

In the normal turn of events, lieutenants don't have arguments with generals. Pershing, not known to encourage disagreements with his ideas—especially from junior officers—rarely changed his mind. The discussion between the general and his aide noted the personal (as well as professional) relationship the two enjoyed.

On December 3, Patton wrote Beatrice:

Collins and I dined with the 13th Cav. this evening. They have a nice regimental mess hall and tin dishes. It was very pleasant, afterwards we sat around a big fire place and talked shop. It is quite obvious that the effect of so many troops together has in making men take their profession seriously.

In his letter to his wife on December 8, Patton wrote of the freezing temperatures that had fallen on Dublán, but his only concern was how "the poor horses will suffer." He also instructed Beatrice, "Don't lose the poems as I have no more copies." The next day he again wrote about his poetry, saying he had written another "very ghastly poem" on a typewriter, but because he had "put the carbon paper in wrong I can't send you a copy until tomorrow."

Patton's letters to Beatrice on December 11 and 13 focused primarily on polo matches in which he had participated. He proudly reported that he had scored several goals but that "it was so dusty that it is not too much fun." He concluded, "The troops here are really in fine shape and the best trained we have ever had. Gen. P. is certainly a fine leader and tireless worker."

In addition to correspondence from Beatrice and other family members, Patton received letters from friends and acquaintances. On December 13, Joseph R. Anderson, the historian of the Virginia Military Institute, wrote with the salutation "My dear George":

I feel I must address you thus for the love I bear your father. I have watched your brilliant career, my dear fellow with the keenest interest and rejoiced that another of your glowing name had become distinguished. That was a "narrow call" you had with those devils in Mexico.

I am distressed that your father was defeated in his candidacy for the Senate but suppose it was a very difficult thing to "buck against" that seasoned politician Governor Johnson.

You may not be a full graduate of the old V.M.I. but you are one of her most cherished alumni.

In preparation for the approaching Christmas season, Patton wrote Beatrice on December 14 with instructions on gifts:

I don't want any present if I am still in Mexico at Christmas. And the only thing I could send you would be something I picked out of a catalogue which would not be nice so I will not send you anything.

Send cards to people for us both.

I want to give Gen. P. a present. If there are any shaving sets for Durham Duplex razors. This is a set with brush soap razor and blades. Get one and send it to me for him. Marked J. J. P. Get me a pipe in a case for Shallenberger and a whip for Collins. If you see some little things for Maj. Hines, Capt. Viner, Capt. Campanole, Maj. Wilton, Col. C. get them but very trifling affairs as they would not give me anything and might feel badly.

Patton obviously did not want to flaunt his wealth to his fellow officers when directing that presents be "very trifling affairs." The exception was the gift for Pershing. With the claim of "Razor Sharp since 1910," the Durham Duplex company produced the era's most popular shaving device, its duel-combed blade providing a more efficient and safer shave than the traditional straight razor.

On December 17, Patton dwelt briefly on the politics of the Expedition. He likely recalled his readings of Carl Von Clausewitz, who wrote, "War is mere continuation of policy by other means," when he wrote Beatrice, "We rather think that Carranza wants us to stay for a while as our presence keeps Villa out of this part of Chihuahua." He also showed his understanding of the responsibilities of leadership, saying, "There is no use in Ma's asking Gen. P. for Christmas as he could not possibly leave here while he is in command."

With the approach of Christmas, Patton's letters to Beatrice demonstrated his loneliness, increased frustrations with the army, and concerns about the future. On December 19, he wrote:

This will probably get to you the day before Christmas, and I wish I could come with it but I can't. Last Christmas was not much but we were together and I enjoyed it for I fear I am still and ever will be jealous of B. Jr. and R. E. [daughters]. Still I had hoped to be with you this year. If we were doing any good here I would not mind but to just sit and see things go to hell . . . is not very pleasant.

He was even more morose, and expressed doubts about his previous perceived destiny, in his letter to his wife the next day when he penned:

It is just about a year since we had that wind storm at Sierra Blanca and you cried and wished I would resign. It has been awful here for the last two days. I have never seen such dust. And it made me wish I was out of it. If I could only be sure of the future I would get out. That is if I was sure that I would never be above the average army officer I would for I don't like the dirt and all except as a means to fame. If I knew that I would never be famous I would settle down and raise horses and have a good time. It is a great gamble to spoil your and my own happiness for the hope of greatness. I wish I was less ambitious, then too sometimes I think I am not ambitious at all, only a dreamer. That I don't really do my damnedest even when I think I do.

This job I now have is not good as I have not enough to do and get lazy. Well this is not much of a Christmas letter. I hope you have a nice time and stay young.

Christmas marked the 285th day of the deployment of the Punitive Expedition into Mexico. Detailed plans were made to celebrate the day and to make it as happy as possible for the soldiers far from home and family. The *El Paso Times* interviewed Colonel William H. Allaire, West Point class of 1882 and decorated veteran of the Philippines, and published the following article on December 25:

United States troops are to observe Christmas today as American soldiers have never observed Christmas before. Games, races, an elaborate Christmas dinner, and fireworks will be included in the program of the soldiers in Mexico today.

Colonel William H. Allaire, of the Sixteenth Infantry whose regiment is stationed "somewhere in Mexico," reached El Paso Saturday on a brief leave of absence, after nine months of service in Mexico.

Colonel Allaire tells of the plans which have been made for the obser-
vance of Christmas today by his and other troops.

"At the sound of reveille Sunday morning, the Fifth cavalry band
will march through the different camps at our field base, playing patri-
otic airs," said Colonel Allaire yesterday. "The band will play in the
camp of every regiment before it returns to the Fifth Cavalry camp.

"At 9:30 o'clock in the morning, there will be an exhibition foot-
ball game between picked teams. One eleven will be chosen from the
cavalry and artillery, and the other from the infantry and engineers.

"At 11 o'clock a number of horse and mule races will be staged.
Prizes will be offered to all winners. The rider of the slowest mule
as well as the fastest will receive a prize in the mule race. A number
of different mule races will be run, including one in which the riders
will change mounts, and will prevent one another, if possible, from
attaining the finish line. The horse races will include one-fourth mile
and one-half mile race and hurdle races. These last named races will
not be open to the cavalry, as the cavalrymen would have a decided
advantage in the hurdle races.

"Four hundred and fifty dollars in prize money will be offered to
the winners of the various contests. This money was raised through
contributions from the officers and the various company funds.

"The Christmas dinner will be served at 12:30 o'clock. Turkeys
furnished by the government and other table luxuries from the com-
pany funds will make up the spread. Christmas gifts will be distrib-
uted at the table, and the Red Cross gifts will be given out.

"At 2 o'clock this afternoon a Mexican bull fight will be given for
the entertainment of the soldiers. It will be followed by cock fights.
These exhibitions will be in charge of Mexicans near the field base.

"At 7 o'clock in the evening a concert will be given by a Mexican
band. During the concert moving pictures will be shown.

"At 8 o'clock the climax of the entertainment of the day will be
given. This is to be an elaborate fireworks display. Several trucks
loaded with fireworks have been brought to the base. A fund for the
purchase of the fireworks, totaling $265, raised by contributions from
the officers and the various company funds, was expended.

"This will be but one of the Christmas entertainments. At another camp an enormous Christmas tree will be provided, and a barbecue will be held."

Unfortunately, Mother Nature did not cooperative with the plans—at least not in the Mexican desert. Major Tompkins would later write:

The 25th of December was ushered in by a cold northerner and Christmas dinner with its accompanying festivities, which had been long planned, was entirely spoiled by the tremendous wind storm that will long be remembered by everyone who was in Mexico at that time. Whole steers that were being barbecued were so covered with dust that they were unfit for food, and the troops had to seek what shelter they could. Very few men ate at all for twenty-four hours.

Once the wind finally abated, a half-inch of dust draped the camp. Tents were shredded, building roofs blown into the desert. Although the planned feast had been destroyed and other festivities canceled or postponed, Pershing saw to it that every man received a gift, most of which were supplied by the Red Cross and delivered from Columbus. The Red Cross also provided forty-one thousand cigars and eleven thousand pounds of candy. Books were also distributed.

Patton made little comment about the disastrous storm in a letter written to Beatrice late Christmas night. His primary comments were brief as he wrote, "All my presents were fine. The phonograph is really wonderful and Gen. P. came in and we had a concert."

There is no record of what recordings Beatrice sent along with her gift of the phonograph, for she had many popular tunes from which to choose—both patriotic ones (such as "America" and the British "It's a Long, Long Way to Tipperary") and sentimental songs (such as "My Old Kentucky Home," "Carry Me Back to Old Virginny," and "My Home Sweet Home"). It is doubtful that Beatrice would have sent a copy of "I Didn't Raise My Boy to Be a Soldier," which was a best seller at the time.

Patton concluded the letter, "The Gen. told me tonight that he would probably go to Columbus about the middle of January and would take me. He is going to invite Nita too. Get her to accept as then he will surely take me."

In a letter to his father at the end of the year, Patton exposed his declining opinion of humanity and thoughts on the war in Europe. On December 30, he wrote:

> *Only in epochs where the state is dominant has men advanced. Individualism is the theory of decay. Individual man has habitually failed to run himself for himself. He must be run. Germany has the only true idea. The few must run the many for the latter's good. To hell with the people!*
>
> *As to your jocular assertion that the Central Powers are on the point of ruin, even the aftereffects of Christmas cannot justify such a belief. The Allies are on the point of rupture and another year of war will see their shadow policy an utter failure.*

Patton concluded the letter with a request that indicated his boredom as well as his continued desire to advance his language skills. He wrote, "Please get me a medium sized Spanish–English dictionary. And a couple of simple Spanish stories like Nick Carter or Robinson Crusoe."

He repeated some of these sentiments in a letter on the same day to Beatrice: "There is very little to do just now and time passes slowly. I certainly am sick of this but so is everyone else so there is no good growling."

CHAPTER SEVENTEEN

January 1917

The new year brought no change to the Expedition other than the turning of a calendar page. In a letter to Beatrice on the first day of 1917, Patton wrote of a match with the City Troop Philadelphia polo team, a group from one of the National Guard border units. The letter revealed his confidence in his own abilities as well as his pettiness in desiring his own team lose to the visitors.

> *We selected a team to play them. I was on the team but at [No.] three which I can't play. We had a practice game with a second team this morning and they beat us with the result that Anderson got put on in my place. At first they were going to put me on at four but finally decided to let Erwin stay in my place. I think this is a mistake as I am a better four than he so I hope they will be beaten.*

The new year also saw the publication of the article Patton had completed the previous month, the one with Pershing's supervision and agreement to include use of the saber. The article emphasized the offensive mindset shared by Patton and his commanding general. Appearing in the January 1917 edition of the *U.S. Cavalry Journal*, and titled "Cavalry Work of the Punitive Expedition," the article opened:

> *"Cavalry can fight anywhere except at sea and only the fact the horse is not web-footed restricts is prowess even there." The limitation of a*

field library prevents an exact quotation but something like the above is the goal toward which American cavalry has ever aspired.

Patton's writing continued with a detailed explanation of the training Pershing had initiated within his command. This progressive training had begun with teaching or refining the individual skills of marksmanship and personal care of oneself, his horse, and equipment. This process then merged into training at the squad, platoon, and squadron level before advancing to maneuvers as a regiment. The final training phase united the cavalry regiment with infantry, artillery, and engineers to form a combined arms team. This training model is still followed by today's army.

The article continued with Patton quoting Pershing:

The Cavalry Service Regulations say that "mounted action is the principal method of fighting of cavalry." By adopting that view and inserting it in the drill book, the cavalry had done itself irreparable harm . . . [as it] creates the impression that cavalry is no longer to be considered for dismounted work.

I do not subscribe to any such narrow conception of the role of cavalry. If our cavalry is to be limited to mounted work, then it has failed to profit by the lessons of the Civil War. For open warfare, under modern conditions, it is more necessary than ever to have troops that are able to move rapidly from one place to another over any kind of country and arrive at the point of action fit for a fight. In addition to the important functions of reconnoitering and screening and the dashing sphere of mounted combat, the cavalry must know how to fight on foot. Perfect control of the horse and expert use of the pistol or saber are demanded for successful mounted attack, while thorough training in rifle firing and mastery of the principles of fire tactics are equally essential in the dismounted fight.

Patton concluded the article in his usual flowery style with references to mythology as well as historical characters. Some of his readers may have had to consult their reference library to learn that the "Fates" were three Greek goddesses who assigned individual destinies to mortals at birth, or that Joachim Murat was a French cavalry leader during the Napoleonic Wars, and to brush up on the backgrounds of others cited in the article. Patton summarized the purpose of the cavalry:

To be able to fight anywhere, anytime, and to do it better than our opponent. So that should the Fates and Mars call on us to meet the thundering squadrons of a civilized foe, we may charge them as head-long in ardor as ever animated the troops of Seidlitz or Murat; or, if we are required to hold the foe in play while our citizens arm, we may do so as well as did the men of Forrest or DeWitt; or, if we are called to pursue an enemy, as cruel and elusive as the coyote, we may be able to dislodge him from the mountain fastness with our perfected fire attack, to saber and pistol him as he flees vainly seeking fresh cover.

In a letter dated January 4, 1917, to Beatrice, Patton acknowledged a book she had sent and mentioned that he had borrowed several books "on war" from fellow officers. He added a P.S. stating, "Gen. P. was much tickled with B's [daughter] letter [wishing the general a Merry Christmas] and then seemed to think of his dead children and his eyes filled with tears."

Patton did not reveal the titles of the books sent by his wife, but, in addition to those "on war," he likely read the best sellers of the time. These included *The Art of Public Speaking* by Dale Carnegie, *Victory* by Joseph Conrad, and the more cerebral *Metamorphosis* by Franz Kafka and *Relativity: The Special and General Theory* by Albert Einstein. Other best-selling authors of the period included W. Somerset Maugham, Virginia Woolf, Willa Cather, James Joyce, Robert Frost, and Edgar Rice Burroughs.

Patton also found other ways to pass the time. On January 6, he wrote Beatrice that he found bullfighting an interesting sport but "a little hard on the bulls. Still I should like to see a real good one."

On January 9, Patton wrote Beatrice:

When this reaches you, you will have had a birthday and I shall not have been there. I am very sorry both for your having a birthday and also for my absence. I hate to get old and also for you to get old. It is true you look just as young as you did when I went to West Point but I hate to have us out of the twenties. Since we have lost a year of each other it almost seems that we should not age.

Patton's daughter Ruth Ellen later wrote in her memoir of her mother, "Getting older was always a worry to Georgie. He worried about losing his hair. He worried about losing his figure and used to try on his cadet uniform to see if he could still get into it."

Meanwhile, Pershing continued his rigid schedule of training and inspections. In his January 10 letter to Beatrice, Patton noted:

We worked from eight thirty to twelve thirty and from two to five inspecting today. It is very tedious work but gets the results. I had to open all the horses' mouths in four regiments of cavalry which is some job. It is really surprising that in nearly three thousand horses you hardly find any who make any trouble about opening their mouths. In the morning we will inspect the infantry and artillery which will be an easier job for me as there are fewer horses.

The 10th Cav. had the best equipments and altogether put up the best show. You never saw anything like their stony gaze when at attention. I asked one why he had a certain strap on his bridle. He replied, "I don't know sar, it is de regulation." It was not but I let it go at that as he was so sure of it.

In a letter the next day to his wife, Patton noted the increase in the number of desertions among the troops despite a ten-year prison sentence for those apprehended. He also admitted, "I am getting fat in a disgusting rate but hope to reduce soon."

General Frederick Funston, commander of the U.S. Southern Department at San Antonio and Pershing's immediate boss, arrived in Dublán for an inspection tour and a pass in review. Patton wrote Beatrice, on January 14, about the visit and said that he and the general would not be able to join her and Nita in Columbus as planned because of Funston's arrival. He added that he had been notified that he would be examined for promotion to captain on March 1 but that "no action would probably be taken until July 1 at the earliest." He concluded with a response to her appreciation for her birthday flowers: "I am glad you got the roses, they were not much but the best I could do from here."

Funston's presence accelerated the already rapidly spreading rumors about when the Expedition would be withdrawn from Mexico and the speculation about where the regiments would be assigned once back across the border. On January 15, Patton wrote his wife:

> *Collins swears that the Eleventh will go to El Paso. I wrote Gen. Scott a personal letter asking if he could transfer me to it [the Regiment]. If Pa goes to Washington, I will get him to go see Gen. Scott also.*
>
> *Gen. Funston has a Medal of Honor but he is afraid of a horse. Coming in from the review his horse fidgeted a little and he squealed just like a puppy.*

In a single letter of a few paragraphs, Patton admitted to skipping every level in the chain of command possible in directly corresponding with General Hugh L. Scott, the highest-ranking officer in the army and its chief of staff. Not only had he breached protocol, but he had also questioned the courage of a senior officer. It showed that once again Patton was relying on his social contacts to advance his own career while at the same time uninhibitedly stating his negative observations.

As an infantry officer, Funston would not have had the experience on horseback equivalent to that of the Expedition's cavalrymen, but there was no question about his bravery and leadership. After failing to gain admission to West Point because of his diminutive size of only five feet four and weighing 120 pounds, he had joined the Cuban revolutionaries in their fight for independence from Spain. He later secured an infantry commission in the Kansas militia to continue his fight in Cuba and then earned the Medal of Honor in the Philippines. In 1906, Funston, as the commander of the Presidio, took charge after the San Francisco earthquake aftermath to stop the spreading of fires and looting, a heroic effort that secured him the title of "Savior of the City." By the time of his visit to Mexico, Funston had the full backing of the American military and civilians, most believing that he would lead the American Expeditionary Force (AEF) if and when it was committed to the war in Europe.

Once Funston departed, the drudgery of camp life resumed at Dublán. On January 16, Patton wrote Beatrice, "There is absolutely nothing to write about. And I have one of my worthless streaks on when I don't seem to do or care to do anything. I guess I have been here too long."

Two days later, Patton wrote Beatrice, stating, "Some damn fools are trying to get cuts put in the saber manual so I wrote an indorsement . . . I hope they all die. Ignorance is more profound on the saber than on anything else yet every ass has an idea."

Patton was unrelenting in his beliefs about the importance of the saber, and he enthusiastically defended the manual he had written, considering himself the absolute expert on the weapon and one who would not shy away from standing behind his views. Hoping that his opponents "all die" is a bit of the Patton hyperbole but is nonetheless the way he expressed his adamant convictions on the subject.

Basically, the changes in the manual focused on emphasizing the use of the saber to slash rather than stab. He began his endorsement:

Each point, lunge, and the charge saber taught in the Saber Manual 1914 is also a complete parry for any cut or thrust delivered from the direction of attack. This being the case it is clearly better to use the lunges now taught which are also parries than it would be to use simple negative parries.

Patton saved his deepest stab of criticism for those who wanted to replace parts of the Saber Manual, writing that the current change to slashing would not threaten the enemy in any way and would simply raise the morale of opponents. He added "that all the attacks taught are also parries is a fact which is not understood by the vast majority of officers whose only knowledge of fencing comes from reading the manual, not from practicing it."

Patton continued writing about the proposed changes in the manual, regretting "so much time in devoting to running at dummies and so little time to combats between men" and claiming, "In the charge the point will always beat the edge. It gets there first."

In his conclusion, Patton followed his usual pattern of including quotes from earlier warriors and military leaders. He ended the piece, however, with a statement far less emotional and more logical than his earlier comments. "I respectfully suggest," he wrote, "that the present manual be continued in force till after the close of the war in Europe when in company with most other manuals may have to undergo changes to lessons there to be learned."

Then suddenly, and without fanfare, on January 20, Patton wrote Beatrice that everyone was "packing and rushing about" in preparation to "come out" of Mexico. He seemed rather detached from the activities, reporting, "I am going to a bull fight. If you divest yourself of the foolish sentiment of the bull's feelings it is a fine sight and takes a lot of nerve."

Patton again wrote his wife on January 23, this time saying that, although nothing was yet definite, she should plan to make lodging arrangements in Columbus. On January 25, when the withdrawal orders were made official, he wrote that he expected to be back across the border on February 4. He added that she should also reserve a room for Nita if she planned to join them.

Pershing did not cease training his troops despite their preparations to depart Mexico. The cavalry regiments participated in a series of attack exercises. Patton acted as an observer and "respectfully" offered a detailed report of his observations. He criticized the regiments' use of scouts and patrols—both in leading the assault and during the attack, writing that "the guides seemed more intent on cautioning men to go fast and not shoot anyone than on the gait and direction."

Patton included his philosophy of "attack, attack, attack":

Had any of the troops which pulled up to fire been opposed by a real enemy, they would have been ridden down as happened to the Austrians at Luthen. A bullet fired into a charging horse at ten yards will not stop him unless he is struck in the brain.

During training and withdrawal preparations, Patton continued to focus on his next duty assignment as well as note the refugees fleeing Mexico alongside withdrawing Americans. On January 28, he wrote to Beatrice:

I also got a letter from Gen. Scott saying he could not transfer me. So I felt very blue expecting to have to ride in with the 10th. I went to the General and asked him if he would give me a leave so I could go to El Paso and pack. He said that it was his intention to take me there with him if he could as he said he did not want to "loose me."

So I guess we will get to keep our house a little while anyway. If I do get to be a captain in July, I will have a fine chance of getting to a decent regiment. So cheer up.

Gen. P. and I went out to see the refugees today. There were over a hundred wagons of them. It was the most pathetic sight I ever saw. Women and children and old men and young men with all they had in rickety old wagons. Leaving a country where neither life nor virtue is respected.

One family was all mounted on burros. One old man limped after the thinnest cow and calf you ever saw. All he had. It was very cold and they were shaking. There in the midst were two wagons full of painted whores under guard.

I expect that all the Carranzistas will follow us out. All the Mormons are leaving too and they had better.

In the last days of January, orders came for the assignment of each regiment on return to the United States. Patton was scheduled to return to the Tenth Cavalry and accompany them to Nogales, Arizona. He quickly took measures to ensure his return to Fort Bliss. Patton met with First Lieutenant Pearson M. Menoher of the Seventh Cavalry, who preferred Arizona over Texas, and the two quickly gained the approval of their commanders to trade assignments. Patton was happy to be joining Beatrice at their Fort Bliss quarters and to become a member of the Seventh Cavalry Regiment, which, he wrote, "had some nice people in it."

On January 29, he wrote to his Aunt Nannie, commenting on the destruction of the adobe buildings they had erected around Dublán:

Beatrice has probably told you that I am sure of getting transferred to the Seventh Cavalry which will be in El Paso.

We have been busting up houses all day. We do it in a funny way simply pull the roof off and then back a truck against the wall. It pushes them over as nice as you please.

CHAPTER EIGHTEEN

February 1917

On February 5, 1917, the Punitive Expedition—with regimental bands playing "When Johnny Comes Marching Home"—crossed the International Border at Palomas and marched into Columbus and Camp Furlong. General Pershing, along with Patton and the rest of the staff, rode at the front of the long column consisting of 10,690 officers and men, 9,305 animals, and more than 500 trucks and automobiles. At the end of the column were 2,030 Mexican, Mormon, and Chinese refugees.

From Columbus the regiments went by rail to their new duty assignments along the U.S.–Mexican border. Within weeks the bustling logistical center at Columbus was dismantled, its assets transferred elsewhere, and the town returned to its pre-Expedition idleness. El Paso and Fort Bliss welcomed Pershing, the Expedition staff, and the Seventh Cavalry. Otherwise, there was little acknowledgment or celebration of the return of the Punitive Expedition. Most Americans were far more focused on the possibility of entry into World War I than on what many believed to have been a failed operation in Mexico.

Indeed, the public opinion was that the Mexican Punitive Expedition was a failure, for Villa was neither in chains nor buried in a desert grave. However, Pershing had never been charged with the mission of killing or capturing Villa. Instead, his telegraphed orders from the War Department had stated:

The President desires that your attention be especially and earnestly called to his determination that the Expedition into Mexico is limited to the purposes originally stated, namely the pursuit and dispersion of the band or bands that attacked Columbus, N.M.

By those orders and most other measures, the Expedition was, in fact, successful. Despite opposition from Villa's bandits, the Mexican government, as well as limitations placed by President Wilson and senior army officials, Pershing and his men succeeded in "the pursuit and dispersion of the band or bands" that had attacked U.S. soil. From the early hours when Major Tompkins and the Thirteenth Cavalry pursued the fleeing bandits from Columbus, the Villistas never reformed an effective fighting force while the Americans were in Mexico. Villa remained hidden in the mountains recovering from wounds and did not reorganize his band to resume operations until the Expedition crossed back into New Mexico ten months later. The "band" that attacked Columbus was effectively dispersed in accordance with the Expedition's orders.

Numbers alone support the claim of the Expedition's success. Exact totals of those bandits who participated in the Columbus raid and later became casualties are lost in the fog of war. The most accurate figures, however, are found in the "Report of Operations of 'General' Francisco Villa Since November 1915, Headquarters Punitive Expedition in the Field, Mexico, July 31, 1916," a document on file in the National Archives.

According to the report, Villa observed the attack on Columbus from a nearby hill with an estimated eighty men who comprised his staff and guards. About 485 bandits, organized into six detachments based mostly on their home area of origin in Mexico, made the actual attack. Of this number, 248 were killed in their retreat from Columbus or during the operations by the Expedition. An additional 33 were captured by the U.S. or Mexican government, for a total of 281 of the Villistas either killed or captured and imprisoned. Given that this sum of 281 accounts for nearly one-half of the entire Columbus raider force, this event marked the zenith of Villa's military career and was the beginning of the end of his influence on Mexico and the U.S. border region.

In their fights with the Villistas and Federal troops, the Expedition suffered remarkably few casualties. Only thirty-seven American soldiers died in Mexico.

The Punitive Expedition's departure from Mexico also exhibited one of the classic principles of withdrawal from enemy territory. With only a few days' notice, the troops destroyed buildings and other assets rather than leaving them behind.

Another principle Pershing applied was in his treatment of the non-combatants who had assisted the Expedition. No man or woman who wanted to leave Mexico—military or civilian—was left behind when the column marched north.

Finally, in the actual withdrawal back to the United States, Pershing deployed flank and rear guards as well as frontal reconnaissance. Despite threats from the Mexican army and Villa's bandits, the withdrawal did not suffer a single casualty.

In his departure message to the members of the Expedition, General Pershing said:

> *The splendid services that the regular troops comprising this Expedition have performed under most adverse conditions, again proves that for natural ability, physical endurance, unflinching persistence, general efficiency, and unquestioned loyalty and devotion to duty, the well-trained officers and men of the regular army are excelled by the troops of no other nation.*

Perhaps the best summation of the performance of the Expedition came from Lieutenant Colonel James D. Glennan, Pershing's chief surgeon. According to Tompkins's book, Glennan said:

> *The Punitive Expedition lived nearer to the earth and learned to get along with less than any command in our experience. It was hardened by active service, and profitably interested and occupied by professional work and training. It has been cheerful and has maintained the good health and sanitation that goes with good discipline. The country has never had a more thoroughly trained and fit command.*

Pershing sincerely appreciated the performance of his men but was not satisfied with the overall accomplishments. In a letter on January 20, 1917, to his father-in-law, Senator Francis Warren, he wrote:

> *When the true history of the Expedition, especially the diplomatic side of it, is written, it will not be a very inspiring chapter for school children or even grownups to contemplate. Having dashed into Mexico with the intention of eating the Mexicans raw, we turn back at the very first repulse and are now sneaking home under cover like a whipped cur with his tail between his legs. I would not dare write this to anybody but you nor repeat it before anybody but a confidential stenographer.*

The far more significant aspect of the Mexican Punitive Expedition than the applications of principles or the after-action assessments was what the operation accomplished in the preparation for the upcoming war in Europe. Having units in Mexico offered the military a platform for mobilizing and training the National Guard, for integrating aircraft into strategies, for refining the use of motorized transportation and resupply, and for employing electronic communications. These innovations formed the foundation of the American Expeditionary Force and its effectiveness in World War I. Of the forty-three divisions that made up the AEF, seventeen were veterans of service in Mexico or along the U.S.–Mexican border. Senior commanders of the Putative Expedition led divisions and corps on the battlefields of France. Junior officers, including Patton, gained more experiences in the First World War that would elevate them to senior command positions in World War II.

H. A. Toulmin, in his book *With Pershing in Mexico*, published in 1935, wrote of the Expedition, "Historically it is the first real blend of new devices of the new army and the best devices and equipment of the old army."

CHAPTER NINETEEN

Conclusions

On January 29, 1917, First Lieutenant George S. Patton wrote to his wife, Beatrice, "This is the last letter I shall write you from Mexico. I have learned a lot about my profession and a lot how much I love you. The first was necessary, the second was not."

The absence from his wife was not necessary for Patton to realize his love for her. His time in Mexico, however, was essential for the experience and education that he received that "made Patton become Patton."

Most enlisted men entering the army find their role models in the ranks of their drill instructors and their first sergeants. Young officers are influenced by their initial company and battalion commanders. Patton's mentorship was unusual. Instead of a captain or lieutenant colonel, he was taken under the wing of one of the army's highest-ranking officers. In addition to having a general as his mentor, Patton spent his time in Mexico surrounded by senior officers who were veterans of the Indian Wars, Cuba, and the Philippines.

Patton learned from Pershing that no detail was too small to go unsupervised. He later wrote:

Under the personal supervision of the General every unit, every horse and every man was fit; weaklings were gone; baggage was still at the minimum; and discipline was perfect. When I speak of supervision, I do not mean that nebulous staff control so frequently connected with the work. General Pershing knew to the minutest detail each of the subjects in which he demanded practice and by his physical presence and personal example and explanation insured himself that they were correctly carried out.

Patton, in turn, contributed to the overall performance of the Punitive Expedition indirectly through his assistance to Pershing and his staff. He directly impacted the results through his personal combat at San Miguel Ranch, where he was responsible for the deaths of one of Villa's senior lieutenants and two of his men.

Patton never forgot the role Pershing played in his development as a military officer. In a letter he wrote to his mentor on February 18, 1919, following his second assignment to Pershing's staff in World War I, Patton stated, "I like to appear well in your eyes." Then, five days later, Patton would again write the general, this time expressing his regret that he was not able to say goodbye in person on his departure from France to return home. Patton thanked his mentor for "all your kindness and consideration" and concluded, "I have attempted in a small way to model myself on you and whatever success I have had has been due to you as an inspiration."

On April 10, 1941, President Franklin Roosevelt nominated, and the U.S. Senate approved, Patton's promotion to major general. When the War Department issued the order, it also announced his assignment to command the Second Armored Division. On receipt of the announcement, Patton wrote Pershing, stating, "Whatever qualities of execution I possess are due to my service under your immediate command. I shall always try to live up to the ideas of military perfection of which you are the embodiment."

Two years later, Patton expanded on the influence of Pershing in a letter dated May 30, 1943, to the general. Patton wrote:

Whatever ability I have shown or shall show as a soldier is the result of a studious endeavor to copy the greatest American soldier, namely yourself. I consider it a priceless privilege to have served with you in Mexico and in France.

Your ability to put away worry has been of inestimable value to me. The night we landed in Morocco I deliberately went to bed (in full pack of course) and slept for two hours after we sighted the coast to prove to myself that I could emulate you.

During our fight in Tunisia, I studiously avoided worrying. One night, about 2:00 a.m., it was necessary to make a most momentous decision. I gave this my careful consideration, issued the orders, went back to bed, and went to sleep. I could never have done this if it had not been for the inspiring memory of what you have done under similar, although much more difficult, circumstances.

By any standard, Lieutenant George S. Patton had not been destined for greatness except in his own arrogant imagination. He had learning difficulties, a weak command voice, and even an aversion to the dirt and hardships of field duty. Before joining the Punitive Expedition, his primary contributions as a soldier had been as an Olympian athlete and teacher and writer devoted to the soon-to-be-antiquated saber. His two senior commanders in the European Theater during World War II— Dwight Eisenhower and Omar Bradley—both graduated in the West Point class of 1915, six years after Patton, and initially overshadowed him.

Of the three senior U.S. Army officers in the European Theater, Eisenhower was the organizer and coordinator of the Allies, while Bradley excelled in supervising large field units, but Patton was the "fighting general" who possessed and exhibited the warrior characteristics.

What Patton experienced and learned in Mexico made him into the Patton heralded by his country, respected by his allies, and feared by his enemies. Mexico was truly Patton's prelude to destiny.

Chapter Twenty

Epilogue

George S. Patton: After his return from Mexico, Patton joined General Pershing at Fort Bliss, Texas, and shortly thereafter accompanied the general to France. There, Patton became interested in tanks and assumed the duties as the organizer of U.S. armor units and wrote the first *Tank Drill and Training Manual*. He then accompanied his tanks against the Germans in their initial combat, where he was wounded. Patton also designed a distinctive triangular shoulder patch for his tankers that remains the basis of the insignia of armor units today.

After the war, Patton performed various staff and command duties as he advanced in rank to colonel. In a paper he wrote in 1926 titled "Secret of Victory," he stated, "The fixed determination to acquire the warrior soul, and have acquired it to either conquer or perish with honor, is the secret of victory."

Patton returned to the U.S.–Mexico border in 1938 to command the Fifth Cavalry Regiment at Fort Clark, Texas. Two years later, in July 1940, he took command of the Second Armored Brigade of the Second Armored Division at Fort Benning, Georgia. On his promotion to major general the following April, he assumed command of the division. In March 1942, he organized and commanded the Desert Training Center in Southern California to prepare armored units for the invasion of North Africa.

During this time, he maintained his letter writing to General Pershing and visited him at his Washington, D.C., apartment whenever possible. Pershing also came to the Pattons when they were stationed at

Fort Myer in 1932 for dinner, where, according to Ruth Ellen, "he and Georgie talked about the old days at Fort Bliss and in Mexico."

Patton's last visit with Pershing came on October 21, 1942, just before his deployment to North Africa. In his diary Patton recorded:

Called on General Pershing. He did not recognize me until I spoke. Then his mind seemed quite clear. He looks very old. It is possibly the last time I shall see him, but he may outlive me. I said that when he took me to Mexico in 1916, he gave me my start. He replied, "I can always pick a fighting man and God knows there are few of them. I am happy they are sending you to the front at once. I like generals so bold that they are dangerous. I hope they give you a free hand." He recalled my killing the Mexicans and when I told him I was taking the same pistol, he said, "I hope you kill some Germans with it."

He said that at the start of the war he was hurt because no one consulted him but was now resigned to sit on the sidelines with his feet hanging over. He almost cried. It is pathetic how little he knows of the war. When I left I kissed his hand and asked for his blessing. He squeezed my hand and said, "Goodbye George, God bless and keep you and give you victory."

Patton commanded II Corps in Tunisia in the African campaign. In a letter to Nita on December 22, 1942, he wrote that Morocco reminded him of California. He added, "The Moroccan psychology is very similar to that of the Mexicans and I find my memory of dealing with Mexicans to be of inestimable value in dealing with the potentates here."

Next, Patton commanded the Seventh Army in the capture of Messina in Sicily. However, he was removed from command for slapping two soldiers suffering from battle fatigue whom he accused of malingering. Patton again took the field in August 1944 in command of the Third Army as they began the historic sweep across Europe that made him an international hero.

The slapping incidents also ended the relationship between Patton and Pershing. While many of Patton's friends and comrades supported (or at least excused) his actions, Pershing did not. He condemned Patton for abusing the soldiers. Patton responded by not responding. He ended his correspondence with the old general and had no further contact with his former mentor.

On December 9, 1945, Patton decided to take one last hunting trip with Major General Hobart "Hap" Gay and visit some old Roman ruins before departing Germany for the United States. On the outskirts of Mannheim, a GMC two-and-a-half-ton truck struck Patton's 1938 Cadillac 75 Special Limousine, causing the general to be thrown forward from the back seat and hit his head on the railing above the rear of the driver's seat. The impact separated Patton's spinal column.

Beatrice arrived from the United States two days after Patton was evacuated to a hospital in Heidelberg, conveyed by the driver who had been at the wheel in Patton's accident. The young soldier, who had substituted for Patton's regular driver, was being brutally criticized even though the wreck was not his fault. Patton ended the criticism of the soldier by requesting that he drive the car that met Beatrice at the airport and brought her to his hospital bed.

Beatrice remained at his side and read to him. Paralyzed from the neck down, Patton deteriorated over the following weeks and on December 23 died of a pulmonary embolism brought on by his paralysis. His last words, spoken to Beatrice while she was reading to him, were "It's too dark. I mean too late." He peacefully died a short time later in his sleep.

Several days earlier, Patton had said to Beatrice, "I guess I wasn't good enough." He was referring to his belief that a professional soldier should "die of the last bullet in the last battle of the last war."

At the time of Patton's death, no fallen soldier had been sent back to the United States for burial since the beginning of the war. When the widow began making plans to fly her husband's remains home, officials approached Beatrice and cautioned her that it would have a negative effect on American families who had lost loved ones if the general, unlike their sons, was returned home for burial. She replied, "Of course he must be buried here. Why didn't I think of it? Furthermore, I know George would want to be beside the men of his Army who have fallen."

On December 24, 1945, during a cold rainstorm, Patton was laid to rest in the American Military Cemetery at Hamm, Luxembourg, alongside many of the dead of the Third Army. A simple white cross, containing only his name, rank, unit, home state, and date of death, just like those of his fellow soldiers, marks the site. Two years later, his remains were moved to the front of the cemetery to accommodate the multitudes of visitors who wished to pay homage.

Supreme Allied Commander General Dwight Eisenhower wrote:

> *He gave me a certainty that the boldest plan could be even more daringly executed. It is no exaggeration to say that Patton's name struck terror in the heart of the enemy. . . . No one but Patton could exert such an extraordinary and ruthless driving power at critical moments or demonstrate the ability of getting the utmost out of soldiers in offensive operations.*

General Alfred Jodl, German army chief of staff, said, "He was very bold and preferred large movements. He took big risks and won big successes."

The United States War Department in Washington, D.C., released General Order 121 the day after Patton's death. It read, in part,

> *General Patton as Commanding General, Third Army, inscribed his name in the annals of military history by bold and brilliant leadership of troops in Africa, and Sicily, and from the Normandy Peninsula across France, Germany, and Austria, inspiring them to many brilliant victories. His sound tactical knowledge, skillful farsighted judgement, and masterful generalship contributed in the highest degree to the success of the Allied arms.*

The Patton Family: George and Beatrice had a son in 1923, whom they named George Smith Patton IV. Although General Patton had been named Jr., he was actually the third to bear the name. Both of their daughters married West Point graduates.

Young George also attended the Military Academy and, like his father, had to repeat his plebe year because of academic deficiencies. The senior Patton understood the pressures on his son and on October 6,

1943, wrote to him, saying, "Naturally with the publicity I've gotten, you are a marked man. It's a good thing to be a marked man if you live up to the reputation."

George IV later commanded a tank company in the latter days of the Korean War. On July 15, 1968, Colonel George Patton assumed command of the Eleventh Armored Cavalry Regiment in Vietnam. According to Brian M. Sobel in his *The Fighting Pattons*, Patton stated in an interview, "'I realized that I would be subject to media attention and therefore I would have to maintain the highest possible standards to keep from getting criticism connected with the achievements of my father and curious relatives stretching back through Army history.'"

While in Vietnam, Patton showed that he was his father's son in proficiently leading the Eleventh Armored Cavalry in the field. He also emulated his father's tendency to disregard civilian sensitivities. The Christmas card he sent in 1968 read "Peace on Earth" above a photograph of a pile of dead Viet Cong bodies.

The younger Patton also shared his father's penchant toward accidents. In 1970, while stationed in Germany, he fell off a walkway on a stone wall and fractured his hip. Lingering effects of the accident continued for the rest of his life.

Despite the injury, Patton recovered sufficiently to assume command of his father's old Second Armored Division in 1975. He later told Sobel, the biographer, about his first day at the division at Fort Hood, Texas: "I went to the chapel by myself and prayed on my knees asking the Lord to let me do a good job and to be a credit to the Army and my family. I could really sense my dad's presence in that chapel with me. My reaction to his presence was simply intense pride."

Patton IV retired from the army in 1980. He died in 2004.

George S. Patton Jr. and his entire family believed in reincarnation. In an interview for Sobel's book *The Fighting Pattons*, Ruth Ellen said, "It never occurred to me until later in life that everyone didn't believe in it. My father used to say it was the only explanation for inequality and injustice."

According to Sobel, she said, "It never seemed at all strange to me. Just strange that more people didn't believe it." She then went on to say that her father recalled being with Hannibal at Carthage. She added, "He remembered being carried on a shield by four Vikings after being wounded, and hearing one Viking saying, 'He will live, he's not ready to go to Valhalla yet.'" Ruth Ellen concluded that on a cold day in Virginia he said that the last time he had been so chilled was during "Napoleon's retreat from Moscow."

Patton never wrote about reincarnation while in Mexico, but he did say that he had lived previous lives on the battlefields of Europe. He stated in his diary, "I generally believe in reincarnation, I always have. I feel I fought in the Napoleonic period. I'm not even sure which side I was on. But I can say that I'm intimately familiar with the area in and around Regensburg, Germany. When I got there for the first time I had complete and total comfort with the area."

As of this writing, no one has stepped forward to claim to be the reincarnated Patton, nor has anyone matched his accomplishments. Time will tell.

John J. Pershing: "Black Jack" Pershing was neither President Wilson's nor Secretary of War Newton D. Baker's first choice to lead the American army into France in World War I. That command was to go to Frederick Funston, commander of the Southern Department, who was Pershing's superior during the Punitive Expedition. However, on February 19, 1917, Funston died of a heart attack at age fifty-one. Pershing was ordered to go to San Antonio as his replacement.

A short time later, Pershing visited the Patton family at Lake Vineyard. The relationship between the general and Nita Patton had grown during their brief visits before and during the Punitive Expedition. Patton recognized the attraction and wrote from Mexico to Beatrice on September 18, 1916, that the general often talked about Nita and concluded that Nita might outrank them all if the two married.

While in California, Pershing received notice to report to Washington to meet with officials about the command of the American Expeditionary Force. Before departing, he wrote his sister May in Lincoln, Nebraska:

I am ordered to Washington for consultation. No one knows what it means. May, do you remember Miss Patton? She is here for a few days. Well, May dear, she is the finest and best woman. I had thought I could never love, but she had made a place all her own. I am telling you all this, May, you and Sister, very confidentially. So please do not mention it to a single soul in the world. I have been so wholly broken-hearted and bereft. It will make a home for little Warren.

Pershing was not successful in keeping his relationship with Nita confidential. An article from an unidentified newspaper from the period in the *Patton Papers* states, "Miss Anita W. Patton, daughter of George S. Patton, a Los Angeles lawyer, is to be the bride of Gen. Pershing after the war, according to rumor."

In little more than a year, Pershing went from leading ten thousand men in Mexico to commanding more than one million soldiers in France. Along with the responsibility came the rank. Promoted from major general to full general, he once again skipped a rank, going directly from two stars to four stars. His organizational, training, and supply skills quickly molded the volunteer and conscripted force into a competent combat army. Over the following months, the Second Battle of the Marne, Saint-Mihiel, and Meuse-Argonne became a part of the legacy of the US. Army and its commander John J. Pershing.

President Wilson and Secretary Baker gave Pershing great latitude in the operations of the AEF. He repaid them by not engaging in politics with other Allied leaders and focusing strictly on his military mission. The only time he went beyond his responsibilities was near the end of the war. Much as he had in Mexico, Pershing believed in completing the mission. He demanded that the Allied Supreme War Council not agree to an armistice and that the Germans should be forced to surrender unconditionally.

This demand brought him criticism from Washington and others who thought he had overstepped his authority. Pershing apologized but continued his fight against the Germans until the last minute before the armistice went into effect. He received even more negative assessments for the 3,500 American casualties inflicted in the last day of the war. Pershing explained his actions to the House Committee on Military Affairs on November 5, 1919:

> *When the subject of the armistice was under discussion, we did not know what the purpose of it was definitely, whether it was something proposed by the German High Command to gain time or whether they were sincere in their desire to have an armistice; and the mere discussion of an armistice would not be sufficient grounds for any judicious commander to relax his military activities. No one could possibly know when the armistice was to be signed, or what hour be fixed for the cessation of hostilities so that the only thing for us to do, and which I did as commander in chief of the American forces, and which Marshal Foch did as commander in chief of the Allied armies was to continue military activities.*

Pershing survived a bout of the Spanish flu to lead the AEF on horseback down the streets of Paris in the victory parade. By his return to the United States from France, Pershing was among the best known and most popular men in America. The president and Congress promoted him to General of the Armies of the United States, the highest rank in the armed forces—a position created especially for him. The Republican Party sought him as a candidate in the 1920 presidential election. Pershing declined to campaign while still in uniform but showed some interest before the Republicans decided the general had too many ties to the Democratic Party and selected future president Warren G. Harding instead.

In 1921, Pershing assumed the duties of the U.S. Army Chief of Staff. He remained in that position until his mandatory retirement at age sixty-four on September 13, 1924. He spent much of his final days in uniform at activities recognizing veterans of the AEF. He also established the Reserve Officers Association and developed the "Pershing Map" composed of a network of proposed military and civilian highways. The eventual Interstate Highway System adopted in 1956 closely resembles his proposal.

After his retirement, Pershing resided in Washington, D.C., and kept a fairly low profile. When he did go out in public, he did it in style; in fact, the *Washington Post* declared him the "Best Dressed Man" in the city. He always went in a chauffeured automobile, as the general never learned to drive. After much work and many rewrites, he published *My Experiences in the World War.* Although described by some critics as "unreadable," it earned him the Pulitzer Prize for History in 1932.

Pershing's relationship with Nita Patton did not survive the war. On February 7, 1919, George wrote Beatrice, "As to J. [Pershing] and Nita. It is possible that the game is up. You see he could get anyone in the world and they are after him. Ambition is a great thing and without soul."

Nita had spent much of the war in Washington, but in the spring of 1918 she sailed to London, where she stayed with her sister-in-law Kay Merrill. Pershing wrote her there, saying that "the feeling" for her had gone and they should not announce their engagement until it returned. The general added that he was concerned about the age difference, that he still had deep feelings for his deceased wife, and that he questioned how well Nita would get along with his son, Warren. He emphasized his rejection by not sending her a ticket to the great victory gala scheduled for July 3, 1919, in Paris. Nita responded by returning the ring Pershing had given her after his return from Mexico in 1917.

Ruth Ellen later wrote:

There are two sides to every story, even to the prejudiced. General Pershing had been under a terrible strain for the war years and had done a fantastic job. As the war drew to its successful close he was wined and dined and flattered and praised by the great and near great; some of the most beautiful women in Europe were not above falling at his feet to gain something for their hearts' interest. He had a Caesar's triumph. Nita with her blond Viking looks and carriage and her predominately good sense, was just there and could be more or less propped in a corner until he had time to regroup and reconsider. Only Nita removed herself with all flags flying.

After returning to the United States, Patton wrote his mother from Fort Meade, Maryland, about Pershing and the breakup:

My own opinion is that he is being purely selfish wanting to let the affair rest for a while to see if his feeling revived. It is perfectly possible that his mind, driven as it was for nearly three years, is incapable of emotion. Or it may be that the war has aged his mind so that like a very old man he can only live in the past. . . . I am not in a position to judge what Nita's action should be. . . . She has acted so well thus far that I feel sure she will always do right.

Most of the extended Patton family were saddened by the breakup between the general and Nita. Not so with her always social status–conscious father. Ruth Ellen wrote:

Bumps was the only person really pleased by the breakup. He did not consider General Pershing good enough for Nita. Among other reasons, he said that Pershing's father had been a brakeman on the railroad. Georgie was relieved too, at having the taint of favoritism or nepotism removed from whatever his future might hold.

The friendship between Pershing and Patton and his wife did not diminish following his breakup with Nita. Ruth Ellen recalled that after one visit by the general, her sister Bee asked their mother how Nita could have ever been in love with such a "silly old man." With a sad look on her face, Beatrice responded:

The John J. Pershing you children know is not the Black Jack Pershing that Nita fell in love with. Lots of men die in wars, but some of them who have very strong bodies go on living long after the person inside of them, the real them, is dead. They are dead because they used themselves all up in the war. That's one of the most terrible things about war.

Despite the thoughts of Patton and his family about Pershing being used up by the war, there is overwhelming evidence that his interest in women did not fade with his service in France. Although a report in a Chicago newspaper that claimed Pershing became engaged to twenty-nine women during his time in France certainly was an exaggeration, he did have an active social life with the opposite sex. An American socialite, Elizabeth Hoyt, was on his arm at several social events. A more intense relationship developed with Louie Cromwell Brooks, an American heiress who had three children and was in the process of a divorce. The relationship eventually waned, but the two remained friends. Brooks later became the first wife of future general Douglas MacArthur.

Pershing first met Micheline Resco when the French government commissioned her to paint the general's portrait. The blonde, twenty-three-year-old Resco, Romanian by birth and of slight build, soon became more than the general's artist. His staff log of visitors began regularly recording that Pershing spent his evenings "studying French." He corresponded with Resco when he was away from Paris. During the Meuse-Argonne Offensive on September 29, 1918, he wrote to her, saying, "I send you a million kisses and I embrace you tenderly."

After his retirement in Washington, D.C., Resco was a frequent visitor in the capital city. Pershing also made regular voyages to France to honor the war's dead and to visit her. Resco had a good relationship with Pershing's son, Warren, and other members of his family. The 1940 U.S. Census shows Resco residing in Washington. The two, however, continued to keep their relationship secret from the public.

In his final days, Pershing moved to a suite at Walter Reed Hospital. There, on September 2, 1946, Catholic priest Jules A. Baisaee blessed the marriage between Pershing and Resco. Her mother, Mathilde, acted as a witness. Perishing died on July 15, 1948, with Resco at his side. He is buried in Arlington National Cemetery.

Pershing left behind a "sizeable check" and a letter he had composed sometime earlier to Resco. It said, "What a beautiful love has been ours. As my companion in life, you will be with me through eternity. So, do not weep, be brave. Say not goodbye but say good night. In all the future, the lingering fragrance of your kisses shall be fresh on my lips."

Resco returned to Paris, where she died in 1968. In Pershing's effects was a locket containing two photographs—one of Warren, the other of Micheline.

With Patton's proximity to Pershing and his headquarters, it is unlikely that he did not know of his boss's relationship with Resco. But he made no mention of the relationship in his diary or letters.

Francis Warren Pershing: After his father's return from France, Warren Pershing accompanied him on many of his trips across the United States and back to France to honor war veterans, often wearing a miniature uniform that brought him minor celebrity in his own right. Warren attended Phillips Exeter Academy in New Hampshire before sailing to Europe to enroll in the Institut Carnall in Rolle, Switzerland.

Warren, with no interest in following his father to West Point or into a military career, attended Yale University before joining Wall Street to seek his fortune—or rather to increase his fortune, as he was the only heir to his father's estate. More important, he was the only surviving grandchild of his namesake, Francis Emory Warren—his mother's father—who was one of the wealthiest men in the state of Wyoming.

Despite the challenges of the Depression, Warren found success on Wall Street. He also, like his father, married well. In 1938, he wed Muriel Bache Richards, the granddaughter of Jules S. Bache, a wealthy banker and financier who reputedly owned one the finest art collections in the world.

Two months after the Japanese attack on Pearl Harbor, Warren Pershing enlisted in the army as a buck private. After basic training, he attended Officer Candidate School and in August 1942 graduated as a second lieutenant in the Corps of Engineers. After an assignment to Fort Leonard Wood in Missouri, he sailed to Europe in early 1944 and advanced in rank to major before the war ended. He then returned to New York and his successful stockbroker career. He died there in 1980.

Warren and Muriel had two sons before his deployment overseas. The older, John (Jack) Warren Pershing, graduated from Boston University and received a commission as a second lieutenant from their Reserve Officers Training Corps. He served in the Special Forces both on active duty and in the U.S. Army Reserves before retiring as a full colonel. He died of cardiovascular disease in 1999.

Richard (Dick) Warren Pershing graduated from Yale in 1966 with a degree in English, the same major as his brother. Dick Pershing earned his second lieutenant bars in Officer Candidate School and joined the 502nd Infantry Regiment of the 101st Airborne Division in Vietnam. He was killed in action on February 17, 1968.

Both brothers are buried with their grandfather in Arlington National Cemetery. Neither had any children. The long line of Pershing men serving their country ended with their generation.

Anne Wilson "Nita" Patton: On July 19, 1919, Nita stood on a London sidewalk observing the International Peace Parade, also known as the Peace Day Parade. General Pershing passed in a procession, standing in an open vehicle with two British officers waving to the cheering crowd. Nita waved back and later wrote that she was sure the general saw her but made no acknowledgment.

A short time later, Nita wrote her parents that she was looking forward to returning home to Southern California. She said, "We were young there once. I suppose all this boom has spoiled us a little, as fame and prosperity spoils us all." Nita informed her parents that she would devote her life to their happiness. In return, concerning her relationship with Pershing, she added, "Let us never speak of it again."

Nita had a serious relationship with Englishman Harry Brain before leaving London. In a letter to her aunt Nannie Wilson on June 25, 1922, she wrote:

I am fated to be free, for this day I have definitely told Harry Brain that never can I be his wife. He is such a dear, so good, true, and tender, that I d----- near said "yes" but my guardian angel came to me and showed me a vision of the night; that unless I could mate with a master, I'd better stay clear of the shoals. So, you'll have me back on your hands for keeps. And the worst of it is I'm glad. Love is not for such as I. But life is so full of a number of things that I'm like the jolly miller on the river Dee.

The reference to the jolly miller offers more insight into Nita's thoughts. The ditty includes these lines:

I care for nobody, no, not I,
If nobody cares for me.
A coin or two I've in my purse,
To help a needy friend,
A little I can give the poor,
And still have some to spend.

Like the jolly miller, Nita dedicated herself to assisting various charities. She also worked with the California Democratic Party and traveled extensively around the world. In the early 1930s, she adopted two sons, Peter and David, a rare occurrence by a single woman at the time. Ruth Ellen wrote, "She spent the rest of her life taking care of everyone."

Nita Patton died on March 14, 1971, in San Marino, California. She is buried in the San Gabriel Cemetery in San Gabriel, California.

Beatrice Banning Ayer Patton: Beatrice returned to the family home, Green Meadows (named for its lush surrounding fields), in Hamilton, Massachusetts. Her siblings had bought the estate for the Pattons in 1928 for their use as a "home base" during their many assignments. From there she began a lifelong effort to maintain, and even enhance, the accomplishments, myths, and legends of her husband.

In 1947, the Houghton Mifflin Company published *War as I Knew It*, by General George S. Patton Jr. Beatrice, along with the help of her husband's chief of staff, Colonel Paul D. Harkins (later commander of the Military Assistance Command in Vietnam from 1962 to 1964), used Patton's diary and notebooks to present the story of his participation in World War II. The book's back cover proclaimed:

War As I Knew It is the captivating memoir of George S. Patton, Jr., the legendary American general, incendiary warrior, and unparalleled military tactician of World War II. Drawing on his vivid memories of battle and detailed diaries, Patton dramatically recounts his celebrated Third Army's sweeping campaign across Western Europe right up to the final Allied casualty report. The result is a remarkable frontline view of daily strategies and heroic drives including the rescue of the Battle of the Bulge from Allied infamy and the triumphant Palatinate Campaign—revealing a fascinating portrait of the full-of-vinegar, controversial commander. With selected prefatory letters from Patton's earlier ventures in North Africa and Sicily and a powerful concluding retrospective, War As I Knew It *is a classic of American military history.*

Beatrice recruited Douglas Southall Freeman, the renowned biographer of George Washington and Robert E. Lee, to write the book's foreword. She had planned for him to write Patton's complete biography, but he died before being able to do so.

In 1950, Beatrice dedicated a bronze statue of her husband at West Point done by the artist James Earle Frazer, who was the best-known sculptor in the country, having designed the iconic *End of the Trail*, the World War II Victory Medal, and the Buffalo Nickle, as well as dozens of other works in Washington, D.C., and across the country.

Beatrice attended ceremonies honoring her husband in Russia, Luxembourg, and France. Back home, she was a strong advocate and speaker for universal military service. She also traveled to various army posts across the United States and Panama to visit her children and grandchildren. While in Panama she continued her lifelong passion for deep sea fishing and caught a record sailfish.

On September 30, 1953, Beatrice suffered an aortic aneurysm while on a fox hunt near Hamilton. She fell dead from her horse. After a brief Episcopal service, her remains were cremated. Several years after her death, her children spread her ashes over the grave of their father in Luxembourg.

Major General Charles D. Herron, in a letter to the editor at the *Washington Post*, wrote on October 6:

In her great qualities of heart and head, and even in courage, she was not overshadowed by her distinguished husband, General George Patton, the foremost battle leader of his rank in the Second World War.

Beatrice Ayer Patton Walters: "Little B," as she was known in the family, grew up overshadowed by her younger sister and baby brother. She attended the exclusive Foxcroft School in Virginia before marrying John K. Walters, West Point class of 1931, in 1934. The Germans captured Walters in Tunisia in 1943, and he sat out the remainder of the war in a prison camp in Germany. Released, he continued his military career and advanced in rank to brigadier general (later full general). Beatrice died of a heart attack at age forty-one at their home near Highland Falls, New York, on October 24, 1952, while her husband was serving in Korea. She is buried in the Immanuel Episcopal Church Cemetery in Baltimore County, Maryland.

Her sister, Ruth Ellen, wrote that Beatrice "was only forty-one years old. It isn't only soldiers who are casualties of war."

Ruth Ellen Patton Totten: Ruth Ellen wrote that in her and her siblings' minds, "There was never a moment in our lives that we were not reminded that our father was the finest, bravest, most gallant, and best-looking man who ever lived and that he was destined for unimaginable glory." She also noted, "Georgie had a lifelong conviction that he would die and be buried in a foreign land. He talked about it, quoting Napoleon, 'The boundaries of an empire are the graves of her soldiers.'"

As the family historian, Ruth Ellen took charge of the *Patton Papers* after the deaths of her sister and mother. It was not until the early 1970s, however, that she provided the documents to Martin Blumenson, who produced two books summarizing the papers. In 1985, he again used the papers to write *Patton: The Man Behind the Legend, 1885–1945*, which he dedicated to Ruth Ellen.

In her book *The Button Box*, Ruth Ellen revealed why the papers were finally made public:

> *We felt his story had to be preserved as a whole someplace because the jackals have and will continue to drag out the bones. And each jackal is going to try and prove something by which bone he pulls out. People who have theories will take three things the old man said and take them out of context, and the next will take five and do the same. So*

*no matter how they spread the skeleton around, we still wanted to
have the context.*

Ruth Ellen founded the Army Distaff Association in 1959. She
later became a speaker and writer on George Armstrong Custer, Native
Americans of the Plains, and customs and traditions of the army. She
died at age seventy-eight on November 25, 1993.

Sheriff Dave Allison: Sheriff Allison, one of Patton's favorite western
characters from his border days, left Sierra Blanca and joined the Texas
Cattle Raisers Association as a detective. On April 1, 1923, Allison and
fellow detective Horace Roberson were sitting in the lobby of the Gaines
Hotel in Seminole, Texas, waiting to testify in the trial of suspected cattle
rustlers Hill Lotis and Milton Good, when the two thieves entered the
lobby with a pistol and shotgun and shot both detectives dead. As the two
started to make their escape, Allison's wife, Martha, came down the hotel
staircase and wounded both outlaws with her own pistol. They were later
apprehended and brought to justice. Allison is buried in the South Park
Cemetery in Roswell, New Mexico.

Apache Scouts: The number of scouts was reduced to twenty-two following the return of the Expedition to the United States. Assigned to
Fort Apache in Arizona, they transferred to Fort Huachuca in 1922
and continued to support U.S. Army operations along the border before
finally being disbanded in 1947. During their service, the scouts wore
crossed arrows as their "branch" insignia. In 1984, the U.S. Special Forces
adopted the insignia as their own.

James L. Collins: Collins again served as Pershing's aide in the early
days of World War I before assuming command of an artillery battalion
in the First Infantry Division. Although in his sixties, he commanded
the Puerto Rico Department and then Fifth Service Command in
Ohio during World War II before retiring in 1946 as a major general.
He died at age eighty in 1963 and is buried in Arlington National
Cemetery. One son, Major General Michael Collins, was an astronaut

on *Apollo 11*, and another son also reached flag rank as a brigadier general. His brother General J. Lawton Collins served as the army chief of staff during the Korean War.

Columbus, New Mexico: Following the return of the Expedition and the closing of Camp Furlong, the economy of the town collapsed. Buildings, including the new brick hotel, were dismantled and moved elsewhere. In 1928, many of the town lots were sold for delinquent taxes. Train service to the town ceased in 1958 and its population dwindled to 350. In the 1990s, Columbus began to revitalize with the development of city and state parks, a museum, RV facilities, and other attractions to draw visitors to its historic past. More recently, it has drawn artists and groups seeking distance from more complex environments, increasing its population to nearly 1,700. However, some things about Columbus seem determined to stay the same. The bandit element once again appeared on the scene in the 1960s and early 1970s in the form of the "Columbus Air Force," a cartel-based operation that was to have "airmen" flying drugs into the country from Mexico. A joint New Mexico and Federal task force shut down the operation in October 1973. In July 2011, the U.S. attorney from El Paso brought charges against the mayor of Columbus, a former police chief, a town trustee, and nine others in a gun-smuggling operation into Mexico. Ten pled guilty and served federal prison time.

Fort Bliss, Texas: Today, Fort Bliss is the home of the First Armored Division and the U.S. Army Air Defense Center and School. It contains about 1.12 million acres of land in Texas and New Mexico and is the home of 38,000 soldiers, 39,000 family members, and 1,000 civilian employees.

Mexico: "Poor Mexico, so far from God, so close to the United States." This quote from Porfirio Díaz, Mexican president in the early twentieth century, may still be true, but the country's problems today are far greater than anything that can be blamed on the United States. Although the Mexican government became somewhat more stable as the Revolution concluded in the 1920s, vast portions of the country today, including much of the territory occupied by the Punitive Expedition, is under the control of cartels. These cartels not only smuggle drugs into the United States but also control much of the illegal immigration crossing the border. Within the country they assassinate government and law enforcement officials and kidnap citizens for ransom. Corruption among politicians and the police at all levels remains rampant.

Álvaro Obregón: Obregón later served as minister of war in Carranza's cabinet before retiring to his Sonora ranch and farm in 1917, where he became quite wealthy in producing and exporting chickpeas. He was easily elected to the presidency when Carranza stepped down in 1920. He instituted education and land reforms, rebuilt the Mexican economy, and encouraged the emerging oil industry. He also settled old scores, including having military and political rivals executed and, it was rumored, ordering the assassination of Pancho Villa. Obregón returned to his ranch after serving as president for four years but then returned yet again to politics in 1927. Although opposed by the Catholic Church, he once again assumed the presidency in 1928. He served only briefly before being assassinated by a "Catholic fanatic" on July 17.

Pershing's Chinese: When the Expedition withdrew back to the United States, Pershing realized his Chinese helpers would be severely punished or killed for their assistance to the Americans by one or the other of the opposing Mexican forces. He sought and received permission to bring the Chinese with him across the border. More than four hundred Chinese eventually made their way to San Antonio, where many went to work at twenty cents an hour for the Quartermaster Corps, clearing the land and building what became Camp Travis during the buildup for the First World War. Others found employment in the laundries and mess halls of Fort Sam Houston. Pershing did not forget "his Chinese." On his triumphant return from Europe after the war, he campaigned for them to remain permanently. President Warren G. Harding signed Public Law 29 on November 23, 1921, granting the Chinese residency rights. On May 27, 2011, a marker was dedicated at Fort Sam Houston honoring the Chinese for their service, with several descendents of the original "Pershing's Chinese" in attendance.

Pancho Villa: After the Punitive Expedition left Mexico, Villa continued his revolt against the Federal government, unsuccessfully attacking Juárez again as well as other border towns. He and his bandits remained so troublesome that Adolfo de la Huerta, who became president after the assassination of Carranza on May 20, 1920, extended amnesty to Villa and his followers in an effort to finally bring peace to Mexico. In exchange for disbanding his army, Villa received an annual pension, a 25,000-acre ranch outside of Parral, and permission to maintain fifty of his Dorados as security. Villa's retirement did not last long. In spite of his bodyguards, he was gunned down in the streets of Parral on June 23, 1923, at the age of forty-five. The assailants were never identified. Although from all evidence Villa was killed instantly in the ambush, later reports claimed he died saying, "Don't let it end like this. Tell them I said something." Interestingly, just seven years after the Putative Expedition, Villa had given up horseback for a modern automobile. When killed, he was riding in a 1919 Dodge touring car. Initially buried in Parral, his remains were removed to the Monument to the Revolution in Mexico City in 1976. His legend lives on in stories and songs.

Sierra Blanca: The town remains but a pitstop along Interstate 10 between Dallas and El Paso. Its population in 2014 was 567. In recent years its significance has become that it is a literal dumping ground for waste from other areas, including treated sewage from New York City, delivered by train. A proposal for a radioactive waste disposal site was proposed and turned down in the 1990s. More recently, Sierra Blanca has been newsworthy for its Border Patrol check station, located just west of town. Tour buses of entertainers Willie Nelson, Snoop Dogg, Armie Hammer, Fiona Apple, and Nelly have all been detained there for possession of illegal drugs.

United States Cavalry: The Punitive Expedition marked the last large-scale use of horse cavalry by the U.S. Army. By the time the United States entered World War I, the conflict had morphed into static lines dominated by trenches, barbed wire, machine guns, and artillery. Cavalry regiments continued to patrol along the Mexican border after the armistice, but over the years horses were exchanged for motorized and mechanized vehicles. The last cavalry charge took place in the Philippines on the Bataan Peninsula when the Twenty-Sixth Cavalry Regiment attacked a Japanese position on January 16, 1942. Unfortunately, the troopers of the Twenty-Sixth Cavalry, besieged and facing starvation and overwhelming numbers of the enemy, were forced to slaughter their horses for food before their surrender. Today, cavalry divisions and regiments still fight under the colors of their forebearers. Instead of horses, however, they fight with helicopters, wheeled and mechanized vehicles, and tanks. The only horses in today's army are found in ceremonial units and burial details.

Sources/Bibliography

The primary sources for this book are George S. Patton's diaries and letters on file in the National Archives and John J. Pershing's "Punitive Expedition Report" in the archives of the Army War College. A visit to Columbus, New Mexico; Palomas, Mexico; Fort Bliss, El Paso; and Sierra Blanca, Texas, offered insights into the territory on and near the border, while a train ride from El Paso to Chihuahua and an automobile excursion across much of the land where Pancho Villa rode and the U.S. Cavalry pursued provided the author's understanding of the Expedition's area of operations. Tours of the General George Patton Museum of Cavalry and Armor at Fort Knox, Kentucky, and the General Patton Memorial Museum at Chiriaco Summit, California, added to the appreciation of the Patton legend. A visit to Patton's grave in Luxembourg completed the circle. The author also had the privilege of serving under George Patton IV at Fort Knox and in Germany in the early 1970s. Finally, the experiences of the author as a lieutenant infantry platoon leader, reconnaissance platoon leader, and rifle company commander in the Vietnam War contributed to the insights and understanding of the influences of the Expedition on Lieutenant Patton.

BOOKS

Alexander, Bob. *Fearless Dave Allison: Border Lawman.* Silver City, NM: High Lonesome Books, 2003.

Allen, Robert S. *Lucky Forward.* New York: Vanguard, 1947.

Asplund, Carol A. *A Soldier's Perspective: 1916–1919.* Pittsburgh, PA: Dorrance, 2021.

Axelrod, Alan. *Patton: A Biography.* London: Palgrave Macmillan, 2006.

Ayer, Fred, Jr. *Before the Colors Fade: Portrait of a Soldier, George S. Patton, Jr.* Boston: Houghton Mifflin, 1964.

Banks, Stephen A. *Doing My Duty: Corporal Elmer Dewey, One National Guard Doughboy's Experiences during the Pancho Villa Punitive Campaign and World War I.* Springfield, VA: Stephen A. Banks, 2011.

Baron, Richard. *Raid! The Untold Story of Patton's Secret Mission.* New York: Putnam, 1981.

Blumenson, Martin. *Patton: The Man Behind the Legend.* New York: William Morrow, 1985.

———. *The Patton Papers: 1885–1940.* Boston: Houghton Mifflin, 1972.

———. *The Patton Papers: 1940–1945.* Boston: Houghton Mifflin, 1974.

Braddy, Haldeen. *Pancho Villa at Columbus: The Raid of 1916*. El Paso: Texas Western Press, 1980.

———. *The Paradox of Pancho Villa*. El Paso: Texas Western Press, 1960.

———. *Pershing's Expedition in Mexico*. El Paso: Texas Western Press, 1966.

Buchenau, Jurgen. *The Last Caudillo: Alvaro Obregon and the Mexican Revolution*. Hoboken, NJ: Wiley-Blackwell, 2011.

Carew, Harold C. *History of Pasadena and the San Gabriel Valley*. 3 vols. Pasadena, CA: S. J. Clark Publishing, 1930.

Carpenter, Allan. *George Smith Patton, Jr.* Vero Beach, FL: Rourke Publishing, 1987.

Clendenen, Clarence C. *Blood on the Border: The United States Army and the Mexican Irregulars*. Toronto, Canada: Macmillan, 1969.

D'Este, Carlo. *Patton: A Genius for War*. New York: HarperCollins, 2002.

Easterling, Stuart. *The Mexican Revolution: A Short History*. Chicago: Haymarket Books, 2013.

Eisenhower, John S. D. *Intervention: The United States and the Mexican Revolution*. New York: Norton, 1993.

Essame, Hubert. *Patton: A Study in Command*. New York: Charles Scribner's Sons, 1974.

Farago, Ladislas. *The Last Days of Patton*. New York: McGraw-Hill, 1981.

———. *Patton: Ordeal and Triumph*. Yardley, PA: Westholme, 2005.

Gilly, Adolfo. *The Mexican Revolution*. New York: New Press, 2006.

Guinn, Jeff. *War on the Border: Villa, Pershing, the Texas Rangers, and an American Invasion*. New York: Simon & Schuster, 2021.

Guzman, Martin L. *The Eagle and the Serpent*. New York: Doubleday, 1965.

Harris, Charles H. III, and Louis R. Sadler. *The Great Call-Up: The Guard, the Border, and the Mexican Revolution*. Norman: University of Oklahoma Press, 2015.

———. *The Texas Rangers and the Mexican Revolution: The Bloodiest Decade, 1910–1920*. Albuquerque: University of New Mexico Press, 2004.

Harris, Larry A. *Pancho Villa and the Columbus Raid*. El Paso, TX: McMath, 1949.

Hatch, Alden. *George Patton, General in Spurs*. New York: Julian Messner, 1950.

Hirshson, Stanley. *General Patton: A Soldier's Life*. New York: Harper Perennial, 2003.

Horne, Gerald. *Black and Brown: African Americans and the Mexican Revolution, 1910–1920*. New York: New York University Press, 2005.

Howe, Jerome W. *Campaigning in Mexico, 1916, Adventures of a Young Officer in General Pershing's Punitive Expedition*. Tucson: Arizona Pioneers Historical Society, 1968.

Hurst, James W. *Pancho Villa and Black Jack Pershing: The Punitive Expedition in Mexico*. Westport, CT: Praeger, 2008.

———. *The Villista Prisoners of 1916–1917*. Las Cruces, NM: Yucca Tree Press, 2000.

Justice, Glenn. *Revolution on the Rio Grande: Mexican Raids and Army Pursuits, 1916–1919*. El Paso: Texas Western Press, 1992.

Katz, Frederick. *The Life and Times of Pancho Villa*. Palo Alto, CA: Stanford University Press, 1998.

Knight, Alan. *The Mexican Revolution*. 2 vols. Cambridge: Cambridge University Press, 1986.

Lacey, Jim. *Pershing: A Biography: Lessons in Leadership.* New York: St. Martin's Griffin, 2009.

Lansford, William D. *Pancho Villa.* Los Angeles: Shelbourne Press, 1965.

Machado, Manuel A., Jr. *The Centaur of the North.* Austin, TX: Eakin Press, 1998.

Mason, Herbert Molloy, Jr. *The Great Pursuit.* New York: Random House, 1970.

McLynn, Frank. *Villa and Zapata: A History of the Mexican Revolution.* New York: Carroll and Graf, 2000.

Mellor, William B. *Patton: Fighting Man.* New York: Putnam, 1946.

Miller, Roger G. *A Preliminary to War: The 1st Aero Squadron and the Mexican Punitive Expedition of 1916.* Washington, DC: Air Force History and Museums Program, 2003.

Nye, Roger H. *The Patton Mind.* Garden City, NY: Avery, 1993.

Palmer, Frederick. *John J. Pershing.* Harrisburg, PA: Military Service Publishing Company, 1948.

Patton, George S., Jr. *War as I Knew It.* New York: Houghton Mifflin, 1995.

Patton, Robert H. *The Pattons.* New York: Crown, 1994.

Pearl, Jack. *Blood and Guts Patton.* New York: Monarch, 1961.

Peck, Ira. *Patton.* New York: Scholastic Books, 1970.

Perry, Milton F., and Barbara W. Parke. *Patton and His Pistols.* Harrisburg, PA: Stackpole, 1957.

Pershing, John J. *My Experiences in the World War.* 2 vols. New York: Frederick A. Stokes, 1931.

———. *My Life Before the World War, 1860–1917: A Memoir.* Lexington: University Press of Kentucky, 2013.

Pinchon, Edgcumb. *Viva Villa!* New York: Harcourt, Brace, and Company, 1933.

Prioli, Carmine A. *Lines of Fire: The Poetry of General George S. Patton, Jr.* Lewiston, NY: Edwin Mellen, 1991.

Province, Charles M. *The Unknown Patton.* New York: Hippocrene Books, 1983.

Quick, Robert E. *An Affair of Honor: Woodrow Wilson and the Occupation of Vera Cruz.* Lexington: University of Kentucky Press, 1962.

Rouverol, Jean. *Pancho Villa.* Garden City, NY: Doubleday, 1972.

Semmes, Harry H. *Portrait of Patton.* New York: Appleton-Century-Crofts, 1955.

Smith, Gene. *Until the Last Trumpet Sounds: The Life of General John J. Pershing.* New York: John Wiley & Sons, 1998.

Smythe, Donald. *Pershing: General of the Armies.* Bloomington: Indiana University Press, 2007.

Sobel, Brian M. *The Fighting Pattons.* Westport, CT: Praeger, 1997.

Stillman, Richard J. *General Patton's Timeless Leadership Principles.* New Orleans, LA: Richard J. Stillman, 1998.

Stout, Joseph A. *Border Conflict: Villistas, Carrancistas, and the Punitive Expedition, 1915–1920.* Fort Worth: Texas Christian University Press, 1999.

Sweetman, Jack. *The Landing a Vera Cruz: 1914.* Annapolis, MD: U.S. Naval Institute, 1968.

Thomas, Robert S., and Inez V. Allen. *The Punitive Expedition Under Brigadier General John J. Pershing, United States Army, 1916–1917.* Washington, DC: Department of the Army, Office of the Chief of Military History, 1954.
Thompkins, Frank. *Chasing Villa: The Last Campaign of the U.S. Cavalry.* Silver City, NM: High-Lonesome Books, 1996.
Torres, Elias L. *Twenty Episodes in the Life of Pancho Villa.* Austin, TX: Encino Press, 1973.
Totten, Ruth Ellen Patton. *The Button Box: A Daughter's Loving Memoir of Mrs. George S. Patton.* Columbia: University of Missouri Press, 2005.
Toulmin, H. A. *With Pershing in Mexico.* Harrisburg, PA: Military Service Publishing, 1935.
Tuck, Jim. *Pancho Villa and John Reed.* Tucson: University of Arizona Press, 1984.
Vanderwood, Paul J., and Frank N. Samponaro. *Border Fury.* Albuquerque: University of New Mexico Press, 1988.
Vandiver, Frank E. *Black Jack.* College Station: Texas A&M University Press, 1977.
Wellard, James. *The Man in the Helmet: The Life of General Patton.* London: Eyre & Spottiswood, 1947.
Williams, Vernon L. *Lieutenant Patton: George S. Patton, Jr. and the American Army in the Mexican Punitive Expedition, 1915–1916.* Abilene, TX: Old Segundo Productions, 2003.

PERIODICALS
Adams, Cyrus C. "Northern Mexico, the Scene of Our Army's Hunt for Villa." *Review of Reviews* (April 1916).
Andrews, Marshall. "Our First Aerial Combat Force." *Washington Post Magazine*, May 26, 1929.
Ash, Marinell. "Columbus: Nostalgia and Community Spirit." *New Mexico Magazine* (March 1986).
Blumenson, Martin. "Patton in Mexico: The Punitive Expedition." *American History Illustrated* (October 1977).
Braddy, Haldeen. "Myths of Pershing's Mexican Campaign." *Southern Folklore Quarterly* (September 1963).
Brenner, Sylvia, and Randal R. Bridgeman. "San Joaquin Canyon and the 1916 Punitive Expedition." *Journal of the Southwest* (Spring 2012).
Briscoe, Edward E. "Pershing's Chinese Refugees in Texas." *Southwestern Historical Quarterly* (April 1959).
Coggeshall, Helen R. "The Happy Invasion of 1916." *Password* (Fall 1961).
Collins, Whit. "Patton: Guns That Made Him Great." *Guns and Ammo* (August 1971).
Crouch, James L. "Wings South: The First Foreign Employment of Air Power by the United States." *Aerospace Historian* (March 1972).
Dallam, Samuel F. "The Punitive Expedition of 1916." *Journal of the U.S. Cavalry Association* (July 1927).
Deluca, Leo. "The Trailblazer: Col. Charles Young." *Ohio Magazine* (February 2019).

Dickinson, J. J. "The True Story of the Villa Raid." *Mississippi Valley Magazine* (December 1919).

Dunn, Robert. "With Pershing's Cavalry." *Colliers*, September 13, 1916.

Elser, Frank B. "General Pershing's Mexican Campaign." *The Century* (February 1920).

———. "Pershing's Lost Cause." *American Legion Monthly* (July 1932).

Glines, C. V. "In Pursuit of Villa." *Air Force Magazine* (February 1991).

Harris, Charles H. III, and Louis R. Sadler. "Pancho Villa and the Columbus Raid: The Missing Documents." *New Mexico Historical Review* (Fall 1975).

Hopper, James. "The Little Mexican Expedition." *Collier's*, July 15, 1916.

Howe, Jerome W. "How Villa Evaded the American Troops." *Literary Digest*, July 15, 1916.

Klohr, James E. "Chasing the Greatest Bandido." *Old West Magazine* (Spring 1971).

Mahoney, Tom. "The Columbus Raid." *Southwest Review* (Winter 1932).

———. "When Villa Raided New Mexico." *American Legion Magazine* (September 1964).

McGaw, Bill. "Lt. Lucas' 'Hunch' Cost Lives of Many Villistas at Columbus." *The Southwesterner* (February 1962).

———. "Was Pancho Villa Paid $80,000 For Making Raid on Columbus?" *The Southwesterner* (May 1964).

Morey, Lewis. "The Cavalry Fight at Carrizal." *Journal of the U.S. Cavalry Association* (January 1917).

Morgan, Brandon. "Columbus, New Mexico: The Creation of a Border Place Myth, 1888–1916." *New Mexico Historical Review* 89, no. 4 (2014).

Munch, Francis J. "Villa's Columbus Raid: Practical Politics or German Design." *U.S. Cavalry Journal* (July 1969).

Patton, George S., Jr. "Cavalry Work of the Punitive Expedition." *Journal of the U.S. Cavalry Association* (January 1917).

Pool, William C. "Military Aviation in Texas, 1913–1917." *Southwestern Historical Quarterly* (1955).

Porter, John A. "The Punitive Expedition." *Quartermaster Review* (January–February 1933).

Sarber, Mary A. "W. H. Horne and the Mexican War Photo Postcard." *Password* (Spring 1986).

Shannon, James A. "With the Apache Scouts in Mexico." *Journal of the U.S. Cavalry Association* (April 1917).

Skelton, Skeeter. "Pancho Villa: Merchant of Death." *Shooting Times Magazine* (December 1971).

Smith, Gene. "In Search of 'Black Jack' Pershing." *American Heritage* (Fall 2018).

Smyser, Craig. "The Columbus Raid." *Southwest Review* (Winter 1983).

Stivison, Roy E., and Della M. McDonnell. "When Villa Raided Columbus." *New Mexico Magazine* (December 1950).

Troxel, O. C. "The Tenth Cavalry in Mexico." *Journal of the U.S. Cavalry Association* (January 1917).

Yockelson, Mitchell. "The United States Armed Forces and the Mexican Punitive Expedition: Part 1." *Prologue Magazine* (Winter 1997).

————. "The United States Armed Forces and the Mexican Punitive Expedition: Part 2." *Prologue Magazine* (Fall 1997).

DOCUMENTS

Bruce, Stephen A. "The Punitive Expedition: A Military, Diplomatic, and Political History of Pershing's Chase After Pancho Villa, 1916–1917" (PhD diss., University of Southern California, 1964).

Camacho, Lawrence F. "The Leadership Development of Dwight D. Eisenhower and George S. Patton" (master's thesis, U.S. Army Command and General Staff College, 2009).

Johnson, Donald D. "Alvaro Obregon and the Mexican Revolution" (PhD diss., University of Southern California, 1946).

Patton, George S. "Diary, Letters, and Papers: 1916–1917." National Archives.

Pershing, John J. "Punitive Expedition Report: October 19, 1916." Army War College.

"Report of Operations of 'General' Francisco Villa Since November 1915, Headquarters Punitive Expedition in the Field, Mexico, July 31, 1916." National Archives.

Rice, Laura LeAnn. "The Experience of an Enlisted U.S. Army Soldier During and After the Punitive Expedition and World War I: Thomas F. Cunningham, a Case Study" (master's thesis, University of Maryland, 2011).

Rodriguez, Ismael. "George S. Patton Jr. and the Lost Cause Legacy" (master's thesis, University of North Texas, 2014).

About the Author

Michael Lee Lanning is the author of thirty nonfiction books on military history, sports, and health. More than 1.1 million copies of his books are in print in fifteen countries, and editions have been translated into twelve languages. He has appeared on major television networks and the History Channel as an expert on the individual soldier on both sides of the Vietnam War. The *New York Times Book Review* declared Lanning's *Vietnam 1969–1970: A Company Commander's Journal* "one of the most honest and horrifying accounts of a combat soldier's life to come out of the Vietnam War." The *London Sunday Times* devoted an entire page to review his *The Military 100: A Ranking of the Most Influential Military Leaders of All Time*. According to the *San Francisco Journal*, Lanning's *Inside the VC and the NVA* is "a well-researched, groundbreaking work that fills a huge gap in the historiography of the Vietnam War."

A veteran of more than twenty years in the U.S. Army, Lanning is a retired lieutenant colonel. During the Vietnam War he served as an infantry platoon leader, a reconnaissance platoon leader, and an infantry company commander. In addition to having earned the Combat Infantryman's Badge and Bronze Star with "V" device with two oak leaf clusters, Lanning is Ranger-qualified and a senior parachutist.

Lanning was born in Sweetwater, Texas. He is a 1964 graduate of Trent High School and has a BS from Texas A&M University and an MS from East Texas State University. He currently resides in Lampasas, Texas.